Mastering
Spanish
Vocabulary

A THEMATIC APPROACH

José María Navarro
and Axel J. Navarro Ramil

BARRON'S

Photos on pages 36, 61, 73, 77, 193, 226 reprinted by permission from
UPI/Bettmann.
Photos on pages 15, 97, 123, 151, 174, 175, 181, 199, 204, 206, 225, 254, 270,
274, 279, 297, 355, 363 reprinted by permission from the Spanish Tourist Office in
New York.

Address all inquiries to:
Barron's Educational Series, Inc.
250 Wireless Boulevard
Hauppauge, New York 11788

Library of Congress Catalog Number 95-75993
International Standard Book Number 0-8120-9110-8

Printed in the United States of America

5678 8800 9876543

Contents

Introduction

For whom was this Spanish thematic vocabulary written, and what is its objective?

Mastering a Spanish Vocabulary is intended for young people and adults with previous knowledge of Spanish. It can be used:

- to acquire a vocabulary of basic and more advanced terms and expressions;
- to systematically increase, strengthen, review, and check your knowledge of Spanish;
- to prepare for exams;
- to prepare intensively for a stay abroad in Spanish-speaking countries.

This book can be used in *schools* and *colleges,* in *adult* and *continuing education* courses, and for *self-study*. It is compatible with relevant Spanish textbooks now in use, as well as with every type of course and every method of instruction.

What does this book contain?

Mastering a Spanish Vocabulary is organized according to selected subjects or themes. It consists of 41 groups of interrelated topics and a final chapter devoted to the most current Latin American variants.

Most of the subject areas are broken down into subsections dealing with separate aspects of the overall theme. The key words in each chapter are divided into two levels: basic vocabulary and more advanced vocabulary. The sequence in which the words appear is a logical outcome of the subject matter and associated ideas.

The entire thematic vocabulary contains 5,245 key words, of which 2,547 are part of the basic vocabulary, 2,562 are more advanced terms, and 136 are Latin American variations.

Breaking down the vocabulary according to subject makes it possible for you to learn in small, easy-to-handle units of knowledge relating to a single topic. As a result, you can express yourself in a certain thematic context even before you have acquired the complete vocabulary. In addition, a vocabulary organized by subject matter gives you several options: you can begin with topics that are important to you, required by your course syllabus, related to the subject matter you're studying, or related to each other, and omit other topics or return to them later.

What makes this book a learner-friendly tool?

- Its subject-based structure and the concept of small building blocks containing a wealth of related information
- The up-to-date selection of topics, based on current usage
- The use of illustrative sentences, word arrangement within sentences, and idiomatic English equivalents to understand better the meaning of every Spanish word
- The inclusion of the most common Americanisms, listed in accordance with the subjects covered
- An alphabetical index of all the key words from the basic and more advanced vocabularies. All the key words of the basic vocabulary appear

in **boldface** in the index, while the more advanced words are in Roman type. All Americanisms appear in *italics*.

What sources were used in the selection of terms and expressions?

Complete alphabetical lists of key words were produced by consulting and comparing a large number of sources. Some of the major sources of reference were:
- vocabulary lists
- frequency counts
- word lists of the Council of Europe
- word lists compiled from various adult evening schools
- word lists of most frequently used Spanish textbooks

How was *Mastering a Spanish Vocabulary* produced?

The alphabetical lists mentioned above were evaluated and revised according to the incidence of the words in the sources, their usage in modern standard speech, and their usefulness. Newly coined words, or neologisms, were added for some subjects.

How is this vocabulary presented by subject?

- The thematic vocabulary is organized under 41 subject headings, most of which have several subsections.
- The Spanish key words appear in **boldface** in the left column, the English equivalents in Roman type in the right column.
- No abbreviations of grammatical and lexicographic terms were used. Noun gender is indicated by the article. Feminine nouns that for phonetic reasons are used with the article *el* are designated by an italic *f*. The article *la* should be used with these nouns when another word appears between the article and the noun. The feminine forms of the adjectives are given.
- In the 3,658 examples, typical arrangements of words, idiomatic phrases, grammatical pecularities, and geographical information are presented. The examples contain only words that also are included among the 5,245 key words.
- Each subsection consists of basic vocabulary and more advanced vocabulary. The basic vocabulary is presented first, followed by the more advanced terms, which appear in a gray-shaded box.

How can you use this book to learn better Spanish?

The vocabulary is meant to be acquired according to topic, although the sequence in which you study the topics is irrelevant. However, we recommend studying each individual chapter in the order in which it is presented, because the words are arranged in a meaningful sequence.

First, acquire the basic vocabulary before going on to the more advanced words and phrases. At regular intervals, review the section you have already studied. Daily vocabulary drill is helpful, with the amount you choose to practice determined by your individual learning goals or your course of instruction.

The Editors

Pronunciation Guide

Read aloud both the English and the Spanish examples, pronouncing them carefully. The similarity between the English and the Spanish pronunciations is shown in bold type. Note that the English examples are the closest approximations possible.

	English Example	*Spanish Example*

Vowels

	English Example	*Spanish Example*
a	m**a**ma, y**a**cht	**ca**ma
e	t**e**n, d**e**sk	t**e**l**e**
i	tr**i**o, ch**i**c, el**i**te	s**í**, v**i**v**i**r
o	**o**bey	s**o**l**o**
u	l**u**nar	**u**so
y (alone)	man**y**, penn**y**	**y**

Common Dipthongs

	English Example	*Spanish Example*
ai, ay	**i**ce	b**ai**le, ¡**ay**!
ei, ey	v**ei**n	v**ei**nte, l**ey**
oi, oy	**oi**l, j**oy**	**oi**go, s**oy**
au	c**ow**, h**ow**	**au**to

Consonants

	English Example	*Spanish Example*
b and **v**	**b**at (at beginning of a breath group, and after *m* and *n*)	**b**amba, **v**amos un **b**eso un **v**als
	vat (between vowels)	e**v**itar, i**b**a
c before *a, o, u*	**c**at (c but without a puff of air)	**c**asa, **c**osa
c *before* e, i	**c**ent, **c**ity (in most of Spanish America)	**c**elos, **c**inco

10

	theater, **th**in (in a large part of Spain, especially in central and northern Spain)	**c**elos, **c**inco
ch	**ch**eck	**ch**ico
d	**d**o (at beginning of a breath group and after *l* and *n*—tongue touches back of upper teeth)	**d**onde, al**d**ea
	though (between vowels—with tongue between upper and lower teeth)	i**d**a
f	**f**ame	**f**ama
g before *a, o, u*	**g**as, **g**o, **g**un	**g**ala, **g**oma, **g**ustar
g before *e, i* **h**	**h**ot (heavy aspirant *h*) silent as in **h**our **h**onest, **h**onor	**g**esto, **G**il **h**asta
j before all vowels	**h**ot (heavily aspirated **h**)	**j**ota, **j**efe
k	**k**it (not used in words of Spanish origin)	**k**iosko (Russian origin; also, quiosco)
l	similar, although not identical to English	**l**ento
ll	mi**ll**ion, bu**ll**ion	**ll**ama, e**ll**a
m	similar in most articulations	**m**i
n	similar in most articulations	**n**o
ñ	o**ñ**ion, u**ñ**ion	u**ñ**a, a**ñ**o
p	similar to English, but without puff of air	**p**an, **p**ap**e**l
qu used only before *e* or *i*	cli**qu**e (similar to English **k**, but without puff of air)	**qu**e, **qu**ien
r	"th**rr**ee"—trilled r (tongue tip flutter against boney ridge behind upper teeth)	a**r**oma
rr and **R** at beginning of a breath group	doubly trilled r	a**rr**oz, **R**osa
s	similar, although often not identical to English	**s**in

t	similar, although often not identical to English	tu
w	not used in words of Spanish origin	
x	similar, although not identical to English	excepto
z	**s** sound in most of Latin America	**z**ona
	th as in **th**in in a large part of Spain, especially in central and northern Spain	**z**ona

Where to stress or emphasize Spanish words

Rule One: Spanish speakers normally emphasize the last syllable of the word when the word ends in a consonant, provided that it is not an **n** or an **s**. *Example:* alrede**dor**, pa**pel**, ac**triz**.

Rule Two: When the last syllable ends in **n, s,** or a vowel, the *next to the last syllable* receives the stress or emphasis. *Example:* re**su**men, **ro**sas, **ca**sa.

The Accent Mark: Some Spanish words do not follow Rule One or Rule Two. These words show us where to place the stress or emphasis by using a mark over the vowel in the stressed syllable. That mark is called an accent mark; it looks like this ´. *Examples*: **lám**para, **lá**piz, de**trás,** reu**nión.**

The accent mark has other uses. It distinguishes meanings between words that otherwise have the same spelling, for example, **el** (the) and **él** (he). The accent mark also causes **i** and **u** to be pronounced apart from the vowel near them, breaking the dipthong or semi-consonant, for example, pa**ís**, poli**cí**a, a**ún.** Finally, the accent mark appears on the stressed vowel of every question word (interrogative), for example, ¿**dón**de? (where), ¿**có**mo? (how).

la **persona**

person; human being

ser

be; exist

el **nombre**
¿Cuál es su nombre?

first name; given name
What is your first name?

el **apellido**
Los españoles tienen dos apellidos.

last name; family name
Spaniards have two last names.

llamarse
Me llamo Julio Martín Iglesias.

be named or called
My name is Julio Martín Iglesias.

¿Cuántos años tienes?

How old are you?

el **hombre**
Tu hijo está hecho un hombre.

man; human being
Your son is already a man.

la **mujer**
Rosa Montero es una mujer
extraordinaria.

woman
Rosa Montero is an
extraordinary woman.

el **niño**; la **niña**

boy; girl

el **señor**; la **señora**
Los señores Sánchez tienen dos
hijas.

Mr.; Mrs.
Mr. and Mrs. Sánchez have two
daughters.

la **señorita**

Miss

don; **doña**

¿Cómo es el nombre completo del
señor Martín? —Señor Don Julio
Martín Iglesias.

polite form of address used
only in combination with the
first name and without the article.
What is Mr. Martín's full name?
—Mr. Julio Martin Iglesias.

estar

be

soltero, a
¿Todavía estás soltero?
—No, ya me he
casado pero mi hermana es soltera.

single
Are you still single? —
No, I'm married now,
but my sister is single.

casado, a

married

divorciado, a
No se han divorciado.

divorced
They didn't get a divorce.

el **viudo**; la **viuda**
Su madre se quedó muy joven
viuda.

widower; widow
His mother was widowed very
young.

¿Dónde has nacido?
He nacido en Sevilla.

Where were you born?
I was born in Seville.

¿De dónde es usted?
Soy española.

Where are you from?
I'm a Spaniard.

el **extranjero**; la **extranjera**
En España viven muchos extranjeros.

foreigner; alien
Many foreigners live in Spain.

la **dirección**
Te doy mi dirección para que me
puedas escribir.

address
I'll give you my address, so that
you can write to me.

vivir
¿Dónde vivís? —Vivimos en
Sabadell pero somos de Jaén.

live; dwell
Where do you live? —We live in
Sabadell, but we come from Jaén.

la **calle**
Perdone, ¿dónde está la calle
Matías Perelló?—Lo siento,
no tengo ni idea.

street
Excuse me, please, where is Matías
Perelló Street? —I'm sorry, I have
no idea.

el **número de teléfono**
Dame tu número de teléfono para
yo llamarte mañana.

telephone number
Give me your telephone number, so
that I can call you tomorrow.

el **documento de identidad**
¿Lleva usted el documento de
identidad?

identification card
Do you have an identification card
with you?

el **pasaporte**
Para viajar por Latinoamérica es
necesario llevar el pasaporte.

passport
A passport is required for
traveling in Latin America.

la **profesión**
¿Cuál es su profesión?

profession
What is your profession?

la **identidad**

identity

la **edad**
Ya soy mayor de edad.
Probido para menores de edad.

age
I am of full legal age.
Off limits to minors.

la **tercera edad**
Hay descuento en los viajes para
la tercera edad.

senior citizens
There are travel discounts for
senior citizens.

el **sexo**

sex

separado, a
Se han separado.

separated
They are separated.

el **lugar de nacimiento**
¿Cuál es tu lugar de nacimiento?

place of birth
What is your place of birth?

la **nacionalidad**

nationality

14

la **ciudad de origen**	native town
Mi ciudad de origen es Córdoba.	My home town is Córdoba.
la **residencia**	residence
el **domicilio**	domicile
la **región**	region
Mayte viene de la región andaluza.	Mayte comes from the Andalusian region.
el, la **emigrante**	emigrant
Hay emigrantes gallegos en muchos países hispanoamericanos.	There are Galician emigrants in many Latin American countries.
el, la **inmigrante**	immigrant
el **permiso de residencia**	residence permit
válido, a	valid

IBERIA IB
LINEAS AEREAS DE ESPAÑA   E S P A Ñ A

Apellidos ....
Surname
Nom
Name

Nombre ....
Name
Prenom
Vorname

Nacionalidad ....
Nationality
Nationalité
Staatsangehörigkeit

Fecha de nacimiento............................
Date of Birth
Date de Naissance
Geburtsdatum

Pasaporte expedido en ....
Passport issued at
Passeport delivré a
Reisepass ausgestellt in

1-89 Printed in Spain - IB 617

15

2 | The Human Body

Body Parts and Organs

la **piel**
skin

el **hueso**
bone

Me he quedado en la piel y los huesos.
I'm just skin and bones.

la **cabeza**
head

Juan tiene la cabeza muy grande.
Juan has a very large head.

el **pelo**
hair

Tengo poco pelo.
I don't have much hair.

la **cara**
face

Ponte crema en la cara para no quemarte.
Put cream on your face, so that you don't get sunburned.

la **frente**
forehead

Cuando Miguel se acordó otra vez, se dio en la frente.
When Miguel remembered it it again, he slapped his forehead.

el **ojo**
eye

Teresa tiene unos ojos muy bonitos.
Teresa has very pretty eyes.

la **oreja**
ear

Si te portas mal, te tiraré de las orejas.
If you don't behave, I'll pull your ears.

la **nariz**
nose

¡No te metas el dedo en la nariz!
Don't pick your nose!

la **boca**
mouth

Tienes una boca muy bonita.
You have a very pretty mouth.

la **lengua**
tongue

Al probar la sopa caliente me he quemado la lengua.
I burned my tongue when I tasted the hot soup.

el **diente**
tooth

El azúcar es malo para los dientes.
Sugar is bad for the teeth.

la **muela**
molar

Gema tiene dolor de muelas.
Gema has a toothache.

el **brazo**
arm

Paco tiene un brazo enyesado.
Paco has his arm in a cast.

la **mano**
hand

Los españoles no se dan la mano cada vez que saludan.
Spaniards don't always shake hands when they greet one another.

el **dedo**
Pilar se chupa el dedo.

finger
Pilar sucks her finger.

el **pecho**
Lola tiene un niño de pecho.

breast, chest
Lola has a newborn.

el **corazón**
Tomás tiene el corazón delicado.

heart
Tomás has a weak heart.

la **sangre**
El herido está muy pálido porque ha perdido mucha sangre.

blood
The injured man is very pale because he has lost a great deal of blood.

el **estómago**
Me duele el estómago.

stomach
I have a stomachache.

la **espalda**
Perdone que le dé la espalda.

back
Excuse me for turning my back to you.

la **pierna**
Cuando subo a un avión me tiemblan las piernas.

leg
When I get in an airplane my knees shake.

el **pie**
Me canso de estar de pie.

foot
I'm tired of standing.

el **cuerpo**
Hacer deporte es bueno para la constitución del cuerpo.

body
Doing sports helps get your body in good condition.

corporal

bodily

físico, a

physical

el **esqueleto**
Debajo de la ruina encontraron un esqueleto humano.

skeleton
Beneath the ruin they found a human skeleton.

el **cerebro**
El cerebro dirige las actividades y los sentidos del hombre.

brain
The brain controls a person's motions and senses.

el **cuello**
Es muy práctico llevar la cámara fotográfica al cuello.

neck
Wearing your camera around your neck is very practical.

la **ceja**
De aquella caída tengo la cicatriz sobre las cejas.

eyebrow
I got the scar above my eyebrows from that fall.

el **labio**

lip

la **mejilla**
Las españolas saludan con un beso en cada mejilla.

cheek
Spanish women greet one another with a kiss on each cheek.

la **barbilla** Cuando mi padre está pensando se acaricia la barbilla.	chin When my father is thinking, he strokes his chin.
la **garganta** Me duele la garganta.	throat I have a sore throat.
el **hombro** Si pesa la maleta, la llevo a hombro.	shoulder If the suitcase is heavy, I'll carry it on my shoulder.
la **barriga**	belly
la **cadera** Ana tiene caderas anchas y Clara estrechas.	hip; hipbone Ana has broad hips and Clara has narrow ones.
el **codo** Me he dado un golpe en el codo.	elbow I bumped my elbow.
la **muñeca** Se me ha torcido la muñeca.	wrist I sprained my wrist.
el **puño**	fist
la **uña** Benito se come las uñas.	fingernail Benito bites his fingernails.
el **pulmón** El tabaco daña los pulmones.	lung Tobacco damages the lungs.
respirar Quiero respirar aire puro.	breathe I want to breathe fresh air.
la **respiración** Para bucear hay que contener la respiración.	respiration; breathing When you dive you have to hold your breath.
el **vientre** En general, vientre significa el interior de la barriga. Popularmente "hacer de vientre" significa hacer las necesidades.	belly; abdomen; bowels Generally "vientre" refers to the interior of the abdomen. Colloquially "hacer de vientre" means to relieve oneself.
el **riñón** Pablo tiene piedras en el riñón.	kidney Pablo has kidney stones.
el **hígado** El alcohol es malo para el hígado.	liver Alcohol is harmful to the liver.
el **apéndice**	appendix
digerir Todo lo que comemos, lo digerimos.	digest Everything we eat, we digest.
la **digestión** Hago la digestión muy pesada.	digestion I have digestive trouble.

el **trasero**
Le duele el trasero de estar sentada.

buttocks
Her bottom hurts from sitting.

la **rodilla**
Víctor se ha puesto de rodillas en
la iglesia.

knee
Victor knelt in the church.

el **tobillo**
Isabel se ha torcido el tobillo.

ankle
Isabel has sprained her ankle.

el **nervio**
El paciente sufrió un ataque de nervios.

nerve
The patient suffered a nervous
breakdown.

la **vena**
El médico me sacó sangre de la vena.

blood vessel; vein
The doctor took blood from my
vein.

el **músculo**
El deportista tiene músculos de acero.

muscle
The athlete has muscles of steel.

el **sudor**
Cámbiate los calcetines que te
huelen a sudor.

sweat
Change your socks; they
smell sweaty.

Senses and Perceptions

sentir
Siento frío.

feel
I feel cold.

tocar
Por favor, no toquen el género.

touch
Please don't touch the
fabric.

duro, a
Esto está duro como una piedra.

hard
It's as hard as a rock.

blando, a
Mayte tiene la piel muy blanda.

soft
Mayte has very soft skin.

ver
Hoy no quiero ver a nadie.

see
Today I don't want to see
anyone.

mirar
Mira Carlos, ahí hay un bar.

look
Look, Carlos, there's a bar.

oír
Pedro está oyendo las noticias.

hear; listen to
Pedro is listening to the news.

19

escuchar
Clara escucha la radio.

listen to
Clara is listening to the radio.

el ruido
Con tanto ruido no puedo dormir.

noise
I can't sleep when there's so much noise.

el silencio
¡Silencio que hay un enfermo!

quiet; silence
Quiet! There's a sick man here.

el olor
El olor del café me despierta.

smell; stench
The smell of coffee wakes me up.

oler
Tu perfume huele muy bien.

smell
Your perfume smells very good.

gustar
Me gusta mucho la paella.

taste; be pleasing
I like the paella very much.

dulce
No me gustan los pasteles muy dulces.

sweet
I don't like very sweet pastries.

salado, a
Me parece que el agua está salada.

salty
I think the water is salty.

caliente
Tienes las manos calientes.

warm
You have warm hands.

el frío
Tengo frío.

cold
I am cold.

el calor
¡Que calor tengo! ¿Vamos a bañarnos?

heat
I'm so hot! Are we going swimming?

---

el sentido
Estoy con los cinco sentidos en el asunto.

sense
I am in it with heart and soul.

notar
Hemos notado la vida más cara.

notice; observe
We've noticed that life has become more expensive.

percibir
Ricardo percibió una sensación de paz.

perceive; sense; feel
Ricardo felt a sense of peace.

la vista
Rafael perdió la vista en un accidente.

sight; vision
Rafael lost his sight in an accident.

el oído
Carmen canta de oído.
Ana me lo ha dicho al oído.

sense of hearing; ear
Carmen sings by ear.
Ana whispered it in my ear.

el **tacto**
Los ciegos leen por el tacto.

sense of touch
The blind read by touch.

la **mirada**
¡Eche una mirada al periódico!

look; glance
Have a look at the newspaper.

bello, a

pretty

reconocer
He visto a Norma pero no
me ha reconocido.

recognize
I saw Norma, but she didn't
recognize me.

el **gusto**
Hay gustos que merecen palos.

taste
There is no accounting for tastes!

el **sabor**

taste; flavor

amargo, a
El café solo es amargo.

bitter
Coffee without anything is bitter.

agrio, a
La leche está agria.

sour
The milk is sour.

agridulce

bittersweet

gozar
El público goza con el espectáculo.

enjoy
The audience enjoys the
performance.

Activities

la **actividad**
España ofrece muchas actividades
deportivas.

activity
Spain offers many opportunities
for sports.

la **acción**
A Pablo le gustan las películas
de acción.

action; deed
Pablo likes action films.

hacer
¿Qué hiciste el sábado?—Nada
especial.
Me quedé en casa estudiando
y leyendo.

make; do
What did you do on Saturday?—
Nothing special.
I stayed at home, studying and
reading.

sonreír
¡Sonría, por favor!

smile
Smile, please!

la **sonrisa**
Tienes una sonrisa muy simpática.

smile
You have a nice smile.

reírse
Nos reímos mucho del chiste.

laugh
We laughed heartily at the joke.

la **risa**
Es para morirse de risa.

laugh
It's too funny for words.

acariciar
El gato no se dejó acariciar.

stroke; pet
The cat didn't let itself be petted.

moverse
Lola se mueve mucho.

move; travel
Lola travels a lot.

quedarse
Mi mujer se ha quedado embarazada.

remain
My wife is pregnant.

ir
Voy a la playa.

go; travel; walk
I'm going to the beach.

irse
Se va a casa.

go away; leave; go on a trip
She is going home.

venir
¿Vienes conmigo?

come from; come
Are you coming with me?

llegar
Llegaré el domingo.

arrive
I will arrive on Sunday.

regresar

return

pasar
¡Pase usted primero, señora!—
Muchas gracias.—
De nada.
¡Hola! Pasa y siéntate.

go in; enter
You go first, ma'am!—Thanks
very much.—
You're welcome.
Hello! Come in and sit down.

entrar
¿Podemos entrar por aquí?—No,
es mejor que entren por
aquella puerta.

enter
May we enter here?—No, it's
better for you to enter through
that door.

salir
Maruja ha salido.

leave; go out
Maruja has gone out.

volver
Volverá a las diez.

return; come back
He will return at 10 o'clock.

andar
Carmen anda siempre descalza.

go; walk
Carmen always goes barefoot.

correr
¡Corre, que llegamos tarde!

run; race
Make it snappy, we're going to be
late!

darse prisa
Tenemos que darnos prisa.

hurry
We have to hurry.

tener prisa
Tengo mucha prisa.

be in a hurry
I'm in a great hurry.

pisar
Perdone que le haya pisado.

step on someone
Please excuse me for stepping on you.

caerse
Pedro se ha caído.

tumble; fall down
Pedro fell down.

levantarse
¿A qué hora se levanta?

rise; get up
What time do you get up?

sentarse
¡Siéntese!

sit down
Sit down!

estar sentado, a

sit

acostarse
Ana se acuesta tarde.

go to bed; lie down
Ana goes to bed late.

dormir
Los sábados duermo hasta las once.

sleep
On Saturday I sleep until 11 o'clock.

el **gesto**
Mi padre tenía un gesto muy severo.

facial expression; look; gesture
My father had a very stern facial expression.

Tu gesto ha sido muy generoso.

Your gesture was very generous.

el **esfuerzo**

effort; strong endeavor

bostezar
Julio bosteza porque tiene sueño.

yawn
Julio is yawning because he is tired.

temblar

tremble

rascarse
Me pica la espalda pero no me puedo rascar.

scratch oneself
My back itches, but I'm not able to scratch myself.

chupar
Eres muy mayor para chuparte el dedo.

suck
You are too old to suck your thumb.

tragar
Me duele la garganta al tragar.

swallow
My throat hurts when I swallow.

volverse
La gente se volvió al oír la sirena.

turn around
People turned around when they heard the siren.

caminar

go; journey

el **paso**

step

pararse
En Hispanoamérica pararse significa ponerse de pie.

stop, halt
In Spanish America, "pararse" means to stand up.

apoyarse	lean
Por favor, no se apoye en la pared.	Please don't lean against the wall.
la **caída**	fall
agacharse	bend over
Paco se ata los zapatos sin agacharse.	Paco ties his shoelaces without bending over.
echarse	lie down
Ricardo se ha echado un rato.	Ricardo is lying down for a while.
madrugar	get up early
quieto, a	quiet
descansar	rest; take a rest
¡Que descanse!	Sleep well!
relajarse	relax
Relájate para tranquilizarte.	Relax, so that you can calm down.
dormirse	go to sleep
la **siesta**	afternoon nap
Todos los días duermo la siesta.	I take an afternoon nap every day.
despertarse	wake up

Activities Related to Objects

tomar	take
Toma este paquete y dáselo a tu tío.	Take this package and give it to your uncle.
coger	grasp; take
¿Qué autobús cojo?	Which bus do I take?
usar	use; wear
No uso cinturón.	I don't wear a belt.
emplear	use; employ
¿Cómo se ha de emplear este producto?	How does one use this product?
dar	give
Déme un kilo de peras.	Give me a kilo of pears.

entregar	hand over; deliver
poner	put; set; lay
Cecilia pone la mesa.	Cecilia lays (sets) the table.
meter	put in(to); insert
He metido las maletas en el coche.	I put the suitcases in the car.
echar	throw; put in(to)
¿Has echado las cartas al buzón?	Did you put the letters in the mailbox?
sacar	take out; remove
Raúl quiere sacar la moto del garaje.	Raúl wants to take the motorcycle out of the garage.
traer	bring
Lucía me ha traído flores.	Lucía brought me flowers.
llevar	take
Voy a llevar el tractor al mecánico.	I'm going to take the tractor to the mechanic.
llevarse	take along
agitar	shake
¡Agítese antes de usar!	Shake before use!
abrir	open
¡Abra la maleta!	Open the suitcase!
cerrar	close
Por favor, cierre la ventana.	Please close the window.
apretar	press; push
¡Aprieta el interruptor de la luz!	Press the light switch!
encender	turn on; light
Han encendido las luces.	They have turned on the lights.
apagar	turn off; extinguish
¡Apague el cigarrillo!	Put out your cigarette!
dejar	leave (behind)
He dejado los guantes en el coche.	I left the gloves in the car.
quitar	take away; put away; take off
romper	tear; break; smash

el **uso**	use; usage
aplicar	apply
examinar	examine; investigate
Tenemos que examinar bien cada una de las piezas de la máquina.	We have to examine each part of the machine thoroughly.
señalar	stamp; mark; point out; indicate
pinchar	pierce; puncture
llenar	fill (up)
mojar	dampen; wet
buscar	seek; search for
Quien busca, halla.	He who seeks will find.
hallar	find
recoger	pick up; collect; clean out
¿A qué hora recogen el buzón?	When is the mail collected?
levantar	raise; lift
Sólo levanto veinte kilos.	I can lift only 20 kilograms.
colocar	arrange; put in order; place
colgar	hang; hang up
¿Dónde cuelgo este cuadro?	Where do I hang this picture?
fijar	fix; fasten; post; determine
Prohibido fijar carteles.	Post no bills!
mover	move
No muevas los muebles, por favor.	Please don't move the furniture.
atar	tie; fasten; bind
soltar	untie; turn loose
cubrir	cover (up)
esconder	hide; conceal
envolver	wrap
¿Has envuelto el regalo?	Have you wrapped the gift?
tirar	pull; throw away
En Hispanoamérica en las puertas no ponen "tirar" sino "halar".	In Spanish America they put "halar" (pull), not "tirar" (pull), on the doors.
guardar	store; keep in a safe place
empujar	push; shove
¡No empujen!	Please don't shove!

retener	retain; withhold
la **instrucción**	instruction; instructions for use

Frames of Mind

cansado, a
Estoy cansada de planchar.

tired
I'm tired of ironing.

despierto, a
Juan, ¿estás despierto?

awake
Juan, are you awake?

soñar
He soñado anoche contigo.

dream
I dreamed about you last night.

el **sueño**
El niño tiene sueño.

dream; sleep
The child is sleepy.

el cansancio
Por las mañanas noto mucho cansancio.

tiredness; fatigue
I feel very tired in the morning.

cansar

weary, tire

cansarse
Me canso cuando subo escaleras.

become weary or tired
I get tired when I climb stairs.

la **pesadilla**

nightmare

Appearance

alto, a
Carolina está muy alta para su edad.

tall; big
Carolina is very tall for her age.

bajo, a
Don Isidro es bajito y gordo.

short; small
Mr. Isidro is short and fat.

gordo, a
Felipe está cada día más gordo.

fat
Felipe gets fatter every day.

delgado, a
Luisa es muy delgada.

slender
Luisa is very slender.

fuerte
Pepe está delgado pero es muy
fuerte.

strong
Pepe is slender, but very strong.

la **belleza**

beauty

guapo, a
Las valencianas son muy guapas.

pretty
Valencian women are very pretty.

feo, a
Jorge es feo pero muy simpático.

ugly
Jorge is ugly, but nice.

rubio, a
Lucía tiene el pelo rubio como su
madre pero Angel es pelirrojo como
su abuelo.

blond
Lucía has blond hair like her
mother, but Angel is red-haired
like his grandfather.

castaño, a
Muchos canarios tienen el pelo castaño.

dark-haired
Many Canary Islanders are dark-
haired.

moreno, a
¡Qué moreno te has puesto!

brown; sun-tanned
How brown you've gotten!

negro, a
Nicolás Guillén es un escritor cubano
negro.

black; dark-skinned
Nicolás Guillén is a black Cuban
writer.

blanco, a
Estás muy blanca.

white; light-skinned
You are very pale.

el **tipo**
María tiene buen tipo.

figure
María has a good figure.

parecerse
Julián se parece a su padre.

resemble
Julián resembles his father.

adelgazar
Pepa ha adelgazado doce kilos.

lose weight
Pepa has lost 12 kilos.

engordar
Los dulces engordan mucho.

fatten
Sweets are very fattening.

juvenil
Con ese vestido pareces muy
juvenil.

youthful
You look very youthful in this
dress.

atractivo, a
Tu prima es muy atractiva.

attractive
Your cousin is very attractive.

calvo, a

bald

masculino, a
María tiene una voz muy
masculina.

masculine
María has a very masculine voice.

el **bigote**	mustache
la **barba**	beard
Oriol se ha dejado barba.	Oriol has grown a beard.
femenino, a	feminine
Tu prima es muy femenina.	Your cousin is very feminine.
pálido, a	pale
la **arruga**	wrinkle
colorado, a	red; reddish
El niño se ha puesto colorado cuando lo miraron.	The boy turned red when they looked at him.
pelirrojo, a	red-haired
rizado, a	wavy; curly
Marisa tiene el pelo muy rizado.	Marisa has very curly hair.

Cosmetics and Personal Grooming

lavarse
Antes de comer me lavo las manos.

wash (oneself)
Before eating I wash my hands.

bañarse
Vamos a bañarnos.

take a bath
We're going to take a bath.

ducharse
Clara se ducha a diario.

take a shower
Clara showers every day.

el **jabón**
Me gusta el jabón español.

soap
I like Spanish soap.

limpio, a
¿Tienes las manos limpias?

clean
Are your hands clean?

sucio, a
No, las tengo sucias.

dirty
No, they are dirty.

mancharse
Me he manchado de tinta el pantalón.

get oneself dirty
I got an ink stain on my trousers.

secarse
Isabel se seca las manos.

dry oneself
Isabel dries her hands.

la **toalla**
Necesito toallas porque me voy a duchar.

towel
I need towels because I'm going to take a shower.

limpiarse los dientes
Me limpio los dientes tres veces al día.

brush one's teeth
I brush my teeth three times a day.

lavarse la cabeza
Aquí hay que lavarse la cabeza todos los días.

wash one's hair
Here you have to wash your hair every day.

el champú
Quisiera un champú para niños.

shampoo
I would like a children's shampoo.

el peine
Quiero un peine de bolsillo.

comb
I would like a pocket comb.

peinarse
Prefiero cepillarme el pelo a peinármelo.

comb one's hair
I prefer brushing my hair to combing it.

afeitarse
Como se me ha roto la máquina de afeitar, me afeito con cuchilla.

shave oneself
Because my electric shaver is broken, I have to use a safety razor.

la máquina de afeitar

electric shaver

la cuchilla de afeitar

safety razor

la brocha
Las mejores brochas son de pelo natural.

shaving brush
The best shaving brushes are made of natural bristles.

la crema
Déme crema para el sol.

cream
Please give me some suntan cream.

el aseo personal

personal grooming

dejarse
Desde que vive solo se ha dejado mucho.

neglect oneself
Since he's been living alone, he has really let himself go.

el cepillo de dientes
Quiero un cepillo de dientes y un tubo de pasta dentífrica.

toothbrush
I would like a toothbrush and a tube of toothpaste.

la pasta dentífrica

toothpaste

el cepillo
¿Tiene cepillos para el pelo?

brush
Do you carry hairbrushes?

cepillarse

brush one's hair

mojado, a
Dame una toalla que estoy mojado y tengo frío.

wet
Give me a towel. I am wet and cold.

el secador
Este secador es muy lento.

hairdryer
This hairdryer is very weak.

el **peinado**
¿Quién te ha hecho ese peinado?
—Yo misma.

hairdo
Who did your hairdo?
—I did it myself.

la **peluquería**
¿Cuándo tienes hora en la
peluquería?—A las cuatro.

ladies' hairdresser; barbershop
When is your appointment
at the hairdresser's?—At
4 o'clock.

teñirse el pelo

dye one's hair

el **corte de pelo**

haircut

maquillarse
Algunas mujeres se maquillan mucho.

put on (apply) makeup
Some women put on a lot of
makeup.

pintarse
Los niños se han pintado las
camisetas.

put on paint
The children have painted their
T-shirts.

la **sombra de ojos**
A mi hermana le he comprado
sombra de ojos y rímel.

eyeshadow
I bought eyeshadow and
mascara for my sister.

el **rímel**

mascara

el **carmín**
Emilia siempre lleva el carmín en
el bolso.

lipstick
Emilia always carries a lipstick in
her purse.

la **laca**
Mi abuela no usa ni laca de
uñas ni laca para el pelo.

nail polish; hairspray
My grandmother uses neither
nail polish nor hairspray.

las **pinzas**
¿Me puedes prestar tus pinzas?

tweezers
Can you lend me your
tweezers?

la **lima**
Al intentar abrir la puerta con
la lima, se me partió.

nail file
When I tried to open the door
with the nail file, it broke off.

el **perfume**
Marta usa un perfume suave.

perfume
Marta uses a light perfume.

perfumarse
No te perfumes demasiado.

perfume oneself
Don't wear too much
perfume.

higiénico, a
¿Dónde venden aquí papel
higiénico?—En la sección de
farmacia. Allí está, al lado de
las compresas higiénicas.

hygienic; sanitary
Where can I buy toilet paper?—In
the pharmacy department. It's
right next to the sanitary
napkins.

la **compresa higiénica**

sanitary napkin

31

el **tampón**	tampon
la **farmacia; droguería**	drugstore

Reproduction and Sexuality

la **mujer**
Hay que luchar por los derechos de la mujer.

woman
We have to fight for women's rights.

el **hombre**
Los hombres también lloran.

man
Men cry too.

el **chico**; la **chica**
La chica de la falda roja es mi hermana.

boy; girl
The girl in the red skirt is my sister.

el **sexo**
Hay ropa para ambos sexos.

sex
Clothing for both sexes is available.

enamorado, a
Yo estoy enamorada de Andrés y Andrés,
por desgracia,
de Marisa.

in love
I am in love with Andrés, and Andrés
is unfortunately in love with Marisa.

querer
Los abuelos quieren mucho a los nietos.
¿Me quieres?

love; desire
Grandparents love their grandchildren very much.
Do you love me?

amar
Te amo.

love
I love you.

el **beso**
Dame un beso.

kiss
Give me a kiss.

besarse
Los novios se besaban con mucho cariño.

kiss each other
The engaged couple kissed very tenderly.

íntimo, a
Lola y Juan tienen relaciones íntimas.

intimate
Lola and Juan have an intimate relationship.

embarazada
Estoy embarazada de cinco meses.

pregnant
I am five months pregnant.

el **varón**
Su mujer ha tenido un varón.

male; man
Your wife has had a baby boy.

la **hembra**

female; woman

el **homosexual**
¿Por qué discriminan a los
homosexuales?

homosexual
Why are homosexuals
discriminated against?

la **lesbiana**
Maria es lesbiana

lesbian
Maria is a lesbian.

enamorarse

fall in love

la **virgen**
Marisa es virgen.

virgin
Marisa is a virgin.

hacer el amor
Mis abuelos hacían el amor.

make love; sleep together
My grandparents made love.

la **píldora**
¡Olvidé tomarme la píldora!

pill
I forgot to take my pill!

el **condón**
Déme un paquete de condones.

condom
Give me a package of condoms.

sexual

sexual

la **pubertad**
Hay chicas que llegan a la pubertad
a los doce años.

puberty
There are girls who reach
puberty at the age of 12.

el **embarazo**
Ofelia tiene un embarazo sin problemas.

pregnancy
Ofelia is having an easy
pregnancy.

el **aborto**
El **aborto** es un tema muy discutido.

abortion
Abortion is a controversial subject.

la **matriz**
Me duele la matriz.

uterus
I have lower abdominal pain.

el **período**
¿Cuándo tuvo el último período?

period; menstruation
When did you have your last period?

Birth, Stages of Life, Death

nacer
Beatriz ha nacido en junio.

be born
Beatriz was born in June.

el cumpleaños
Mañana es mi cumpleaños.

birthday
Tomorrow is my birthday.

vivir
De mis abuelos ya no vive ninguno.

live
Not one of my grandparents is still living.

la **vida**
Así es la vida.

life
That's how life is.

vivo, a
El herido estaba vivo cuando llegó la ambulancia.

alive
The injured man was alive when the ambulance came.

el **bebé**
El bebé despierta a toda la familia cuando llora.

baby
The baby wakes the entire family when he cries.

el **niño**, la **niña**
Todavía no sabemos si será niño o niña.

child; boy, girl
We don't know yet whether it will be a boy or a girl.

el, la **joven**
Muchos jóvenes no tienen trabajo.

youth; young man; young woman
Many young people have no job.

joven
Carmela no es muy joven.

young
Carmela is not very young.

viejo, a
Cuando sea viejo me iré a vivir a España.

old
When I am old, I'll move to Spain.

la **muerte**
¡Peligro de muerte!

death
Grave danger!

morir
Doña Felisa murió de cáncer.

die
Dona Felisa died of cancer.

el **muerto**, la **muerta**
Nadie pudo identificar el muerto.

dead man; dead woman
No one was able to identify the dead man.

Le acompaño en el sentimiento.

You have my heartfelt sympathy.

el **parto**
Ha sido un parto fácil.

delivery; birth
It was an easy delivery.

la **comadrona**

midwife

crecer
Has crecido mucho.

grow
You have grown a lot.

la **infancia**
En mi infancia jugábamos en la calle.

childhood
In my childhood we played in the street.

infantil

childish

la **juventud**
La juventud pasa deprisa.

youth
Youth passes quickly.

el **adulto**, la **adulta**
Hay cursos de español para adultos.

adult man; adult woman
There are Spanish courses for adults.

el **anciano**; la **anciana**

old man; old woman

la **vejez**
No hay que temer la vejez.

old age; declining years
There is no need to fear old age.

morirse

die

mortal
La caída pudo haber sido mortal.

fatal
The fall could have been fatal.

el **suicidio**
Tomar tanto el sol es un suicidio.

suicide
Lying in the sun so long is suicide.

suicidarse
Los drogadictos se suicidan poco a poco.

kill oneself; commit suicide
Drug addicts commit suicide gradually.

ahogarse
¡Me ahogo de calor!

drown; be suffocated
I'm suffocating from heat.

envenenarse
Se ha envenenado con arsénico.

poison oneself
He poisoned himself with arsenic.

el **veneno**
El tabaco es veneno para la salud.

poison
Tobacco is poison for one's health.

el **cadáver**

cadaver; corpse

el **entierro**
El entierro será esta tarde.

burial; funeral
The burial will take place this afternoon.

enterrar
Mis padres están enterrados en Madrid.

bury; inter
My parents are buried in Madrid.

35

el **pésame**
Quiero darle el pésame.

sympathy; condolence
I want to express my condolences to you.

el **luto**
Estoy de luto.

mourning
I am in mourning.

el **duelo**
Carmelo está de duelo por la muerte de su abuelo.

mourning
Carmelo is wearing mourning because his grandfather died.

la **sepultura**
La enterraron en una sepultura individual.

grave
She was buried in a single grave.

la **tumba**
La tumba de Felipe II está en El Escorial.

grave; tomb
The tomb of Philip II is in the Escorial.

El Sr. Carrasco murió. Su entierro fue en el cementerio de San José.
Mr. Carrasco died. His burial was at St. Joseph's Cemetery.

━━━━ General State of Health ━━━━

encontrarse
¿Cómo se encuentra hoy?—
Mucho mejor que la semana pasada.

feel; be; find oneself
How do you feel today?—
Much better than last week.

¿Qué tal?—Muy bien.

How are you?—Fine.

regular
¿Cómo estás?—Pues regular.

fairly good; so-so
How are you?—Fairly good.

¡Que se mejore!

I wish you a speedy recovery!

la **salud**
¿Cómo están tus padres de salud?—
Muy bien. ¿Y los tuyos?

health
How is your parents' health?—
Fine, and your parents'?

sano, a
Es muy sano hacer deporte.

healthy
Engaging in sports is very healthy.

enfermo, a
La televisión me pone enfermo.

ill; sick
Television makes me sick.

doler

hurt; ache

débil
Me encuentro muy débil.

weak; feeble; sickly
I feel very weak.

sentirse
De pronto Luis se sintió mal.

feel
Suddenly Luis felt ill.

el **aspecto**
Marisa tiene mal aspecto hoy.
¿Está enferma?

appearance
Marisa looks awful today. Is
she ill?

el **malestar**
Siento malestar.

indisposition; slight illness
I don't feel well.

enfermar

make ill; become ill

consciente
Estuve consciente todo el tiempo.

conscious
I was conscious the entire time.

Medical Care

el **médico**; la **médica**
Aquí cerca hay un médico.

male doctor; female doctor
There's a doctor nearby.

el, la **dentista**
¿Para cuándo te ha dado hora el
dentista?

male dentist; female dentist
When is your appointment with
the dentist?

la **consulta**
El doctor López no tiene consulta
los lunes.

practice; office hours
Dr. López doesn't have office
hours on Monday.

el **consultorio**
Enfrente de la farmacia está el
consultorio de mi amigo.

medical practice
My friend's medical practice is
across from the pharmacy.

el **hospital**
Los hospitales son estatales.

hospital
The hospitals are public.

el **enfermero**; la **enfermera**
Hay muy pocos enfermeros.

male nurse; female nurse
There are very few male
nurses.

la **ambulancia**
¡Llame a una ambulancia!

ambulance
Call an ambulance!

la **farmacia**
¿Abren las farmacias los domingos?—
Sólo las farmacias de guardia.

pharmacy
Are the pharmacies open on
Sunday?—Only those on
emergency duty.

los **primeros auxilios**
En la Cruz Roja le dieron los
primeros auxilios.

first aid
First aid was provided at the Red
Cross.

la **clínica**
Luis está en una clínica particular.

clinic; doctor's office
Luis is in a private clinic.

Urgencias; **Emergencia**
¿Dónde encuentro un médico de
urgencias?

emergency room
Where can I find an emergency
room physician?

la **urgencia**; **emergencia**
¡Llame a un médico! Es un caso
de emergencia.

emergency
Call a doctor. It's an emergency.

la **sirena**

siren

la **cirugía**
La cirugía ha avanzado mucho.

surgery
Surgery has made great advances.

el, la **cirujano**
Me dan miedo los cirujanos.

surgeon (male, female)
I'm afraid of surgeons.

el **seguro de enfermedad**
Esta operación no la paga el seguro
de enfermedad.

health insurance
This operation is not paid for
by health insurance.

la **casa de socorro**

En la casa de socorro sólo atienden
urgencias y primeros auxilios.

emergency hospital; first-aid
station
At an emergency hospital they
only treat emergency cases and
give first aid.

sanitario, a

health; sanitary; hygienic

Diseases

la **enfermedad**
Muchas enfermedades son
incurables.

disease; illness
Many diseases are incurable.

sufrir
Mi tía sufre de reuma.

suffer; undergo
My aunt suffers from rheumatism.

el **enfermo**; la **enferma**
Hay muchos enfermos en el hospital
y pocas enfermeras.

patient (male, female)
There are many patients in the
hospital and few nurses.

el **dolor**
Tengo dolor de espalda.

pain
I have back pain.

la **herida**
Te has hecho una herida poco
profunda.

injury; wound
You don't have a serious injury.

el **herido**; la **herida**
Llevaron al herido al hospital.

injured man; woman
They brought the injured man to
the hospital.

herido, a
Se llevaron al policía herido en una
ambulancia.

injured
They took the injured policeman
away in an ambulance.

hacerse daño
¿Te has hecho daño?—No,
no ha pasado nada.

injure oneself
Did you injure yourself?—No,
nothing happened.

cortarse
Te vas a cortar con la navaja.

cut oneself
You're going to cut yourself with
that pocketknife.

la **fiebre**
Debo tener fiebre.

fever
I must have fever.

sudar
Lo mejor contra ese resfriado es que te acuestes y sudes.

sweat
The best way to fight this cold is for you to go to bed and sweat it out.

mareado, a
Cuando estoy mareado tengo que vomitar.

dizzy; dazed; seasick
When I'm seasick I have to throw up.

vomitar

throw up; vomit

el **resfriado**
Carmen tiene un resfriado.

chill; cold
Carmen has a cold.

resfriado, a
Yo también estoy resfriado.

afflicted with a cold
I also have a cold.

resfriarse
Cuando me resfrío toso mucho.

catch cold
When I've caught cold, I cough a lot.

la **gripe**
Creo que tienes la gripe.

influenza; flu
I think you have the flu.

la **tos**
¿Tiene algo contra la tos?

cough
Do you have something for a cough?

toser
Estoy tosiendo toda la noche.

cough
I cough all night long.

el **cáncer**
Hoy se puede curar muy pocas veces el cáncer.

cancer
Today cancer is rarely curable.

el **ataque**

attack; fit

loco, a
¿Estás loco?

crazy; insane
Are you crazy?

ciego, a
A consecuencia del accidente me quedé ciego de un ojo.

blind
As a result of the accident I was left blind in one eye.

el **ciego**; la **ciega**
La organización de los ciegos en España se llama la ONCE.

blind man; woman
The organization for the blind in Spain is called ONCE.

sordo, a
¿Estás sordo o es que no me quieres escuchar?

deaf
Are you deaf, or are you unwilling to listen to me?

mudo, a
Se ha quedado muda.

mute
She was left mute.

grave
Juan está grave.

grave; serious; dangerous
Juan is gravely ill.

leve
En el accidente sólo hubo heridos
leves.

slight; minor
Only minor injuries were incurred
in the accident.

¡Ay!
¡Ay! ¡Qué daño me he hecho!

Ow!
Ow! I hurt myself!

doloroso, a
Las picaduras de mosquito son
dolorosas.

painful
Mosquite bites are painful.

la **picadura**

insect bite; sting

la **cicatriz**

scar

el **dolor de cabeza**
Además me duele la cabeza.

headache
Besides, I have a headache.

enfermar

make ill

sangrar
El chico sangraba por la nariz cuando
lo llevaron al médico.

bleed
The boy was bleeding from the
nose when they brought him to the
doctor.

marearse

Cuando voy en barco me mareo.

become dizzy; become
seasick
I get seasick on voyages.

el **mareo**
Cuando no como me dan mareos.

nausea; seasickness
When I don't eat, I feel
queasy.

desmayarse

faint

caer desmayado, a
El enfermo cayó desmayado.

faint; lose consciousness
The sick man lost
consciousness.

el **contagio**
Evita contagios lavándote las manos.

contagion; infection
Prevent contagion by washing
your hands.

contagiarse
No quiero que te contagies.

be infected; catch (a disease)
I don't want you to become
infected.

quemarse
Alejandro se quemó la lengua.

burn oneself
Alejandro burned his tongue.

el **hongo**

fungus (athlete's foot, mold)

la **infección**
Tiene una infección en el dedo.

infection; inflammation
She has an infected finger.

infectarse
Se ha infectado la herida.

become infected
The wound became infected.

el **pus**
Hay que abrir la herida para que
salga el pus.

pus
The wound has to be opened to
let the pus come out.

hinchado, a

swollen

la **inflamación**
El hielo te calmará la inflamación.

swelling; inflammation
The ice will alleviate your
inflammation.

inflamarse
Se me ha inflamado el tobillo.

swell; become inflamed
My ankle has become swollen.

torcerse

sprain; twist

la **fractura**
La fractura de cadera es complicada.

break; fracture
Pelvic fractures are complicated.

complicado, a

complicated

el **apendicitis**

appendicitis

la **diarrea**

diarrhea

el **reuma**

rheumatism

el **Sida**
Mi amiga tiene el Sida.

AIDS
My girlfriend has AIDS.

el **sarampión**
El sarampión es peligroso para adultos.

measles
Measles are dangerous for adults.

la **pulmonía**
Si no te vistes, vas a coger una
pulmonía.

pneumonia
If you don't get dressed, you're
going to catch pneumonia.

el **infarto de corazón**
El clima del Mediterráneo es bueno
para enfermos de infarto.

cardiac infarct
The Mediterranean climate is good
for people with a cardiac infarct.

la **cólera**

cholera

el **tifus**

typhus

la **malaria**

malaria

la **locura**
Rosana tuvo un ataque de locura.

madness; insanity
Rosana had a fit of insanity.

el **minusválido**; la **minusválida** Este aparcamiento está reservado para minusválidos.	handicapped (man, woman) This parking place is reserved for the handicapped.
cruzar la vista Los que cruzan la vista necesitan gafas.	squint; be cross-eyed People who squint need glasses.
miope Mi hermana es miope.	near-sighted; myopic My sister is near-sighted.
la **vista cansada** Con los años se tiene la vista cansada.	far-sightedness As we age we become far-sighted.
el **sordomudo**; la **sordomuda** Algunos sordomudos aprenden a hablar.	deaf-mute (man, woman) Some deaf-mutes learn to speak.
cojo, a ¿Por qué andas cojo?	limping; lame Why do you walk with a limp?
dañar El tabaco le ha dañado los pulmones.	damage; harm Tobacco has damaged his lungs.

■■■ Methods of Treatment and Medications ■■■

prevenir Más vale prevenir que curar.	prevent Prevention is better than cure.
tratar ¿Qué médico le trata?	treat Which doctor is treating you?
curar La herida ya se ha curado del todo.	cure; heal The wound has already healed completely.
la **radiografía** Necesito una radiografía de la rodilla.	X-ray; radiography I need an X-ray of my knee.
la **inyección** La enfermera le pondrá las inyecciones.	injection; shot The nurse will give you the injections.
la **operación** Nunca he visto una operación.	operation I have never watched an operation.
el **medicamento** Prefiero medicamentos naturales.	remedy; medication I prefer natural remedies.

la **receta**
Para la aspirina no hace falta receta.

prescription
You don't need a prescription to
buy aspirin.

la **medicina**
Es mejor no tomar medicinas.

medicine
It is better not to take any
medicines.

la **pastilla**
Tome una pastilla después de comer.

tablet; pill
Take one tablet after eating.

la **aspirina**
Si te duele la cabeza tómate una a
spirina.

aspirin; analgesic
If your head aches, take an
aspirin.

las **gotas**
Estas gotas son inofensivas.

drops
These drops are harmless.

la **venda**
¿Tiene vendas elásticas?

bandage
Do you have elastic
bandages?

las **gafas**
Antonio ha olvidado las gafas en
casa.

(eye)glasses
Antonio left his glasses at
home.

arriesgado, a
Ha sido una operación arriesgada.

dangerous; risky
That was a risky operation.

el **empaste**
Se me ha caído el empaste.

filling
I have lost a filling.

la **sala de operaciones**

operation room, OR

el tratamiento médico
Estoy en tratamiento médico.

medical treatment
I am under medical treatment.

el **reconocimiento**
Le voy a hacer un reconocimiento.

examination
I'm going to examine you.

reconocer
Desnúdese para que la reconozca.

examine
Please undress, so that I can
examine you.

el **análisis de sangre**
Tengo que hacerle un análisis de
sangre.

blood test
I have to give you a blood
test.

inyectar
No sé inyectar en la vena.

inject
I don't know how to inject
intravenously.

la **vacunación**

vaccination

vendar
Le voy a vendar el tobillo.

(apply a) bandage
I'm going to bandage your ankle.

el **esparadrapo** — adhesive tape

operar — operate
Me han operado de apendicitis. — They operated on my appendix.

la **anestesia** — anesthesia
La anestesia hizo efecto en seguida. — The anesthesia took effect immediately.

incurable — incurable
Me parece que el cáncer aún es incurable. — I think cancer is still incurable.

mejorar — recover from a disease; get well
En casa mejorará más de prisa. — He will get well faster at home.

recetar — prescribe
¿Me puede recetar algo contra la diarrea? — Can you prescribe something for my diarrhea?

el **remedio** — remedy

el **calmante** — sedative
Toma un calmante. — Take a sedative.

el **comprimido** — tablet

calmar — alleviate
La aspirina calma dolores. — Aspirin alleviates pain.

la **pomada** — salve
Frótese la pomada en el hombro. — Rub this salve into your shoulder.

frotar — rub

la **tirita** — band-aid
Déme un paquete de tiritas. — Please give me a package of band-aids.

el **régimen** — diet

el **masaje** — massage
¿Te da masajes en la espalda? — Does he massage your back?

el, la **masajista** — masseur; masseuse
Como tenemos dolor de espalda, vamos a ir al masajista. — Since we have back pain, we'll go to the masseur.

Foods

el **pan**
bread

el **pan integral**
dark bread
Prefiero el pan integral.
I prefer dark bread.

la **harina**
flour
Eso es harina de trigo.
That is wheat flour.

el **arroz**
rice
El arroz es la base de la paella.
Rice is the basic ingredient of paella.

la **mantequilla**
butter
Sólo uso mantequilla para desayunar.
I only use butter at breakfast.

el **huevo**
egg
¿Quieres un huevo cocido?—
No, lo quiero pasado por agua.
Do you want a hard-boiled egg?—
No, I would like a soft-boiled one.

el **queso**
cheese
Uvas con queso saben a beso.
Grapes with cheese taste delicious.

el **embutido**
sausage
Muchos embutidos tienen patata cocida.
Many sausages contain cooked potatoes.

el **jamón**
ham
El jamón serrano es más caro que el jamón york.
Cured ham is more expensive than cooked ham.

la **carne**
meat
¿Cómo se prepara la carne?—No lo sé.
How is the meat prepared?—I don't know.

el **bistec**
steak
Dos bistecs de ternera, por favor.
Two veal steaks, please.

el **filete**
filet
Los filetes de magro son buenos.
The lean filets are good.

el **pollo**
chicken
Quiero medio pollo para hacer caldo.
I would like half a chicken for soup.

el **pescado**
fish
Prefiero el pescado a la carne.
I prefer fish to meat.

fresco, a
fresh; cool
¿Está fresco el pescado?—Sí.
Is the fish fresh?—Yes.

el **atún**
Déme una lata de atún.

tuna fish
Please give me a can of
tuna.

la **sardina**
La sardina fresca es muy rica.

sardine
Fresh sardines have a very good
taste.

el **marisco**
El marisco es carísimo.

shellfish
Shellfish is very expensive.

la **gamba**
Me gustan las gambas a la plancha.

prawn
I like grilled prawns.

el **azúcar**
El azúcar moreno es bueno para
el té.

sugar
Rock candy is good in tea.

la **sal**
¿Tiene sal de mar?

salt
Do you have sea salt?

el **aceite**
El aceite de oliva crudo es sano.

oil
Uncooked olive oil is healthy.

la **mermelada**
Me gusta el queso con mermelada.

marmalade; jam
I like the taste of cheese with
marmalade.

el **pastel**
Una docena de pasteles de fresa.

tart; pie
One dozen strawberry tarts.

el **caramelo**
Le gustan los caramelos de limón.

candy
She likes lemon candies.

el **helado**
Póngame un helado de
chocolate con nata.

ice cream
Give me chocolate ice cream with
cream on top.

la **pasta**
El domingo nos trajeron pastas de
su pueblo.

dough; pastries
On Sunday they brought us pastries
from their village.

el **panecillo**
¿Tiene panecillos de leche?—No, pero
en la panadería de la plaza hay.

roll
Do you have French rolls?—No,
but the bakery on the square does.

el **salchichón**
No me gusta el salchichón con
mucha grasa.

salami; hard sausage
I don't like salami with a lot of fat.

la **salchicha**
En España se come más jamón
que salchichas.

small sausage
In Spain they eat more ham than
sausage.

la **rodaja**

(sausage) slice

el **chorizo**
Déme medio kilo de chorizo.

chorizo; spicy (red pork) sausage
Please give me 1 pound of chorizo.

la **carne picada**
Déme medio kilo de carne picada.

ground meat
Please give me 1 pound of ground meat.

la **chuleta**
Ayer comimos unas chuletas riquísimas.

chop; cutlet
Yesterday we ate some delicious chops.

el **salmón**
¿Tiene salmón?

salmon
Do you have any salmon?

el **lenguado**
En Galicia comimos un lenguado muy bueno.

sole
In Galicia we ate an excellent sole.

el **mejillón**
Los mejillones se cocinan sin agua.

mussel
Mussels are cooked without water.

la **merluza**
A mi tío le encanta la merluza.

hake
My uncle is very fond of hake.

el **calamar**
¿Tiene calamares a la romana?

squid
Do you have deep-fried squid?

la **cigala**
Estas cigalas están muy frescas.

crawfish
These crawfish are very fresh.

la **langosta**
La langosta aún está viva.

lobster
The lobster is still alive.

el **langostino**
Ya no hay muchos langostinos en el Mediterráneo.

Norway lobster; crayfish
There are no longer many crayfish in the Mediterranean.

la **pimienta**
¡No eches tanta pimienta!

pepper
Don't put so much pepper on it!

el **pimentón**
El chorizo tiene mucho pimentón.

paprika
Chorizo contains a lot of paprika.

el **vinagre**
¿Le pongo vinagre a la ensalada?

vinegar
Shall I put vinegar on the salad?

la **mostaza**
Esta mostaza pica.

mustard
This mustard is hot.

el **azafrán**
El arroz de la paella se prepara con azafrán.

saffron
The rice for paella is prepared with saffron.

la **miel**
Me gusta la leche con miel.

honey
I like milk with honey.

la **galleta**
¿Quieres una galleta?

cookie
Would you like a cookie?

el **bombón**
Te hemos traído unos bombones
de Suiza.

chocolate; bonbon
We brought you chocolates from
Switzerland.

el **flan**
De postre voy a tomar un flan.

rich custard
For dessert I'm going to have
custard.

la **avellana**

hazelnut

la **nata**
A veces tomo el café con nata
montada.

cream
Sometimes I drink coffee with
whipped cream.

la **nata montada**

whipped cream

la **sacarina**

saccharin; sweetener

Fruits and Vegetables

la **verdura**
En casa comemos mucha verdura.

vegetables
At home we eat a lot of
vegetables.

la **fruta**
Como poca fruta.

fruit
I don't eat much fruit.

el **limón**
El pescado se come con limón.

lemon
Fish is eaten with lemon.

la **naranja**
La naranja valenciana es famosa.

orange
Oranges from Valencia are
famous.

la **manzana**
¿Os gusta el pastel de manzana?

apple
Do you like an apple tart?

la **pera**
La pera de agua está muy madura.

pear
The juicy pear is very ripe.

el **melocotón**
Hay que pelar los melocotones.

peach
Peaches have to be peeled.

la **uva**
Me gusta más la uva blanca que
la negra.

grape
I prefer white grapes to black
ones.

el **melón**
El melón con jamón me encanta.

melon
I am very fond of melon with ham.

el **plátano**
El plátano canario es dulce como el
guineo americano.

banana
The Canary Island banana is as
sweet as the American Guinean
banana.

la **patata**
Las patatas se llaman en Hispanoamérica papas.

potato
In Spanish America, potatoes
are called "papas."

las **judías**
A Cecilia nunca le han gustado las
judías verdes.

beans *(always plural)*
Cecilia has never liked green
beans.

la **zanahoria**
El zumo de zanahoria es sano.

carrot
Carrot juice is healthy.

el **pimiento**
El pimiento frito es mi plato
favorito.

pepper (vegetable)
Fried peppers are my favorite
food.

el **tomate**
¿Te preparo una ensalada de
tomate?

tomato
Shall I make you a tomato salad?

el **pepino**
¿Tiene pepinos naturales?

cucumber
Do you have fresh cucumbers?

la **lechuga**
Hay que lavar la lechuga antes
de comerla.

lettuce
Lettuce has to be washed before it
is eaten.

la **cebolla**
Lloro cuando pelo cebollas.

onion
I cry when I peel onions.

la **aceituna**; la **oliva**
¿Tiene aceitunas rellenas?

olive
Do you have stuffed
olives?

las **legumbres**

legumes; vegetables

maduro, a
La fruta ya está madura.

ripe
The fruit is already ripe.

verde
Estos plátanos están verdes.

unripe; green
These bananas are unripe.

la **ciruela**

plum

el **albaricoque**

apricot

la **cereza**
La niña se pone cerezas como
pendientes.

cherry
The little girl is wearing cherries
as earrings.

la **fresa**
En Cataluña hay fresas grandes.

strawberry
In Catalonia there are large
strawberries.

la **sandía**	watermelon
La sandía es refrescante.	Watermelons are refreshing.
la **piña**	pineapple
la **alcachofa**	artichoke
la **espinaca**	spinach
Las espinacas no se deben calentar otra vez después de cocinarlas.	Spinach should not be reheated after it is cooked.
la **col**	cabbage
¿Necesita la col mucha agua?	Does cabbage need a lot of water?
la **coliflor**	cauliflower
Antes de cocinar la coliflor hay que lavarla muy bien.	Before you cook cauliflower, you need to wash it thoroughly.
el **espárrago**	asparagus
De primero hay sopa de espárragos.	The first course is asparagus soup.
el **haba** *f*	broad bean
Las habas fritas están muy ricas.	Fried beans are quite delicious.
el **guisante**	pea
el garbanzo	chickpea
En la paella hay garbanzos.	The paella contains chickpeas.
el **maíz**	corn
La tortilla mejicana se hace con harina de maíz.	Mexican "tortillas" are made with cornmeal.
el **ajo**	garlic
He puesto tres dientes de ajo.	I put in three cloves of garlic.
el **perejil**	parsley

Beverages

beber	drink
¿Qué quieres beber?	What would you like to drink?
la **sed**	thirst
Estoy muerta de sed.	I'm dying of thirst.
la **bebida**	drink; beverage
Las bebidas están en la nevera.	The drinks are in the refrigerator.

el **café**
Déme un café con leche.

coffee; espresso
Give me coffee with milk.

el **cortado**
Póngame un cortado.

espresso with a dash of milk
Make me an espresso with milk.

el **té**
En España se toma poco té.

tea
In Spain they don't drink much tea.

la **leche**
¡A ver si te tomas la leche de una vez!

milk
I hope you're finally going to
finish your milk!

el **chocolate**
Me gusta el chocolate.

hot chocolate; chocolate
I like chocolate.

el **agua mineral** *f*
Tráiganos un agua mineral con gas
y otra sin gas.

mineral water
Bring us one carbonated mineral
water and one noncarbonated.

el **zumo**; el **jugo**
¿Tiene zumo de naranja natural?

juice
Do you have fresh-squeezed
orange juice?

---

sediento, a
Si como paella estoy sediento todo
el día.

thirsty
When I eat paella, I'm thirsty all
day long.

tomarse

consume; drink; eat

descafeinado, a
Mi abuela sólo debe tomar café
descafeinado.

decaffeinated
My grandmother is allowed to
drink only decaffeinated coffee.

la **infusión**
¿Quieres que te prepare una infusión?

herbal tea
Do you want me to make you
some herbal tea?

el **refresco**
¿Hay refrescos de limón y piña?

refreshment; cold drink
Do you have lemon- and
pineapple-flavored drinks?

refrescante

refreshing

la **naranjada**
¿Cuánto cuesta la naranjada?

orangeade; orange-flavored pop
How much is the orange pop?

la **limonada**
¿Tiene azúcar la limonada?

lemonade; lemon-flavored pop
Does the lemon pop contain
sugar?

la **horchata**

La horchata se hace principalmente
de chufa.

drink made of nuts, sugar, and
water *(typical drink of Valencia)*
"Horchata" is made principally
from "chufas"—ground almonds.

■ Alcohol, Tobacco, and Drugs ■

el **alcohol**
El alcohol al volante es un peligro.

alcohol
Alcohol behind the wheel is dangerous.

la **copa**
¿Vamos de copas?

drink of liquor
Shall we go bar-hopping?

el **vino**
En la Rioja se cultivan vinos blancos y tintos.

wine
In Rioja, red and white wines are cultivated.

el **jerez**
El jerez suave se llama fino.

sherry
Pale, mild sherry is called fino.

seco, a
El cava seco es mejor que el semiseco.

dry; sec (of wines)
Dry (sec) champagne is better than semidry (demisec).

semiseco, a
Este tinto semiseco no es muy bueno.

semidry; demisec (of wines)
This semidry red wine is not very good.

suave
El tabaco rubio es suave.

mild; mellow
Light tobacco is mild.

la **cerveza**
La cerveza española es muy ligera.

beer
Spanish beer is very light.

el **tabaco**
¿Tienes tabaco?

tobacco; cigarettes
Do you have cigarettes?

el **tabaco rubio**
En España el tabaco rubio es más caro que el negro.

light tobacco; cigarettes
In Spain, light tobacco costs more than dark.

fumar
Prohibido fumar.

smoke
No smoking.

el **fumador**; la **fumadora**
El fumador pierde la salud.

smoker (male, female)
Smokers ruin their health.

el **cigarrillo**
¿Me das un cigarrillo?

cigarette
Will you give me a cigarette?

el **cigarro**
Me fumo diez cigarros al día.

cigar; cigarette
I smoke 10 cigars a day.

la **cerilla**
¿Tiene cerillas de madera?

match
Do you have wooden matches?

el **encendedor**
Quiero un encendedor de gas.

cigarette lighter
I would like a gas lighter.

el **cenicero**
El cenicero está lleno.

ashtray
The ashtray is full.

la **droga**
El consumo de drogas aumenta.

drug
Drug use is on the rise.

el **alcohólico,** la **alcohólica**

alcoholic (male, female)

el **trago**
¡Dame un trago!

drink
Give me a drink!

borracho, a
Está borracho pero no es un alcohólico.

drunk
He is drunk, but he is not an alcoholic.

bebido, a
Estais un poco bebidos.

tipsy
You are a little tipsy.

emborracharse
En la fiesta Paco se emborrachó.

get drunk
At the party Paco got drunk.

el **brandy**
El brandy tiene mucho alcohol.

brandy; cognac
Brandy contains a great deal of alcohol.

el **licor**
¿Prefiere usted un licor a un jerez?—No, gracias.

liqueur
Would you prefer a liqueur to sherry?—No, thank you.

el **cava**
El cava catalán es riquísimo.

champagne
Catalonian champagne is quite delicious.

la **caña**
Déme una caña.

draft beer
A draft beer, please.

el **carajillo**

coffee with spirits (*espresso with cognac, for example*)

El carajillo es café con brandy.

The "carajillo" is coffee with brandy.

la **sangría**

sangria (*red wine punch*)

el **ron**

rum

el **puro**
Los puros habanos son los mejores.

cigar
Havana cigars are the best.

la **pipa**
Mi abuelo fumaba pipa.

pipe
My grandfather smoked a pipe.

el **filtro**
Es mejor fumar cigarrillos con filtro.

filter
It is better to smoke cigarettes with a filter.

la **ceniza**
¡Cuidado con la ceniza!

ash(es)
Be careful with the ashes!

el **drogadicto**, la **drogadicta**
Hay muchos jóvenes drogadictos.

drug addict *(male, female)*
There are many young drug addicts.

el **hachis**
El hachis es droga blanda como
la marihuana.

hashish
Hashish, like marijuana, is not a
hard drug.

la **marihuana**

marijuana

la **heroína**
La heroína es tan peligrosa como
la cocaína.

heroin
Heroin is just as dangerous as
cocaine.

la **cocaína**

cocaine

el, la **narcotraficante**
El narcotraficante de drogas es un
delincuente.

drug dealer (male, female)
Drug dealers are criminals.

Shopping

ir de compras
Nos vamos de compras al centro
comercial.

go shopping
We're going shopping at the
shopping center.

comprar
Compro en el supermercado.

buy; shop
I shop at the supermarket.

vender
¿Venden pescado?

sell
Do you sell fish?

pagar
Voy a pagar en metálico.

pay
I'll pay cash.

la **caja**
Hay que abonar el importe total
en la caja.

cash register; cashier's counter
The full amount is due at the cash
register.

el **precio**
Si me hace un buen precio me llevo
toda la caja de naranjas.

price
If you give me a good price,
I'll take the whole crate of oranges.

Los precios están por las nubes.

The prices have risen sky-high.

¿Cuánto es?

How much does that come to?

caro, a
Para muchos españoles la vida se ha
vuelto muy cara.

expensive
For many Spaniards, life has
become very expensive.

barato, a
¿A cuánto están las gambas?—
Hoy están muy baratas.

cheap
How much do the prawns cost?—
Today they're very cheap.

el **supermercado**
Este supermercado no cierra al
mediodía.

supermarket
This supermarket does not close
at midday.

la **tienda**
En España las tiendas abren de nueve
a dos y de cinco a ocho de la tarde.

store; shop
In Spain the stores are open from
9 to 2 o'clock and from 5 to 8
o'clock.

el **estanco**

store that sells tobacco and
postage stamps

el **mercado**
Voy al mercado a comprar la verdura.

market
I'm going to the market to buy
vegetables.

la **panadería**
La panadería abre los domingos.

bakery
The bakery is open on
Sunday.

abierto, a

open

cerrado, a

closed

la **botella**
La botella de tres cuartos es más barata
que la de medio litro.

bottle
The 3/4 liter bottle is cheaper than
the 1/2 liter bottle.

el **paquete**
¿Cuánto cuesta el paquete de
galletas?

package
What does the package of cookies
cost?

la **caja**

box

---

la **compra**
¿Ya has hecho tus compras?

purchase; shopping
Have you already done your
shopping?

el **turno**
¿Le toca el turno a usted?—Sí, es
mi turno.

turn
Is it your turn?—Yes, it's my turn.

el **autoservicio**

self service

el **carrito**
Mi hija se sube al carrito.

shopping cart
My daughter climbs into the
shopping cart.

la **cesta**

basket

la **bodega**
En la bodega el vino es más barato.

wine store; shop
Wine is cheaper at the wine store.

la **variedad**
Hay gran variedad de vinos de Rioja.

variety
A great variety of Rioja wines is
available.

la **carnicería**
Aquí hay una carnicería muy buena.

meat market; butcher's shop
There is a very good butcher's shop here.

la **verdulería**

La verdulería de la esquina es muy económica.

fruit and vegetable shop; greengrocer
The fruit and vegetable shop at the corner is very reasonable.

la **pescadería**
La pescadería cierra los lunes.

fish shop
Fish shops are closed on Monday.

la **conserva**

canned food

el **bote**; la **lata**
Un bote de café y una lata de atún.— No queda atún.—¡Qué lata!

can
A can of coffee and a can of tuna.— We're out of tuna.—What bad luck!

podrido, a
¡Oiga! No me ponga peras podridas.

spoiled; rotten
Now listen! Don't give me any rotten pears!

la **tableta de chocolate**

chocolate bar

Eating and Setting the Table

comer
¿Quiere comer algo?

eat
Would you like something to eat?

el **hambre** *f*
Tengo mucha hambre.

hunger
I'm very hungry.

el **desayuno**
El desayuno español a veces es sólo un café.

breakfast
The Spanish breakfast sometimes consists only of coffee.

desayunar
Sólo desayunan el café bebido.

eat breakfast; have breakfast
They only have coffee for breakfast.

el **almuerzo**
Hoy tenemos un almuerzo en la oficina.

lunch
Today we're having a working lunch in the office.

almorzar
¿A qué hora almuerzas?

eat lunch
What time do you eat lunch?

la **comida**
En casa la comida es a las dos.

meal; food; lunch; dinner
At home we eat dinner at 2 o'clock.

la **cena**
¿Qué te preparo para la cena?

dinner; supper
What shall I fix you for supper?

cenar
¿Qué hay para cenar?

eat dinner; supper
What are we eating for supper?

gustar
Me gusta la tortilla de pimiento.

taste
I like omelets with sweet peppers.

el **mantel**
El mantel y las servilletas
están en el aparador.

tablecloth
The tablecloth and the napkins are
in the sideboard.

la **servilleta**

napkin

el **vaso**
Póngame un vaso de vino.

glass
Give me a glass of wine.

la **taza**
¿Quieres el café en vaso o en taza?

cup
Would you like your coffee in a
glass or in a cup?

el **plato**
Emilia compra platos llanos y
hondos.

plate
Emilia buys flat and deep plates.

el **cubierto**

Camarero, estos cubiertos están
sucios.

(set of) knife, fork, and spoon;
cover (at table)
Waiter, these sets of cutlery are
dirty.

el **cuchillo**
El cuchillo no corta.

knife
The knife doesn't cut.

el **tenedor**
Pincha las aceitunas con el tenedor.

fork
Pierce the olives with the fork.

la **cuchara**
La paella se come con cuchara de
madera.

spoon
Paella is eaten with a wooden
spoon.

la **cucharilla**
Colecciono cucharillas de plata.

teaspoon
I collect silver teaspoons.

el **alimento**
El pescado tiene mucho alimento.

food; nourishment
Fish has great nutritional value.

alimentarse
Mucha gente se alimenta mal.

eat; feed
Many people eat an improper diet.

comer

eat

masticar
Tú no masticas, tú tragas.

chew
You don't chew; you only
swallow.

el **palillo de dientes**

toothpick

hambriento, a
Siempre estás hambriento.

hungry
You are always hungry.

la **merienda**
Hemos preparado la merienda a
los niños.

afternoon snack
We prepared the children's
afternoon snack.

la **copa**
A mí, déme una copa de brandy.

wine; champagne glass
I would like a glass of brandy.

Cooking and Menu Terms

cocinar
No me gusta cocinar.

cook
I don't like to cook.

preparar
¿Preparamos la comida?

prepare; fix
Shall we fix dinner?

probar
Voy a probar la salsa.

try; taste
I'm going to taste the sauce.

freír
Fríe las patatas con mucho aceite.

fry
Fry the potatoes in a lot of oil.

echar
Hay que echar más aceite a la sartén.

throw; put in(to); add
You have to add more oil to the
pan.

cortar
En las comidas su padre cortaba el pan.

cut
At meals his father sliced the
bread.

la **rebanada**

slice (of bread)

mezclar
Para hacer la pasta hay que
mezclar harina con huevos.

mix
To make the dough, you have
to mix flour and eggs.

el **fuego**
La paella se prepara a fuego lento.

fire; heat
Paella is cooked over low heat.

calentar
Virginia calienta el pan en el horno.

heat; warm up
Virginia heats the bread in the
oven.

caliente
Oiga, el agua está caliente y el café frío.

warm; hot
Look here, the water is warm and
the coffee is cold.

la **receta**
La receta del gazpacho se puede
variar de muchas maneras.

recipe
The recipe for gazpacho can be
varied in many ways.

la **ensalada**
Aún no le he puesto aceite y vinagre a la ensalada.

salad
I haven't put oil and vinegar on the salad yet.

la **sopa**
Esto es sopa de sobre.

soup
This is a soup from a packaged mix.

el **gazpacho**
El gazpacho se toma en verano.

cold vegetable soup
Gazpacho is eaten in summer.

la **tortilla**
La tortilla de patata es muy típica para la cocina española.

omelet
The potato omelet is very typical of Spanish cuisine.

típico, a

typical

la **paella**

Esta mañana he encargado una paella para doce personas porque tarda mucho en hacerse.

paella *(typical rice dish of Valencia)*
This morning I ordered a paella for 12 people, because it takes a great deal of time to make.

el **bocadillo**
¿Quieres un bocadillo de queso?

sandwich
Would you like a cheese sandwich?

la **mayonesa**
La mayonesa de ajo se llama alioli.

mayonnaise
Mayonnaise with garlic is called "alioli."

---

cocer
¿Hay que cocer las patatas?—

No, las voy a freír.

cook; boil
Do the potatoes have to be boiled?—

No, I'm going to fry them.

batir
Bate bien los huevos.

beat
Beat the egg whites until frothy.

remover
Mientras remuevo la sopa, exprime dos limones.

stir
Squeeze two lemons while I stir the soup.

exprimir

squeeze

pelar

peel

rico, a
Las patatas asadas con alioli están muy ricas.

delicious
Roasted potatoes with garlic mayonnaise taste delicious.

asar
El cochinillo asado de Segovia es famoso.

roast
The roasted suckling pig of Segovia is famous.

La cocina española es robusta. La gente va a los restaurantes con frecuencia.
Spanish cuisine is robust. People frequently go to restaurants.

pegarse
Si no pones más aceite, se pegarán las patatas.

stick; burn
If you don't add more oil, the potatoes will burn.

picante
La comida española no es muy picante.

spicy; highly seasoned
Spanish cooking is not very spicy.

asar a la parrilla
Hoy hay chuletas a la parrilla.

grill
Today we have grilled chops.

muy hecho, a
¿Cómo desean los bistecs?—Para mi marido muy hecho, para la niña medio hecho y el mío lo quiero poco hecho.

well done
How would you like the steaks?—For my husband, well done; for the young lady, medium well; and I would like mine rare.

poco hecho, a

rare

medio hecho, a

medium well done

crudo, a
Este pollo está todavía crudo.

raw; uncooked
This chicken is still raw.

frito, a

fried

hervir
El agua para el té ya está hirviendo.

boil
The water for the tea is already boiling.

quemar

burn

el **horno**
Hace media hora que he metido el pollo en el horno y todavía no está hecho.

oven
I put the chicken in the oven half an hour ago, and it is still not done.

duro, a
El pan ya está duro.

hard; tough
The bread is already hard.

tierno, a
Este cordero es muy tierno.

tender
This lamb is very tender.

magro, a

lean

soso, a

dull; insipid

sabroso, a
La salsa picante es muy sabrosa.

tasty
The spicy sauce is very tasty.

el **caldo**

(meat) stock

la **salsa**
Se ha quemado la salsa de la carne.

sauce; gravy
The meat gravy burned.

la **patata frita**

French fried potatoes

el **asado**

roast

el **cocido**	stew
el **churro**	pastry fried in olive oil; fritter
A veces desayunamos chocolate con churros.	Sometimes we have hot chocolate with "churros" for breakfast.
la **tostada**	toast (bread)
la **ensaladilla**	potato salad with various ingredients
La ensaladilla se ha hecho mala.	The potato salad turned sour.

Eating Out

el **restaurante**
Ese restaurante es bueno.

restaurant
That restaurant is good.

el **bar**
Tomás desayuna todos los días en el bar.

bar
Tomás eats breakfast in the bar every day.

el **camarero**; la **camarera**
¡Camarero! ¡La cuenta, por favor!

waiter, waitress
Waiter, the check, please!

la **lista**
A la puerta del restaurante está la lista de precios.

list
At the door of the restaurant, the price list is displayed.

servir
¿Quién sirve esta mesa?

serve
Who is serving this table?

traer
Tráiganos cuatro cervezas y aceitunas.

bring; fetch; serve
Bring us four beers and some olives.

¿Qué te pongo?

What do I serve you?

la **carta**
Por favor, déme la carta.

menu
Please bring me the menu.

pedir
No sé que pedir.

order
I don't know what to order.

tomar
¿Qué va a tomar?

take; drink; eat
What will you have?

el **menú**
¿Tienen menú del día?

complete meal; dinner; menu
Do you have a special menu of the day?

el **plato**
¿Qué desean de primer plato?—

Una sopa de verduras.

course; dish
What would you like as a first course?—
Vegetable soup.

favorito, a	favorite
a la plancha	grilled
el **postre**	dessert
Hay fruta de postre.	There is fruit for dessert.
la **tapa**	small snack; appetizer
Déme una cerveza y una tapa de jamón.	Please bring me a beer and a ham appetizer.
la **ración**	serving; portion
Una ración de calamares, por favor.	One serving of squid, please.
otro, a	another
¿Quieres otro café?	Would you like another coffee?
la **jarra**	pitcher; earthen jug; carafe
Traiga otra jarra de cerveza.	Bring another pitcher of beer.
la **cuenta**	bill
La cuenta, por favor.	The bill, please.
incluido, a	included
la **cafetería**	cafeteria; luxurious cafe
En la cafetería se puede tomar un pastel o un helado.	In a cafeteria you can eat cake or ice cream.
la **barra**	bar; counter
el **barman**	bartender
El barman está un poco mareado.	The bartender is a little dizzy.

el **taburete**	stool; barstool
Los taburetes altos están delante de la barra.	The tall barstools are in front of the bar.
la **bandeja**	tray
El camarero pone las tazas sucias en la bandeja.	The waiter puts the dirty cups on the tray.
el **apetito**	appetite
escoger	choose; select
¿Has escogido ya?	Have you already made your selection?
la **especialidad**	specialty
el **aperitivo**	aperitif
¿Quieren un jerez de aperitivo?	Would you like sherry as an aperitif?
¡Qué aproveche!	Bon appétit!
¿Qué tal el pescado?	How does the fish taste?
la **propina**	tip
En España no es obligatorio dar propina.	In Spain, leaving a tip is not compulsory.

Articles of Clothing

la **moda**
El verde está de moda.

fashion
Green is in fashion now.

la **ropa**
En rebajas se puede comprar
ropa barata.

clothing
You can buy low-priced clothing
at sales.

llevar
Llevas un traje muy elegante.

wear
You're wearing a very elegant
suit.

ponerse

get dressed; put on

vestirse
El niño ya se viste solo.

get dressed; dress oneself
The boy already dresses himself.

desnudarse
Cuando estuve en el médico, me
tuve que desnudar.

undress; get undressed
When I was at the doctor's office,
I had to undress.

la **calidad**
La ropa de calidad sienta mejor.

quality
Quality clothing fits better.

el **sombrero**
Los españoles llevan poco sombrero.

hat
Spaniards rarely wear hats.

el **pañuelo**
Si estás resfriado, tienes que
llevar pañuelos.

cloth; scarf; handkerchief
If you have a cold, you need to
carry some handkerchiefs.

el **pijama**
Me gusta dormir sin pijama.

pajamas
I like sleeping without pajamas.

el **bañador**
Joaquín usa bañadores bermuda.

bathing suit; swim trunks
Joaquin wears Bermuda-length
swim trunks.

la **camisa**
Busco una camisa de manga corta.

shirt
I'm looking for a short-sleeved
shirt.

la **blusa**
Has perdido un botón de la blusa.

blouse
You've lost a button off your
blouse.

el **jersey**
Tengo dos jerseys nuevos: uno sueco y
otro inglés.

pullover; sweater
I have two new sweaters: a
Swedish one and an English one.

la **chaqueta**
Tengo una chaqueta de punto.

jacket
I have a knitted jacket.

el **pantalón**
En verano vamos en pantalón corto.

trousers
In summer we wear short trousers.

el **tejano**
Los tejanos dan mucho calor.

jeans
Jeans are very warm.

la **falda**
Está de moda la falda-pantalón.

skirt
Divided skirts are in fashion.

el **vestido**
Margarita lleva un vestido bonito.

dress
Margarita is wearing a pretty dress.

el **traje**
Te sienta bien el traje.

suit
The suit looks good on you.

el **calcetín**
Llevo calcetines de lana.

stocking; sock
I wear wool socks.

la **media**
Las medias no duran nada.

nylon stocking
Nylon stockings don't last long.

el **abrigo**
Fernando se ha comprado un abrigo de piel.

coat
Fernando bought himself a leather coat.

el **guante**
¿Tiene guantes de piel?

glove
Do you carry leather gloves?

el **zapato**
En Mallorca hay fábricas de zapatos.

shoe
In Mallorca there are shoe factories.

la **bota**
Estas botas son para montar a caballo.

boot
These boots are for riding.

la **zapatilla**
Mi suegro usa zapatillas a cuadros.

houseshoe; slipper
My father-in-law wears checkered slippers.

la **tela**
Compré tela para hacerme una blusa.

cloth; fabric
I bought fabric to sew myself a blouse.

---

cambiarse
En verano nos tenemos que cambiar todos los días de ropa.

change (one's clothes)
In summer we have to change clothes every day.

quitarse

undress; get undressed

desnudo, a

naked; nude

los **textiles**

textiles

el **tejido**
Quiero tejido para trajes.

tissue; fabric
I would like some suit fabric.

grueso, a	thick; bulky
rayas, a	striped
Con el vestido a rayas pareces más delgada.	You look thinner in the striped dress.
cuadros, a	checkered; checked
Estoy buscando una camisa a cuadros.	I'm looking for a checked shirt.
liso, a	plain
unicolor	of one color
Me gustan las telas unicolores.	I like fabrics of one color.
la **gorra**	cap
El guardia lleva una gorra.	The policeman wears a cap.
la **boina**	beret
Mi abuelo llevaba siempre boina.	My grandfather always wore a beret.
la **bufanda**	woolen scarf; muffler
Se ha dejado la bufanda en el teatro.	He left his muffler in the theater.
la **corbata**	necktie; cravat
Siempre lleva corbatas a flores.	He always wears flowered neckties.
el **calzoncillo**	underwear; men's undershorts
Mi abuelo usaba calzoncillos largos.	My grandfather wore long underwear.
la **braga**	panties
Clara lleva bragas de seda.	Clara wears silk panties.
el **sostén**; **sujetador**	bra
Se te ven los tirantes del sostén.	Your bra straps are showing.
el **tirante**	straps
el **camisón**	nightshirt; nightgown
El camisón cortito se llama "reconciliación".	The short nightgown is called "reconciliation."
la **camiseta**	undershirt; jersey; T-shirt
Los futbolistas intercambiaron las camisetas.	The soccer players exchanged jerseys.
el **albornoz**	bathrobe
Ponte el albornoz cuando salgas del baño para no resfriarte.	Put your bathrobe on when you leave the bathroom, so that you don't catch cold.
el **suéter**	sweater; pullover
Este suéter es de lana.	This sweater is made of wool.

el **impermeable**	raincoat
la **gabardina**	raincoat
Como está lloviendo me pongo la gabardina.	Since it's raining, I'll put on my raincoat.
el **anorak**	parka; anorak
el **uniforme**	uniform
la **sandalia**	sandal
En verano llevo sandalias para ir a la playa.	In summer I wear sandals to go to the beach.
descalzo, a	barefoot
atarse	tie; lace
¡Átate bien los zapatos!	Tie your shoes correctly.

Shopping

el **almacén**
En los almacenes hay de todo.

department store; warehouse
Everything is available in department stores.

la **zapatería**
En muchas zapaterías españolas los clientes escogen los zapatos que están expuestos en el escaparate.

shoe store
In many Spanish shoe stores, the customers select shoes that are on display in the store window.

el **escaparate**

shop window; showroom window

desear
¿Qué desea usted?

wish; desire
What do you wish?

el, la **cliente**
La dependienta está a disposición del cliente.

customer (male, female)
The saleswoman is at the customer's disposal.

atender
¿Ya le atienden?

wait on; take care of
Are you being waited on?

probarse
¿Quiere probárselo?

try on
Would you like to try it on?

estar bien/mal; **ir bien/mal**
El vestido rojo te está bien.

be becoming/unbecoming
The red dress looks good on you.

gustar
No me gusta nada la camisa que llevas.

like
I don't like the shirt you're wearing at all.

largo, a
Me está largo el pantalón.

long
These slacks are too long for me.

corto, a
La falda te viene corta.

short
The skirt is too short for you.

estrecho, a
Julián lleva pantalones muy estrechos.

tight; small
Julián wears very tight trousers.

ancho, a
Tu nuera me está haciendo un
camisón ancho.

wide; big
Your daughter-in-law is making
me a large nightgown.

bonito, a
Ofelia me ha traído un pañuelo muy
bonito de China.

pretty
Ofelia brought me a very pretty
scarf from China.

demasiado, a
El pijama de seda es demasiado
caro.

too much; excessive(ly)
The silk pajamas are too
expensive.

costar
¿Cuánto cuestan estas medias?

cost
How much do these nylon
stockings cost?

la sección
En la sección de deportes
encontrará balones.

section; department
You'll find balls in the sporting
goods department.

estar a disposición

be available; at (someone's) disposal

la **talla**
¿Cuál es su talla?

standard size
What is your size?

el **probador**
Me he dejado el bolso en el
probador.

dressing room
I left my purse in the dressing
room.

caber
No quepo en estos pantalones.

fit into
I don't fit into these slacks.

el **cuello**
¿Qué ancho de cuello tiene?

collar
What is your collar size?

la **manga**
En verano no llevo camisas de
manga larga.

sleeve
In summer I don't wear long-
sleeved shirts.

calzar
Pepito calza el mismo número
que José.

put on/wear (shoes)
Pepito wears the same shoe size
as José.

el **calzado**
Aquí hay calzado de calidad.

footwear
High-quality footwear is available
here.

el **tacón**
Se me ha roto el tacón otra vez.

heel
My shoe heel has broken off
again.

sentar bien/mal
La boina roja te sienta muy bien.

fit; become; suit
The red beret suits you very
well.

■■■ Jewelry and Accessories ■■■

la **cadena**
Para su bautizo le regalamos
una cadena de oro.

chain
We gave her a gold chain for
her christening.

el **collar**
Tu cuñada tiene muchos collares de
perlas pero ninguno es valioso.

necklace
Your sister-in-law has many pearl
necklaces, but not a single one is
valuable.

el **pendiente**
Sólo llevo un pendiente.

earring
I wear only one earring.

la **pulsera**
Tengo un reloj de pulsera.

bracelet
I have a wristwatch.

el **reloj**

clock; watch

el **anillo**
Siempre se me olvida ponerme el
anillo de boda después de lavarme
las manos.

ring
I always forget to put on my
wedding ring after washing
my hands.

precioso, a
Llevas unos pendientes preciosos.

beautiful; valuable
You're wearing beautiful
earrings.

la **perla**
¿Son perlas naturales?

pearl
Are those real pearls?

las gafas de sol
Uso gafas de sol en verano.

sunglasses
In summer I wear sunglasses.

el **bolso**
¡Me han robado el bolso!

purse; (hand)bag
They stole my handbag!

el **bolsillo**
Tengo un diccionario de bolsillo.

pocket
I have a pocket dictionary.

el **cinturón**
Quiero un cinturón de cuero.

belt
I would like a leather belt.

el **paraguas**
Llevo el paraguas para no
mojarme.

umbrella
I'm taking the umbrella so that I
won't get wet.

los **accesorios**	accessories
valioso, a	valuable
La pulsera es valiosa.	The bracelet is valuable.
la **joya**	piece of jewelry; jewel
¿Dónde deposito las joyas?	Where can I deposit my jewelry?
la **joyería**	jeweler's shop
Me he comprado un reloj en la joyería.	I bought a clock at the jeweler's shop.
la **relojería**	watchmaker's shop
He llevado el reloj a la relojería porque se paraba.	I took the clock to the watchmaker because it stopped.
el **bastón**	(walking) stick; cane
Mi abuelo tiene un bastón de caña de bambú.	My grandfather has a bamboo walking stick.
la **cartera**	wallet
el **monedero**	pocketbook, billfold

Care and Cleaning

la **lavandería**	laundry
Voy a llevar la ropa a la lavandería.	I'm going to take the clothes to the laundry.
la **mancha**	spot
Esa mancha no se quita.	This spot won't come out.
lavar	wash
Como se ha roto la lavadora tengo que lavar a mano.	Since the washing machine broke down, I have to wash by hand.
la **lavadora**	washing machine
Pedro arregla la lavadora.	Pedro is repairing the washing machine.
la **tintorería**	dry cleaner's shop
El traje lo limpian en la tintorería.	The suit is being cleaned at the dry cleaner's.
planchar	iron
A Isabel no le gusta planchar.	Isabel doesn't like to iron.

la **percha** — clothes hanger, coat hanger

coser — sew
No sé coser. — I don't know how to sew.

el **sastre**; la **sastresa** — tailor; seamstress
Me he hecho un traje sastre. — I made myself a tailored suit.

el **botón** — button
¿Te coso el botón de la camisa? — Shall I sew the button on your shirt?

teñir — dye; color
¿Quedará bien si tiñen el abrigo de azul? — Will it be all right if they dye the coat blue?

la **plancha** — iron
Me he quemado con la plancha. — I burned myself on the iron.

lavable — washable

el **detergente** — detergent
No ponga tanto detergente. — Don't use so much detergent.

tender — hang up

colgar la ropa — hang out the laundry; hang the wash out to dry

Carmela cuelga la ropa en el balcón. — Carmela hangs the wash out on the balcony to dry.

la **pinza de la ropa** — clothespin
Cuando cuelgues la ropa, ponle suficientes pinzas para que no se vuele. — When you hang the wash out to dry, use enough clothespins, so that the clothes don't blow away.

la **máquina de coser** — sewing machine
Con la máquina de coser se puede coser muy rápido. — With a sewing maching you can sew very quickly.

remendar — mend; patch; darn
Ya no se remiendan los pantalones. — Trousers aren't mended any longer.

acortar — shorten
Acórteme la falda diez centímetros. — Shorten my skirt by 10 centimeters [4 inches].

el **hilo** — thread
Cuando viajo llevo hilo y aguja. — When I travel I take along a needle and thread.

la **aguja** — needle

el alfiler	pin
Cuidado, no te pinches con los alfileres.	Careful! Don't stick yourself with the pins.
pincharse	stick; prick oneself
la cremallera	zipper
Necesito una cremallera negra.	I need a black zipper.
la sastrería	tailor's shop
En esta sastrería trabaja una modista que hace vestidos muy bonitos.	A dressmaker who makes very pretty dresses works in this tailor's shop.
el, la modista	dressmaker (male, female)
hacer vestidos/ropa	tailor; sew; make clothing
el betún	shoe polish (cream)
¿Tiene betún incoloro?	Do you have colorless shoe polish?

Muchas mujeres latinas prefieren colgar la ropa al sol.
Many Latin women prefer to hang the clothes in the sun.

6 | Living Arrangements

Building a House

construir
Están construyendo mucho.

build; construct
There's a lot of construction.

el arquitecto; la **arquitecta**
El arquitecto firma el plano de
construcción.

architect (male, female)
The architect signs the
construction plan.

el **plano**

plan; drawing

el **fontanero**, la **fontanera**
Es difícil conseguir un
fontanero.

plumber (male, female)
It is hard to get a plumber.

el **grifo**
El grifo no cierra bien.

water faucet
The water faucet is
dripping.

el **clavo**
Estos clavos no sirven porque son
demasiado largos.

nail
These nails won't do, because
they're too long.

el **martillo**
Déme un martillo pequeño.

hammer
Please give me a small
hammer.

el, la **electricista**
¿Puede venir el electricista?

electrician (male, female)
Can the electrician come?

la **electricidad**
No tenemos electricidad.

electricity, current
We have no electricity.

la **luz**
Se ha ido la luz.

current; light
The current has failed.

el **enchufe**
Los enchufes de electrodomésticos
europeos son distintos de los
norteamericanos.

(wall) socket; plug
The electric plugs of
European appliances are
different from North
American plugs.

la **bombilla**; **ampolleta**
Se han fundido las bombillas.

electric light bulb
The light bulbs have burned
out.

fundirse

burn out

la **pintura**
No me gusta esta pintura.

color; paint
I don't like this paint.

el **pintor**; la **pintora**
Busco un pintor.

painter (male, female)
I'm looking for a painter.

pintar
Vamos a pintar la casa.

paint
We're going to paint the house.

reformar
Han reformado el piso (*or*
departamento).

renovate; improve
They have renovated the
apartment.

la **construcción**

Los gastos de construcción suben.

building; act and art of
constructing
Construction costs are rising.

el **solar**
En este solar se va a construir un
hospital.

lot; plot of ground
A hospital will be built on
this lot.

el **albañil**
Los albañiles trabajan a veces con
pico y pala.

mason; bricklayer
Masons sometimes work with a
pick and shovel.

yesar

plaster

la **arquitectura**
Mi nieto estudia arquitectura.

architecture
My nephew is studying
architecture.

el **ladrillo**
Nos hemos hecho una pared de ladrillo.

brick
We built a wall of brick.

la **teja**
Su casa tiene las tejas rojas.

roof tile
Your house has red roof tiles.

la **viga**
Esa casa tiene vigas de madera.

beam; rafter
That house has wooden rafters.

el **pilar**
Los pilares son de hormigón.

pillar; column; post; pile
The piles are made of concrete.

la **grúa**
La grúa hace mucho ruido.

crane
The crane makes a lot of noise.

la **pala**
La pala limpia la playa.

shovel; bulldozer
The bulldozer cleans the
beach.

picar
El fontanero tiene que picar la pared
para cambiar la tubería.

break open; chop
The plumber has to break
open the wall to replace the
piping.

la **tubería**
Se sale la tubería.

piping; pipe
The pipe leaks.

salirse

leak; overflow

el **tubo**
El tubo del gas está roto.

pipe
The gas pipe is broken.

el **azulejo**	tile
Los azulejos están sueltos. Hay que ponerlos otra vez.	The tiles are loose. They have to be relaid.
el **carpintero**	carpenter
El carpintero le arregla las persianas.	The carpenter is repairing your shutters.
la **carpintería**	carpenter's shop
la **sierra**	saw
Se ha roto la hoja de la sierra.	The saw blade broke.
el **cable**	cable; circuit line
Está partido el cable.	The cable is broken.
clavar	nail
el **tornillo**	screw
la **tensión**	tension
el **fusible**	fuse
Ha saltado el fusible.	The fuse popped out.
el **cortocircuito**	short circuit
Fue un cortocircuito.	There was a short circuit.
el **interruptor**	light switch
El interruptor está mal instalado.	The light switch is improperly installed.
instalar	install
Nos vamos a instalar una calefacción en el chalé.	We're going to install a heating system in the vacation house.
pintado, a	painted
El armario está recién pintado.	The cabinet is freshly painted.
recién	recently; newly; freshly (painted)
el **papel pintado**	wallpaper
Pablo ha comprado el papel pintado para el dormitorio.	Pablo has bought wallpaper for the bedroom.
el **pincel**	brush
Quiero un pincel fino y una brocha.	I would like a fine brush and a wall brush.
la **brocha**	wall brush; flat bristle brush
el **aguarrás**	turpentine
¡Quita la pintura con aguarrás!	Remove the paint with turpentine!

El albañil trabaja con ladrillos y cemento.
The bricklayer works with bricks and cement.

Houses

el **edificio**
Es un edificio de ocho pisos.

building
It is an eight-story building.

la **casa**
¿Está tu prima en casa?

house; home
Is your cousin at home?

la **planta**
En la planta baja se oye mucho ruido.

story; floor
On the ground floor it is very noisy.

la **ventana**
El marco de la ventana es de madera.

window
The window frame is made of wood.

el **cristal**
El limpiacristales viene los miércoles.

windowpane; glass
The window cleaner comes on Wednesday.

el **ascensor**
El ascensor no funciona.

elevator
The elevator is out of order.

la **escalera**
Hay que subir por la escalera.

stairs; staircase; ladder
You have to go up the stairs.

el **escalón**
Hasta mi casa hay cincuenta escalones.

step of a stairway
There are 50 steps up to my home.

arriba
Los vecinos de arriba hacen mucho ruido.

above; upstairs
The neighbors upstairs are very noisy.

abajo
En el piso de abajo vive mi tío.

below; downstairs
My uncle lives in the downstairs apartment.

subir
Me gusta subir y bajar andando.

go up; climb
I like to go up and down on foot.

bajar

go down; descend

la **entrada**
En la entrada están los buzones.

entrance; entry
The mailboxes are located in the entry.

la **salida**
Te espero en la salida.

exit
I'm waiting for you at the exit.

el **balcón**
En verano comemos en el balcón.

balcony
In summer we eat on the balcony.

la **terraza**
Felisa está tomando el sol en la
terraza.

terrace
Felisa is sunning herself on the
terrace.

el **patio**
El patio andaluz es muy fresco.

yard; patio; courtyard
Andalucian courtyards are very
cool.

el **jardín**
En Valencia se están haciendo
muchos jardines.

garden
In Valencia many gardens are
being planted.

el **garaje**
El garaje es colectivo.

garage
It is a shared garage.

la **finca**
Esta finca es muy acogedora.

farm; country estate
This farmhouse is very
welcoming.

la **hacienda**
Mi padre trabaja en una
hacienda.

landed property; farm
My father works on a farm.

la **manzana**
Vamos a dar una vuelta a la
manzana.

block (of houses)
We're going to walk around the
block.

el **hogar**
Me he criado en el hogar de mis
padres.

home; hearth
I grew up in my parents' home.

el **chalé**; el **chalet**
Tenemos un chalé en la playa.

vacation house; bungalow
We have a bungalow at the
beach.

la **chabola**; **callampa**
Muchos habitantes de Caracas
viven en chabolas.

hut; slum housing
Many inhabitants of
Caracas live in slum
housing.

el **asilo**
No todos los asilos son de
ancianos.

home; institution
Not all homes are for old
people.

el **portal**
No tengo llave del portal.

gate; main entrance; portico
I don't have a key for the main
entrance.

el **tejado**
El gato está en el tejado.

roof
The cat is on the roof.

la **chimenea**
La chimenea tira bien.

chimney; fireplace
The chimney draws well.

el **pararrayos**

lightning rod

el **muro**
El muro del jardín se está cayendo.

wall
The garden wall is falling down.

la **fachada**
Las fachadas de Gaudí son típicas de Barcelona.

facade
Gaudí's facades are typical of Barcelona.

el **marco**
No te apoyes en el marco de la puerta que está recién pintado.

window, door, or picture frame
Don't lean on the door frame; it's been freshly painted.

el **sótano**
En el sótano tenemos los garajes.

cellar
We have our garages in the cellar.

el **ático**
Los áticos tienen terraza.

attic apartment
The attic apartments have a terrace.

la **barandilla**
¡No te apoyes en la barandilla!

balustrade; railing
Don't lean on the railing!

la **valla**
Tengo que pintar la valla.

fence
I have to paint the fence.

Apartments and Their Rooms

el **apartamento**
En la playa se alquilan unos apartamentos.

apartment
Some apartments on the beach are for rent.

el **piso**
Tenemos un piso en propiedad.

apartment; floor
We own our apartment.

la **puerta**
Hace falta un cierre de seguridad en la puerta.

door
We need a safety lock on the door.

el **cierre**

lock

la **llave**
Conviene cerrar con llave.

key
It is better to lock it with a key.

el **pasillo**
El pasillo es muy largo.

corridor; hall
The corridor is very long.

la **habitación**
El piso tiene tres habitaciones y una sala.

room
The apartment has three rooms and a living room.

la **sala**
La sala es tan grande que sirve también de comedor y despacho.

living room; hall
The living room is so large that it also serves as a dining room and a study.

el **comedor**	dining room
el **dormitorio**	bedroom
El dormitorio más grande es el de los niños.	The largest bedroom is the children's.
la **cocina**	kitchen; cuisine
La cocina tiene unos azulejos muy bonitos.	The kitchen has some very pretty tiles.
el **baño**	bathroom; bath
El baño tiene dos lavabos y una ducha.	The bathroom has two sinks and a shower.
la **ducha**	shower
Se ha roto la ducha. No sale ni gota de agua.	The shower is broken. Not a drop of water comes out.
el **lavabo**	sink; lavatory; washstand
¿Puedo pasar al lavabo?	May I use the lavatory?
el **estudio**	attic apartment; atelier; studio
En Zaragoza son carísimos los estudios.	In Zaragoza, studios are very expensive.
el **timbre**	doorbell
El timbre suena como una campana.	The doorbell has a ring like a bell.
llamar	ring (a doorbell)
¡Llamé a tu casa pero nadie me abrió!	I rang your bell, but no one opened the door.
la **cerradura**	lock
Además de la cerradura de seguridad tenemos una alarma.	In addition to the safety lock, we have an alarm system.
la **alarma**	alarm system; alarm
el **recibidor**	vestibule; hallway
El recibidor es muy estrecho.	The hallway is very narrow.
el **despacho**	study; office
Te he dejado las llaves en la mesa de despacho.	I put your keys on the desk.
el **salón**	salon; large parlor
la **despensa**	pantry
La despensa es demasiado pequeña.	The pantry is too small.
el **lavabo**; **excusado**; **wáter**	toilet
En el lavabo hay una ventana.	There is a window in the lavatory.

81

la **bañera**
Preferimos la ducha a la bañera.

bathtub
We prefer the shower to the bathtub.

el **cielo raso**
En casa los cielos, rasos son altos.

ceiling
We have high ceilings at home.

la **pared**
Las paredes están recién pintadas.

wall
The walls are freshly painted.

el **suelo**
Muchas casas españolas tienen el suelo de ladrillo.

floor
Many Spanish homes have brick floors.

la **calefacción**
Las calefacciones funcionan en invierno.

heating system
The heating systems are turned on in winter.

el **radiador**
Cada habitación tiene un radiador.

radiator
Every room has a radiator.

Furnishings

el **mueble**
Busco muebles usados.

furniture
I'm looking for used furniture.

moderno, a
Los pisos modernos son pequeños.

modern
Modern apartments are small.

antiguo, a
Las casas antiguas son más acogedoras.

antique; old
Old houses are more welcoming.

el **sillón**
Luisa quiere un sillón para ver la tele.

armchair; easy chair
Luisa would like an easy chair for watching TV.

el **sofá**
Ahí venden un sofá de dos asientos.

sofa
A two-seat sofa is for sale there.

cómodo, a

comfortable

Me he comprado un sillón muy cómodo.

I bought myself a very comfortable armchair.

incómodo, a
Tu sofá es incómodo para estar mucho tiempo sentado, pero es cómodo para dormir la siesta.

uncomfortable
Your sofa is uncomfortable to sit on for a long time, but it's comfortable for taking a nap.

la **silla**
¿Tiene sillas de comedor?

chair
Do you have dining room chairs?

la **mesa**
Voy a poner la mesa.

table
I'm going to set the table.

la **cama**
Luego haré la cama.

bed
Later I'll make the bed.

el **armario**
Necesito perchas de armario.

cabinet; armoire; wardrobe
I need coat hangers.

la **lámpara**
La lámpara de pie está en la sala.

lamp
The floor lamp is in the living room.

la **cortina**
Carlos corre las cortinas.

curtain
Carlos closes the curtains.

el **frigorífico**; la **nevera**
Necesitamos un frigorífico mayor.

refrigerator
We need a bigger refrigerator.

el **espejo**
¿Tiene espejos para baño?

mirror
Do you have bathroom mirrors?

la **decoración**
He cambiado la decoración.

interior decor; decoration
I have changed the interior decoration.

amueblar
Quiero un piso sin amueblar.

furnish (a room, a house)
I want an unfurnished apartment.

amueblado, a
Se alquila un piso amueblado.

furnished
Furnished apartment for rent.

acogedor(a)

welcoming; cozy

la **alfombra**
Teníamos una alfombra china.

carpet
We had a Chinese carpet.

la **moqueta**
El gato rompe la moqueta.

wall-to-wall carpet
The cat is tearing the wall-to-wall carpet.

la **persiana**
Julia ha bajado la persiana.

shutter; blind
Julia has lowered the blind.

la **cuna**
En España hay muchas "casas cuna".

cradle; birthplace
In Spain there are many children's homes.

el **despertador**

alarm clock

la **mesilla de noche**
Pon el despertador en la mesilla de noche.

bedside table; nightstand
Put the alarm clock on the nightstand.

el **mosquitero**

mosquito netting

el **aparador**
Me he olvidado de las cartas en el aparador.

sideboard
I left the letters on the sideboard.

la **cómoda**
Esta cómoda es muy práctica.

chest of drawers; bureau
This chest of drawers is very practical.

el **cajón**
Los tenedores están en el primer cajón.

drawer
The forks are in the first drawer.

la **estantería**
La estantería tiene seis estantes.

shelf unit
The shelf unit has six shelves.

el **estante**

board; shelf

el **jarrón**
Tengo un jarrón de porcelana china.

flower vase
I have a Chinese porcelain flower vase.

el **colchón**
Duermo en un colchón incómodo.

mattress
I sleep on an uncomfortable mattress.

la **almohada**
Paco duerme sin almohada.

pillow
Paco sleeps without a pillow.

la **sábana**
En verano duermo sólo con una sábana.

sheet (for a bed)
In summer I sleep with only a sheet.

la **manta**
La manta se llama en Hispanoamérica cobija o frazada.

blanket
In Latin America the word for blanket is "cobija" or "frazada."

el **congelador**
Este congelador hace mucho hielo.

freezer; ice compartment
This ice compartment makes a lot of ice.

congelar
Ayer compramos un pollo congelado.

freeze
Yesterday we bought a frozen chicken.

el **lavavajillas**
El lavavajillas ahorra tiempo.

dishwasher
The dishwasher saves time.

enchufar
Cuando enchufes la plancha apaga la lavadora para que no haya un cortocircuito.

plug in
When you plug in the iron, I unplug the washing machine to prevent a short circuit.

el **microondas**

microwave oven

el **ventilador**	ventilator; fan
la **hamaca**	hammock
la **sombrilla**	sunshade, parasol

■■■■ Housekeeping and Housework ■■■■

el **ama de casa** *f*
Las amas de casa trabajan todo el día.

housewife
Housewives work all day.

la **basura**
En España recogen la basura por la noche.

garbage
In Spain the garbage is picked up at night.

limpiar
Limpio la casa los jueves.

clean
I clean house on Thursday.

especial
Este producto especial es para limpiar plata.

special
This special product is for cleaning silver.

el **polvo**
Los muebles están llenos de polvo.

dust
The furniture is full of dust.

la **escoba**

broom

barrer
Antes de irte a la playa, barre la casa.

sweep
Before you go to the beach, sweep the house.

fregar
Anoche fregué los platos.

wash; scrub; rub
Last night I washed the dishes.

el **abrelatas**
En el chalé falta un abrelatas.

can opener
There's no can opener in the vacation house.

el **abrebotellas**
¿Me pasas el abrebotellas?

bottle opener
Can you hand me the bottle opener?

las **tijeras**
Estas tijeras no cortan.

scissors
These scissors don't cut.

el **sacacorchos**
Se me ha roto el sacacorchos.

corkscrew
My corkscrew broke.

arreglar
Voy a arreglar la sala.

clean up; arrange; adjust
I'm going to clean up the living room.

el **trabajo doméstico** El trabajo doméstico nunca se acaba.	housework Housework never ends.
la **empleada**	maid
la **suciedad**	dirt, filth
la **limpieza** La mujer de la limpieza ayuda al ama de casa en la limpieza a fondo.	cleanness; tidiness The cleaning lady helps the housewife with large-scale housecleaning.
la **batidora** En la batidora se hace el gazpacho.	blender; mixer Gazpacho is made in the blender.
el **cubo** En el cubo grande caben diez litros.	pail; bucket The big bucket holds 10 liters.
el **cubo de basura** Cierre bien el cubo de la basura para que los perros no la saquen.	garbage pail; can Close the garbage can tightly so that the dogs don't take the garbage out of it.
la **papelera** Tiré la carta a la papelera.	wastepaper basket I threw the letter in the wastepaper basket.
el **trapo** Seca los platos con el trapo de cocina.	cloth; rag Dry the dishes with the dish cloth.
la **balleta** Pasa la balleta por el suelo.	floorcloth; scouring cloth Wipe the floor with the floorcloth.
el **aspirador**; la **aspiradora** Ayer no pasé el aspirador.	vacuum cleaner Yesterday I didn't run the vacuum cleaner.
el **fregadero** El fregadero está atascado.	kitchen sink The kitchen sink is clogged.
atascado, a	clogged; blocked
la **sartén** En esta sartén se pega todo y se quema.	skillet; frying pan In this pan, everything sticks and burns.
la **cazuela** El conejo a la cazuela es muy sabroso.	(earthen) pan; saucepan; pot Rabbit prepared in an earthen pan is very tasty.
el **puchero** Es un puchero para cocina eléctrica.	cooking pot It is a pot for an electric stove.

la **olla exprés**; **olla a presión**	pressure cooker
Con la olla exprés se ahorra tiempo y energía.	With a pressure cooker you save time and energy.
la **vela**	candle
Cenar con luz de velas es romántico.	Dining by candlelight is romantic.
ordenar	put in order; put away
¡Ordena tus cosas!	Put away your things!
el **desorden**	disorder; mess
Tengo un desorden total en el despacho.	I have a total mess in my study.
el **limpiacristales**	window cleaner
el **criado**, la **criada**	servant; maid; help
No todas las familias españolas tienen una criada.	Not all Spanish families have a maid.

▬▬ Buying, Renting, and Inhabitants ▬▬

alquilar	rent
Se alquilan apartamentos.	Vacation apartments for rent.
el **alquiler**	rent
Hoy he firmado el contrato de alquiler.	Today I signed the rental contract.
mudarse	move
Me mudo de casa todos los años.	I move every year.
el **dueño**; la **dueña**	owner; lessor
Quisiera hablar con el dueño.	I would like to speak with the owner.
la **venta**	sale
¿Se vende este piso?—No, no está a la venta.	Is this apartment for sale? — No, it is not up for sale.
el **vecino**, la **vecina**	neighbor
El vecino de al lado es muy amable.	The next-door neighbor is very friendly.
el **portero**, la **portera**	superintendent; janitor; doorman; caretaker
El portero es la persona más importante de la casa.	The superintendent is the most important person in the building.
privado, a	private
Por aquí no puede pasar. Es un camino privado.	You can't drive through here. It is a private road.

la **vivienda**	apartment
el **inquilino**; la **inquilina** Somos los inquilinos del chalé.	tenant; renter; lessee We are the tenants of the vacation house.
prolongar Queremos prolongar el contrato de alquiler.	extend; lengthen We want to extend the lease.
la **prolongación** El propietario no aceptó una prolongación del contrato.	extension The owner did not agree to an extension of the contract.
el **propietario**; la **propietaria** El propietario no vive aquí.	owner The owner does not live here.
el **administrador**; la **administradora** Yo soy el administrador.	manager; administrator I'm the manager.
la **propiedad** Es de propiedad privada.	property It is private property.
el **corredor**; la **corredora** ¡No te fíes de los corredores!	real estate agent; broker Don't trust real estate agents!
la **fianza**	deposit
la **escritura notarial** Sólo es válida la escritura notarial.	notarized purchase agreement Only a notarized purchase agreement is valid.
trasladarse	move
la **mudanza** Las mudanzas son caras.	moving (residence) Moving is expensive.
la **portería** Deje el paquete en la portería, por favor.	reception desk; office of doorman or caretaker's office Please leave the package in the caretaker's office.

▬▬▬ Positive Characteristics ▬▬▬

el **carácter**
Tiene un carácter muy fuerte.

character; personality
He has a very strong character.

bueno, a
Es una buena muchacha.

good
She is a good girl.

simpático, a
¡Qué simpática!

nice; friendly
Oh, how nice!

amable
Fueron bastante amables en el
banco.

friendly; kind
In the bank they were rather
friendly.

sensible
Luis es un chico sensible.

sensitive
Luis is a sensitive boy.

cariñoso, a
Tengo una novia muy cariñosa.

tender; loving; affectionate
I have a very affectionate
girlfriend.

alegre
En verano estoy más alegre que en
invierno.

cheerful; happy
In summer I'm happier than in
winter.

ser listo, a
Eres un tío muy listo.

be smart
You're a very smart fellow.

tímido, a

timid; shy

serio, a
¿Por qué estás tan seria?

serious; trustworthy
Why are you so serious?

correcto, a
La señora Galíndez es muy correcta.

polite; correct; proper
Mrs. Galíndez is very polite.

puntual
Sé puntual.

punctual; prompt
Be punctual.

activo, a
Es un comerciante muy activo.

active
He is a very active
businessman.

el **humor**
Paco tiene sentido del humor.

humor
Paco has a sense of humor.

gracioso, a
El cura es muy gracioso.

witty; funny; graceful
The priest is very witty.

la **gracia**
La niña se mueve con gracia.
Este chiste no tiene ninguna
gracia.

wit; grace; witticism
The girl moves with grace.
This joke is not funny at all.

la **característica**
El humor es una característica positiva.

characteristic
Humor is a positive characteristic.

característico, a

characteristic; distinctive

la **personalidad**
Marta tiene personalidad.

personality
Marta has personality.

individual

individual; personal

la **mentalidad**

mentality

la **bondad**
Tenga la bondad de rellenar la ficha.

goodness; kindness
Be so kind as to fill out the form.

la **amabilidad**
Es de gran amabilidad ayudar a las personas mayores.

friendliness; kindness
It is very kind to help older people.

educado, a
Es un chico muy bien educado.

well-bred; courteous
He is a very well-bred boy.

honesto, a

honest; decent

honrado, a

honest; honorable; reputable

En los pueblos la gente es más honrada.

In the villages the people are more honest.

justo, a

just

sincero, a
A serte sincero, no me gusta tu perfume.

sincere; honest
To be honest with you, I don't like your perfume.

atento, a
Eres un chico muy atento.

attentive; courteous
You're a very courteous boy.

prudente

cautious; smart

la **atención**

attention; civility; kindness

Tiene muchas atenciones conmigo.

She shows me many kindnesses.

cuidadoso, a
Alberto es muy cuidadoso.

careful; considerate
Alberto is very careful.

valiente
La madre fue muy valiente salvando a su hijo.

brave; courageous
The mother was very brave when she rescued her child.

callado, a
Rosa es muy callada.

quiet; still
Rosa is very quiet.

romántico, a — romantic

orgulloso, a — proud
Estoy orgulloso de ti. — I am proud of you.

optimista — optimistic

realista — realistic

Negative Characteristics

el **defecto** — defect; imperfection
Los amigos saben comprender los defectos. — Friends can understand imperfections.

malo, a — naughty; bad; wicked
Jaimito es muy malo. — Jaimito is very naughty.

tonto, a — stupid; silly; foolish
¡No seas tonto! — Don't be silly!

furioso, a — furious
Estoy muy furiosa con los vecinos. — I am furious with the neighbors.

curioso, a — curious; inquisitive
Mi vecina es demasiado curiosa. — My neighbor is too curious.

la **curiosidad** — curiosity
Tengo curiosidad por conocer a Luisa. — I am curious to make Luisa's acquaintance.

aburrido, a — boring
Tu marido es muy aburrido. — Your husband is very boring.

perezoso, a — lazy

bruto, a — gross; crude; unpolished
¡Qué bruto! — How crude!

enérgico, a — energetic; lively
La señora enérgica estuvo discutiendo con el policía. — The energetic woman was arguing with the policeman.

severo, a — severe; strict

agresivo, a — hostile; aggressive
La gente se vuelve agresiva al volante. — People get aggressive behind the wheel.

la **malicia** — malice; shrewdness
Su acción es mala pero él ha actuado sin malicia. — His action was bad, but he acted without malice.

el, la **cobarde**   coward

cobarde   cowardly
¡Qué cobardes sois!   How cowardly you are!

arrogante   arrogant

insoportable   unbearable; intolerable
La burocracia es insoportable.   Bureaucracy is intolerable.

avaro, a   greedy; avaricious

la **impuntualidad**   unpunctuality; lateness; tardiness

informal   unreliable; informal
Me fastidia la gente informal.   Unreliable people annoy me.

despistado, a   absent-minded

vago, a   vague; idle; lazy
¡Mira que eres vago!   My, but you're lazy!

el, la **sinvergüenza**   scoundrel; brazen; shameless
                                     person
Los camareros de este hotel son unos The waiters in this hotel are
sinvergüenzas.   scoundrels.

fresco, a   fresh; impertinent; insolent
¡Ese tío es un fresco!   This fellow is impertinent!

terco, a   stubborn
Mi padre es muy terco.   My father is very stubborn.

vulgar   coarse; vulgar
Antonia, ¡no seas vulgar!   Antonia! Don't be vulgar!

confiado, a   trusting; unsuspecting
Rafa es demasiado confiado.   Rafa is too trusting.

vengativo, a   vindictive; vengeful
No hay que ser vengativo.   One shouldn't be vindictive.

abandonado, a   careless; sloppy; abandoned
Juan es muy abandonado.   Juan is very careless.

desordenado, a   disorderly; messy
Eres muy desordenado.   You're very messy.

ambicioso, a   ambitious; greedy

pesimista   pessimistic

━━━━━━━━━━━ **Positive Feelings** ━━━━━━━━━━━

el **sentimiento**
Mis sentimientos hacia ti no han
cambiado.

feeling
My feelings toward you have not
changed.

sentir
Siento que no puedas venir.

feel; regret; be sorry
I'm sorry that you can't
come.

la **sensación**

feeling; sensation

feliz
Feliz Año Nuevo.
Los novios son felices.

happy
Happy New Year.
The bride and groom are happy.

la **alegría**
Me has dado una gran
alegría.

joy; merriment
You have given me great
joy.

alegrarse
Me alegro de volver a verte.
Me alegro de que estés bien.

be glad; be happy
I'm glad to see you again.
I'm glad that you are well.

contento, a
¿Estás contenta de estar en Sevilla?

contented; happy
Are you happy to be in Seville?

tranquilo, a
¡Usted tranquila!

calm; quiet; tranquil
Don't worry!

la **simpatía**

Vale más la simpatía que el dinero.

sympathy; liking; friendly feeling;
charm
Friendly feelings are worth more
than money.

querer
Te quiero.

want; love; like
I love you.

el **amor**
El general se mató por amor a la patria.

love
The general killed himself for love
of his fatherland.

el **cariño**
Te tengo mucho cariño.

fondness; affection; love
I'm very fond of you.

apreciado, a
Su abuelo era muy apreciado como
ingeniero.

appreciated; esteemed; valued
His grandfather was a highly
esteemed engineer.

gustar
Me gustas mucho.

be pleasing; like
I like you very much.

tener ganas
Tengo ganas de volver a Venezuela.

desire; wish to
I wish to return to Venezuela.

loco, a
Estoy loco por ti.

crazy; insane
I'm crazy about you.

la emoción
¡Qué emoción!

tension; emotion
How thrilling!

---

la **felicidad**
Muchas felicidades por tu
cumpleaños.

happiness
Happy birthday.

afectuoso, a
Afectuosos saludos de tu amiga
Irene.

affectionate; cordial; fond
Kind regards from your friend
Irene.

cordial
Vuestras relaciones son muy
cordiales.

cordial; friendly
Your relationship is very cordial.

el **placer**

pleasure

la **confianza**
Ten confianza en mí.

confidence; trust
Have confidence in me.

confiar
Confío poco en los médicos.

trust (in); rely (on)
I don't trust doctors much.

la **esperanza**

hope

encantar

enchant; delight

entusiasmar
A Andrea le entusiasma el teatro.

enrapture
Andrea is enraptured by the
theater.

entusiasmarse
Mi mujer se entusiasma con el
fútbol.

become enthusiastic
My wife gets enthusiastic about
soccer.

alegrar

please; make happy; exhilarate

la **ilusión**
Me hace ilusión ir a cenar contigo.

eagerness; illusion; hopefulness
I'm looking forward to having
dinner with you.

emocionarse
Mi abuelito se emociona cuando
oye tangos.

be moved; touched
My granddad is moved when he
hears tangos.

emocionante
Es una película muy emocionante.

thrilling; moving
It's a very moving film.

tranquilizarse
¡Tranquilícese, no ha pasado
nada!

calm down
Calm down, nothing
happened!

apasionarse
No te apasiones por la política.

become impassioned
Don't get passionate about politics.

la **pasión**
La pasión de mi suegro son los toros.

passion; suffering
Bullfights are my father-in-law's passion.

impresionar
Granada me ha impresionado mucho.

impress; affect
Granada impressed me greatly.

la **impresión**
Tengo la impresión de que me engañas.

impression
I have the impression that you're deceiving me.

atraer
La música atrajo al público.

attract
The music attracted an audience.

la **atracción**
Marta tiene una atracción muy especial.

attraction
Marta has a very special allure.

el **estímulo**
Este premio será el estímulo para seguir trabajando tan bien.

stimulus; inducement
This prize will be an inducement to continue the good work.

la **satisfacción**
Terminar un trabajo bien es una satisfacción.

satisfaction
It is satisfying to finish a task well.

Negative Feelings

triste
No estés triste.

sad
Don't be sad.

la **tristeza**
La lluvia me da tristeza.

sadness
Rain makes me sad.

llorar
Tengo ganas de llorar.

cry
I feel like crying.

la **lágrima**

tear

la **vergüenza**
Me da vergüenza hablar del pasado de mi familia.

shame
I'm ashamed to talk about my family's past.

enfadarse

become angry; become furious

Vicente se ha enfadado contigo.

Vicente is furious with you.

enfadado, a

angry; enraged; furious

aburrirse
Me aburro viendo la tele.

become bored
I get bored watching TV.

preocupado, a
Estoy preocupado por lo que tarda Carolina en volver.

worried; preoccupied
I'm worried because Carolina is slow in returning.

nervioso, a
La impuntualidad me pone nerviosa.

nervous
Tardiness upsets me.

la **envidia**
El jefe se ha puesto verde de envidia.

envy
The boss turned green with envy.

envidioso, a
Lucas está envidioso de su hermanita.

envious
Lucas is envious of his little sister.

el **miedo**
No tengo miedo a la oscuridad.

fear
I'm not afraid of the dark.

temer
Temo que me estás mintiendo.

fear
I fear that you're lying to me.

odiar
Odio las guerras.

hate
I hate war.

---

el **disgusto**

quarrel; unpleasantness; annoyance

Pepa tuvo un disgusto con su primo.

Pepa had a quarrel with her cousin.

el **suspiro**

sigh

soportar
No soporto los gritos.

bear; put up with
I can't bear screaming.

la **preocupación**
Las preocupaciones enferman.

worry; concern
Worry makes you ill.

desesperado, a

desperate; hopeless

desilusionado, a

disappointed; disillusioned

desilusionarse

experience a disappointment; become disillusioned

fastidiar
¿No te fastidia?

annoy; displease
Isn't that enough to annoy you?

la **rabia**

rage; rabies

el **rencor** Margarita no guarda rencor.	rancor; animosity; grudge Margarita doesn't carry a grudge.
tener celos Tengo celos de mi mujer.	be jealous I'm jealous of my wife.
asustarse Los precios de este verano nos han asustado.	be frightened The prices this summer frightened us.
el **susto** ¡Vaya susto!	fright; scare; shock Oh, what a fright!
intranquilo, a	uneasy; restless
la **angustia** Las familias de los heridos esperaban noticias con angustia.	fear; anxiety Full of anxiety, the families of the injured waited for news.
el **odio** No siento odio por nadie.	hatred I don't hate anyone.
tener mal genio	to be ill-tempered

¿Tiene mal genio este niño o alguien lo molestó?
Does this boy have a bad temper or has
somebody annoyed him?

97

9 | Thinking

pensar
Piensa ir mañana.

think
He's thinking about going tomorrow.

saber
Ayer supe que venías.

know; learn; be able (can)
Yesterday I learned that you would come.

No sé ruso.
¿Sabes dónde está Inés?

I don't know Russian.
Do you know where Inés is?

creer
Creo que no me ha comprendido, ¿qué crees?

believe; think
I believe he didn't understand me. What do you think?

entender
No entiendes a tu mujer.

understand
You don't understand your wife.

comprender
No he comprendido su explicación.

understand; comprehend
I didn't understand your explanation.

inteligente
Eres una chica inteligente pero has hecho una tontería enorme.

intelligent; smart
You're a smart girl, but you've done an extremely foolish thing.

la **razón**
Tiene usted razón.

reason; right; sense
You are right.

darse cuenta
No se ha dado cuenta de que soy extranjera.

realize
He didn't realize that I'm a foreigner.

reconocer
No la reconozco.

acknowledge; recognize
I don't recognize her.

decidir
Hemos decidido comprar la casa.

decide; determine
We have decided to buy the house.

resolver
Miguel prefiere resolver sus problemas solo.

solve
Miguel prefers to solve his problems unaided.

imaginarse
Imagínese lo que ha subido el autobús.

imagine
Imagine how expensive riding the bus has become.

inventar
¿Qué inventó Juan de la Cierva?

invent; devise
What did Juan de la Cierva invent?

recordar
No recuerdo el título del libro.

remember
I don't remember the title of the book.

acordarse
No me acuerdo de su nombre.

remember
I don't remember his name.

olvidar
He olvidado la cartera.

forget
I forgot my billfold.

olvidarse
Carmen acabará olvidándose de ti.

forget
Carmen will finally forget you.

dudar
Dudo que venga.

doubt
I doubt that she will come.

equivocarse
Se ha equivocado de número.

be mistaken; make a mistake
You have reached the wrong number.

reflexionar
Tengo que reflexionar sobre esto.

think; reflect
I have to think about it.

analizar

analyze

el **pensamiento**
No se me va del pensamiento.

thought; mind
I can't get it out of my mind.

el **genio**

genius

el **filósofo**; la **filósofa**
Ortega y Gasset fue un filósofo español muy conocido.

philosopher
Ortega y Gasset was a famous Spanish philosopher.

la **inteligencia**
No es cuestión de inteligencia.

intellect; skill; intelligence
It's not a question of intelligence.

intelectual
El trabajo intelectual cansa tanto como el corporal.

intellectual
Intellectual labor is as tiring as physical labor.

razonable
Parece ser una chica razonable.

sensible; reasonable
She seems to be a sensible girl.

sabio, a
Amalia se cree muy sabia.

wise; learned
Amalia considers herself very learned.

culto, a

cultured; cultivated

la **lógica**
Lo que dices no tiene lógica.

logic
There's no logic to what you say.

lógico, a
¡Lógico! ¡Claro que sí!

logical
Logical! Of course it is!

opinar
El ministro opina que hay que ahorrar más.

be of the opinion; think
The minister is of the opinion that we need to save more.

el **punto de vista**
Desde tu punto de vista parece ser razonable.

point of view; standpoint
From your standpoint it seems to be reasonable.

presumir	presume; surmise
comparar	compare
¿Has comparado la copia con el original?	Have you compared the copy with the original?
la **comparación**	comparison
Toda comparación es odiosa.	Every comparison is lame [hateful].
la **previsión**	foresight; prediction; forecast
¿Has oído la previsión del tiempo para mañana?	Have you heard the weather forecast for tomorrow?
el **invento**	invention
El invento de Juan de la Cierva fue el autogiro, un avión con características de helicóptero.	The invention of Juan de la Cierva was the autogiro, an aircraft with helicopter features.
la **idea**	idea
No puedes hacerte ni la idea de lo bien que he pasado las vacaciones.	You can't even imagine what a good time I had on vacation.
la **imaginación**	imagination; fantasy
Paco tiene poca imaginación.	Paco has little imagination.
la **duda**	doubt
No cabe la menor duda de que ha sido una equivocación.	There is not the slightest doubt that it was a mistake.
confundirse	be mixed up; wrong
Disculpe, me he confundido de habitación.	Excuse me, I got the rooms mixed up.
la **equivocación**	mistake; error
solucionar	solve

El primer hombre se pregunta, el segundo duda, el tercero tiene una idea.
The first man asks himself, the second one doubts, the third one has an idea.

Neutral Behavior

el **comportamiento**
Su comportamiento es
irresponsable.

behavior; conduct
Your behavior is
irresponsible.

comportarse
Alfonso se comportó como un
verdadero señor.

behave; conduct oneself
Alfonso behaved like a real
gentleman.

reaccionar

react

¿Cómo reaccionasteis al oír la noticia?

How did you react when you
heard the news?

demostrar
Demuestras poco interés.

demonstrate; show
You show little interest.

el **proyecto**
Tengo el proyecto de conocer
Navarra.

plan; project; intention
I plan to get to know
Navarre.

esperar
Espero que vengas pronto.

hope; wait
I hope you come soon.

fiarse
¿Es que no te fías de nosotros?

trust; depend (on)
Don't you trust us?

la **costumbre**
Es una buena costumbre.

custom; habit
It is a good habit.

acostumbrarse
Nos acostumbramos al ruido.

get used to
We got used to the noise.

la **conducta**
El preso fue puesto en libertad
por buena conducta.

conduct; behavior; deportment
The prisoner was released
for good behavior.

la **actitud**
La actitud de Miguel es muy
extraña.

attitude; position; posture
Miguel's attitude is very
strange.

portarse
Antonio se portó muy bien con
nosotros.

act; behave
Antonio behaved very well
toward us.

habitual

usual; habitual

la **reacción**
No entiendo su reacción.

reaction
I don't understand his reaction.

indiferente
Me es indiferente si te pones el
vestido rojo o el negro.

indifferent
I don't care whether you wear the
red dress or the black one.

espontáneo, a — spontaneous

imitar — imitate
Roberto sabe imitar el canto de los pájaros. — Roberto can imitate birdcalls.

aprovechar — utilize; make good use of
Tiene que aprovechar mejor el tiempo. — You need to utilize your time better.
Juan aprovecha todo a fondo. — Juan utilizes everything thoroughly.

la **oportunidad** — opportunity

▬▬▬ Positive Behavior ▬▬▬

crear — create; establish; found
Dalí creó una obra singular. — Dalí created an unusual work.

intentar — try; attempt; intend
Ana intenta conseguir trabajo. — Ana is trying to get work.

mantener — maintain; keep up (conversation)

la **intención** — intention; purpose
Ha sido sin mala intención. — There was no evil intention.

realizar — carry out; realize

conseguir — attain; get; obtain; succeed in
Conseguimos un vuelo económico. — We got an inexpensive flight.
Al final has conseguido romper con la tradición familiar. — You have finally succeeded in breaking with family tradition.
Conseguí que me devolvieran el dinero. — I got them to return the money to me.

insistir — insist; persist; keep on
Señorita, insista en la llamada. — Miss, insist on getting the call through.

el **éxito** — success
La artista tuvo mucho éxito. — The artist had great success.

el **interés** — interest
Pablo tiene interés en hablar con Luis. — Pablo is interested in talking to Luis.

interesarse — be interested in; take an interest
Me interesa la pintura moderna. — I'm interested in modern painting.

la **atención**
Preste atención a las señales de tráfico.

attention
Pay attention to the road signs.

preocuparse
Nos preocupamos del asunto.
¡No se preocupe, ya vendrá!

worry
We're worried about the matter.
Don't worry, he'll come yet!

respetar

respect

responsable
Usted se hace responsable de lo que pase.

responsible
You're responsible for what might happen.

evitar

avoid

la **calma**

calm; quiet

fijarse

¿Te has fijado en el vestido que lleva la señora?

take notice (of); pay attention (to)
Have you noticed the dress the lady is wearing?

interesado, a
Luisa está interesada en comprar el piso.
Es un tipo muy interesado.
Sólo quiere ganar dinero.

interested; mercenary; selfish
Luisa is interested in buying the apartment.
He's a very mercenary fellow.
All he wants is to earn money.

interesar

interest

el **propósito**
Me he hecho el propósito de estudiar inglés.

intention; purpose; aim
I have made up my mind to study English.

la **voluntad**
¿Lo has hecho por tu propia voluntad?

will
Did you do it of your own free will?

esforzarse
Juan se tiene que esforzar para aprender portugués.

exert oneself; try hard
Juan has to try hard to learn Portuguese.

el **empeño**
Para lograr el éxito hay que poner empeño.

earnest desire; effort
To succeed, you have to make an effort.

empeñarse
Rosa se empeña en que compremos un vídeo.

insist
Rosa insists that we buy a VCR.

procurar
Procuramos estar bien con todo el mundo.

try
We try to get along well with everyone.

lograr
¿Logró hablar por teléfono?

obtain; succeed
Did you succeed in making a
phone call?

la responsabilidad
No cargo con la responsabilidad.

responsibility
I assume no responsibility.

la fidelidad

faithfulness; honesty;
constancy

obedecer
Obedezcan siempre las leyes del
tráfico.

obey
Always obey the traffic
regulations.

salvar

save; rescue

la moral
¿Qué es la moral?

morals; morality
What is morality?

Negative Behavior

la tontería
Estas señoras se pasan el día
hablando de tonterías.

foolishness; nonsense
These women spend all day
talking about nonsensical
things.

Has hecho una tontería vendiendo
la moto tan barata.

You did something foolish by
selling the motorcycle so
cheaply.

amenazar
El ladrón nos amenazó con un cuchillo.

threaten
The thief threatened us with a
knife.

hacer faltas
Cuando hablo deprisa hago faltas.

make mistakes
When I speak fast, I make
mistakes.

fracasar
Si preparas bien el examen no
fracasarás.

fail
If you prepare well for the test,
you won't fail.

ofender
Me siento ofendida.

offend
I feel offended.

burlar
El ladrón burló la vigilancia.

deceive; ridicule
The thief deceived the watchmen.

burlarse
¿Te estás burlando de mí?

make fun of
Are you making fun of me?

oponerse
Los mineros se opusieron al cierre de la mina.

resist; oppose
The miners opposed the closing of the mine.

vengarse
Juan se vengó por el asesinato de su hermano.

take revenge
Juan took revenge for the murder of his brother.

estropear

damage

aprovecharse

take advantage of; make the most of

¡No te aproveches de los amigos!

Don't take advantage of your friends!

abusar
El alcalde abusa de su autoridad.

abuse; take undue advantage of
The mayor abuses his authority.

abandonar
El boxeador abandonó a los tres minutos.

give up; abandon
The boxer gave up after three minutes.

irresponsable
Es irresponsable que mueran tantos niños de hambre.

irresponsible; unaccountable
It is unaccountable that so many children die of hunger.

el **fracaso**
El negocio de tu hermano es un fracaso.

failure; downfall; fiasco
Your brother's business is a failure.

confundir
Casimiro confundió la marcha atrás con la primera.

confuse
Casimiro confused reverse gear with first.

provocar
Me está provocando con sus palabras.

provoke; anger
You're provoking me with your words.

insultar
Perdone, no le he querido insultar.

insult; affront
Forgive me, I didn't mean to insult you.

la **ofensa**
Por una ofensa personal se han declarado guerras.

offense; insult
Wars have been declared on account of a personal insult.

la **amenaza**
Subrayó su amenaza sacando la pistola del bolso.

threat; menace
She underscored her threat by taking the pistol out of her handbag.

el **pretexto**
Marisa no vino a la boda con el pretexto de estar enferma.

pretext
Marisa didn't come to the wedding, under the pretext of being ill.

decepcionar
Nos decepcionó el concierto.

disappoint
The concert disappointed us.

envidiar
Te envidio la suerte que tienes.

envy
I envy you your good fortune.

desconfiar
¡Desconfía de malos amigos!

mistrust; have no confidence in
Have no confidence in false
friends!

la venganza
La venganza será terrible.

revenge
The revenge will be terrible.

el provecho
Sólo piensa en su propio provecho,
es un egoísta.

advantage; gain; profit
He thinks only of his own gain;
he is an egoist.

el abuso
Se acusa al ministro de abuso de poder.

abuse
The minister is accused of abuse
of power.

el abandono
No soporto el abandono.

neglect; sloppiness
I don't tolerate sloppiness.

Criminal Behavior

el crimen

crime

cometer
El crimen se cometió entre las
2 y las 5 de la mañana.

commit
The crime was committed between
2 and 5 A.M.

el ladrón; la **ladrona**

thief

el robo

theft; robbery

robar

steal; rob

asaltar

assault

el asalto

assault

cruel

cruel; remorseless

matar
Durante la guerra mataron a mucha
gente.

kill
During the war many people were
killed.

el contrabando
Actualmente se está haciendo mucho
contrabando de drogas.

smuggling
Nowadays there is a lot of drug
smuggling.

clandestino, a

secret; clandestine

el, la **delincuente**	criminal; delinquent
el **delito**	crime; transgression of the law
asesinar	assassinate; murder
García Lorca fue asesinado.	García Lorca was murdered.
el **asesino**; la **asesina**	murderer; assassin
El asesino fue el jardinero.	The murderer was the gardener.
el **asesinato**	murder
Ha sido un robo con asesinato.	It was murder with robbery.
el **ratero**; la **ratera**	pickpocket
el **atracador**; la **atracadora**	bank-robber; gangster
estafar	swindle
el **estafador**; la **estafadora**	swindler
ilegal	illegal
la **violencia**	violence; force
abusar	rape; abuse
Durante horas abusaron de la chica.	For hours they abused the girl.
violar	rape
Mató a su hermano por violar a su hija.	He killed his brother for raping his daughter.
espantoso, a	frightful, awful
¡Qué espantoso!	How frightful!
el **horror**	horror; frightfulness
Me da horror el aumento del número de delincuentes.	I am horrified by the number of offenders.
el **chantaje**	blackmail
el **atentado**	outrage; crime; transgression

capaz de
Corín es capaz de nadar dos horas
sin parar.

capable (of); able (to)
Corín is able to swim for two
hours without stopping.

hábil
Mi mujer es muy hábil.

skillful; capable; gifted
My wife is very capable.

la **competencia**
Este asunto no es de su competencia.

competence; province
This matter is not within her
province.

planear
¿Ya habéis planeado las vacaciones?

plan
Have you planned your vacation
yet?

impedir
Miguel no pudo impedir que el
almacén se quemara.

prevent; hinder
Miguel could not prevent the
warehouse from burning down.

ordenado, a
No eres muy ordenado pero eres
muy buen organizador.

orderly; neat; tidy
You're not very tidy, but
you are a good organizer.

dinámico, a
Los agentes de bolsa son muy
dinámicos.

dynamic; energetic
Stockbrokers are very dynamic.

violento, a

Como María es un poco violenta,
nos dejó en una situación muy violenta.

violent; impetuous; desperate;
harsh
Since María is a little impetuous,
she got us into a very harsh
situation.

formal
Carlos es un comerciante formal.

reliable; serious
Carlos is a reliable businessman.

franco, a
Para ser franco, no sé cómo me
he olvidado de tu santo.

open; frank
To be frank, I don't know how
I could forget your name [saint's]
day.

diplomático, a
Hay que ser un poco diplomático con
el jefe.

diplomatic
You have to be a little diplomatic
with the boss.

decidirse
Me he decidido a estudiar medicina.

decide; determine
I have decided to study medicine.

decidido, a
Marta es una artista muy decidida.

determined
Marta is a very determined artist.

indeciso, a
Cuando tengo que elegir un
regalo soy muy indeciso.

undecided; hesitant; indecisive
When I have to choose a gift,
I am very indecisive.

considerado, a
Tu comportamiento me parece
poco considerado.

prudent; considerate; thoughtful
Your behavior doesn't seem
very prudent to me.

comprensivo, a
Ayer encontramos un policía
comprensivo.

understanding
Yesterday we met an
understanding policeman.

objetivo, a
Los jueces deberían ser
objetivos e imparciales.

objective; factual; unprejudiced
Judges ought to be objective and
impartial.

imparcial

unprejudiced; impartial

generoso, a
En general los españoles son generosos.

generous
In general, Spaniards are
generous.

divertido, a
La señora Florentino es una persona
muy divertida.

amusing; entertaining
Mrs. Florentino is a very
entertaining person.

confesar
Confieso que no fui prudente.

confess
I confess that I was not
cautious.

revelar
Angeles me reveló un secreto.

reveal, divulge
Angeles divulged a secret to me.

seducir
Es un buen amante porque sabe
seducir a las mujeres.

seduce
He is a good lover because he
knows how to seduce women.

convencer
Tus argumentos no me convencen.

convince
Your arguments don't convince
me.

convencido, a
Miguel está convencido de que tiene
razón.

convinced
Miguel is convinced that he is
right.

la **habilidad**
Pedro tiene mucha habilidad
para el arte.

ability; skill
Pedro has great artistic
ability.

la **capacidad**
Jesús tiene gran capacidad para las
lenguas.

capacity; ability
Jesús has great talent for
languages.

la **facultad**

faculty; power

la **decisión**
Tenemos que tomar una decisión para
que no se repitan estos sucesos.

decision
We have to make a decision, so
that these events don't repeat
themselves.

atreverse
No me atrevo decirte lo que he oído.

dare; venture
I don't dare to tell you what I heard.

la paciencia
Las enfermeras tienen mucha paciencia con algunos enfermos.

patience
Nurses have a lot of patience with some patients.

resistir
Estoy segura de que Pablo resistirá mientras pueda.

resist; bear; endure
I am sure that Pablo will resist as long as he can.

la impaciencia
Tu impaciencia no nos ayuda a resolver este problema.

impatience
Your impatience doesn't help us solve this problem.

el organizador; la **organizadora**

organizer

planificar
La urbanización está bastante bien planificada.

plan; design
The development is fairly well planned.

procurar
Los ecologistas procuran salvar la naturaleza.

endeavor; try; procure
Ecologists are trying to save nature.

competente
Esta profesora no me parece muy competente.

competent; able; qualified
This teacher doesn't seem very competent to me.

luchador(a)
Annalisa se abrirá paso porque es muy luchadora.

combative
Annalisa will get her way because she is very combative.

astuto, a
Rosa no es inteligente pero es astuta como una zorra.

cunning; sly
Rosa is not very intelligent, but she is as cunning as a fox.

distraído, a
Estáis muy distraídos hoy, ¿qué os pasa?

innattentive; absent-minded
You're very absent-minded today; what's wrong with you?

espléndido, a
Teresa siempre ha sido muy espléndida conmigo.

generous; splendid
Teresa has always been very generous to me.

la ignorancia
Tu ignorancia es enorme.

ignorance
Your ignorance is enormous.

ignorante
¡Hombre! ¡No seas tan ignorante!

ignorant; dumb
Man, don't be so stupid!

el creador; la **creadora**
¿Quién es el creador de esta moda?

creator, originator; God
Who is the creator of this fashion?

Speaking

hablar
¿Puedo hablar con el director de la empresa?

speak; talk
May I speak to the company manager?

la **voz**

voice

alto, a
No es necesario que hables tan alto, te oigo muy bien.

loud
It's not necessary for you to talk so loud; I hear you very well.

gritar
¡No me grite!

shout; scream at
Don't shout at me!

el **grito**
Esmeralda habla a gritos.

cry; scream
Esmeralda talks at the top of her voice.

bajo, a
Hablad más bajo que los niños están durmiendo.

low
Talk in a lower voice, the children are sleeping.

la **conversación**
Carlos y Mayte estuvieron de conversación durante toda la hora de clase.

conversation; talk
Carlos and Mayte were holding a conversation during the entire class.

charlar
Ayer estuve charlando con Angel sobre mi viaje.

chat
Yesterday I was chatting with Angel about my trip.

decir
¿Qué quieres que te diga?

say; tell
What do you want me to tell you?

la **palabra**

word

expresar
Honorio expresó su malestar.

express; utter
Honorio expressed his discomfort.

llamar
Te está llamando tu madre.

call
Your mother is calling you.

repetir
¿Puede repetir su pregunta más despacio?

repeat
Can you repeat your question more slowly?

el **asunto**

matter

el **caso**

case

conversar
Estábamos conversando,
cuando sonó el teléfono.

converse; talk; chat
We were talking
when the phone rang.

la charla
Las charlas en la televisión me
aburren.

chat; informal address
The talk shows on TV bore me.

pronunciar
Los canarios pronuncian la "z"
como "s".

pronounce
Canary Islanders pronounce
the Spanish "z" as "s."

el acento

accent

el lenguaje

language; style

el término
Antonia emplea siempre
muchos términos técnicos.

term; word
Antonia always uses a
lot of technical terms.

referirse
Los alumnos no saben a qué
se está refiriendo usted.

refer
The pupils don't know what
you are referring to.

callarse
¡Cállese que no tiene razón!

be silent; still; quiet
Be quiet, you're wrong!

chillar

scream, screech

el discurso

speech; discourse

la discusión
No permito más discusiones.

discussion; argument
I allow no further discussion.

discutir
No tengo úlcera porque nunca
discuto.

discuss; argue
I don't have an ulcer because I
never argue.

etcétera

and so forth

la expresión
¿Me puede explicar esa expresión?

expression
Can you explain this expression to
me?

maldecir

curse; damn

justificar

justify

■■■■■ Informing, Asking, and Answering ■■■■■

informarse
Quiero informarme sobre
las excursiones a Toledo.

inquire (into); find out (about)
I would like to find out about
excursions to Toledo.

la **noticia**

news

informar
Les informaremos cuando
tengamos más noticias.

inform
We will inform you as soon
as we have more news.

la **información**
No puedo darle más informaciones.

information
I can't give you any more
information.

es **decir**
Es decir, que no venís.

that is; that is to say
That is, you aren't coming with us.

anunciar
Ya están anunciando la salida del
vuelo.

announce
The departure of the flight is
already being announced.

proponer

propose; suggest

indicar
¿Me puede indicar la combinación
más rápida a Sevilla?

indicate; show; tell
Can you tell me the quickest
connection to Seville?

avisar

Por favor, avíseme cuando
lleguemos a la Plaza de Catalunya.

Nos avisan que van a quitar la luz.

inform; announce; give notice of;
warn; advise
Please inform me when we
get to Catalunya Square.

They warn us that the lights will
go out.

recomendar
¿Qué restaurante me
puede recomendar?

recommend
Which restaurant can you
recommend to me?

explicar
Llegamos tarde porque nos
explicaron mal el camino.

explain
We're arriving late because they
explained the way to us
incorrectly.

la **explicación**
No tengo que darte ninguna
explicación.

explanation
I don't owe you any
explanation.

describir
Tu cuñada es tal como me la habías
descrito.

describe
Your sister-in-law is just the way
you described her to me.

113

el **comentario**
En esta literatura española se
encuentran comentarios sobre la vida
en diferentes épocas.

commentary
In these Spanish writings we find
commentaries on life in different
epochs.

comentar
La prensa comenta las últimas
publicaciones literarias.

comment; expound
The press comments on the
latest literary arrivals.

la **pregunta**
No entiendo tu pregunta.

question
I don't understand your question.

preguntar
¿Puedo preguntarle una cosa?

ask
May I ask you something?

la **respuesta**
No tengo ninguna respuesta a tales
preguntas.

answer; response
I have no response to such
questions.

responder
¿Por qué no me respondes?

answer; respond
Why don't you answer me?

consistir
¿En qué consiste el problema?

consist
What does the problem consist of?

reciente
Acabo de recibir noticias
recientes de Colombia

new; recent
I have just received recent
information from Colombia.

declarar
El ministro declaró que su
viaje fue un éxito.

declare; make known
The minister declared that
his trip was a success.

la **declaración**
El testigo confirmó sus
declaraciones anteriores.

declaration; statement
The witness confirmed his
previous statements.

el **dato**

datum

el **informe**
En el informe interno de la empresa
sólo hay buenas noticias.

report
In the company's internal report
there is only good news.

la **novedad**

novelty; recent occurrence

comunicar
Me han comunicado que hay
huelga de taxistas.

notify
I've been notified that
there is a taxidrivers' strike.

el **mensaje**

notification; message

aconsejar
¿Qué me aconsejáis?

advise; counsel; recommend
What do you recommend to me?

el **consejo**
Deberías seguir mi consejo.

advice; suggestion
You ought to follow my advice.

la **recomendación** ¿Me puede dar una carta de recomendación?	recommendation Can you give me a letter of recommendation?
el **aviso** ¿Cuándo ha llegado el aviso de correos?	notification; notice; advice When did the postal notice arrive?
enterarse	learn; find out about
el **detalle**	detail
aclarar	explain; make clear
la **cuestión** La cuestión es que no hay dinero.	question; problem The problem is that there is no money.
consultar	consult; ask for advice
contestar Tengo que contestar esta carta hoy mismo.	answer I have to answer this letter today.

▬▬▬ Excusing, Regretting, Consoling ▬▬▬

disculpar Disculpe, ¿está libre este sitio?	excuse Excuse me, is this seat vacant?
disculparse Hugo no se quiso disculpar por lo que había hecho.	apologize Hugo didn't want to apologize for what he had done.
perdonar Perdone que le haya pisado.	pardon; forgive Forgive me for stepping on you.
sentir Lo siento mucho.	feel; regret; be sorry I am very sorry.
lamentar Lamentándolo mucho cerramos el restaurante los domingos.	regret To our great regret, we are closing the restaurant on Sundays.
desgraciadamente	unfortunately
consolar El tío consuela a la viuda.	console The uncle consoles the widow.
consolarse El niño se consoló con un caramelo.	console; comfort oneself The boy consoled himself with a piece of candy.

115

la **lástima**	pity
¡Qué lástima!	What a pity!
¡Qué lástima que vivas tan lejos!	What a pity that you live so far away!

(el) **perdón**	pardon; forgiveness
Le pido perdón por las molestias.	I ask your forgiveness for the disturbance.
la **disculpa**	apology; excuse
No me vengas con disculpas.	Don't come to me with excuses.
la **excusa**	apology; excuse
Siempre tienes excusas para llegar tarde.	You always find an excuse for arriving late.
¡Qué pena!	What a pity!
¡Qué pena que no puedas venir a la fiesta!	What a pity that you can't come to the party!
el **consuelo**	consolation
Es un consuelo que no llevaras dinero cuando te robaron.	It is a consolation that you carried no money when you were robbed.

Agreeing, Rejecting, Forbidding, Allowing

sí	yes
¿Fumas?—Yo sí pero mi hermana no.	Do you smoke?—Yes, but my sister doesn't.
estar de acuerdo	agree; be in agreement, accordance
No estamos de acuerdo con la política del gobierno. ¿Estamos de acuerdo?	We are not in agreement with the government's policy. Do we agree?
aceptar	accept
está bien	fine; (it's) all right, okay
Está bien que suban los precios pero no tanto.	It's all right that they raise prices, but not so much.
¡Vale!	All right!; Okay!; Agreed!
¿Vamos al cine esta noche?—Sí, ¡vale!	Are we going to the movies this evening?—Yes, all right!
por supuesto	of course; naturally
¿Me acompañas a casa?—Por supuesto.	Will you escort me home?—Of course.

claro
¿Te vienes con nosotros?—Claro
que voy.
¿Estáis de acuerdo?—¡Claro
que no!

of course; certainly
Are you coming with us?—Of
course I'm coming.
Do you agree?—Certainly
not!

rechazar
Hay que rechazar la destrucción de
la naturaleza.

reject; repel; resist
The destruction of nature has to
be resisted.

no

no; not

nada
¿Desea algo más?—No, nada más.
Es todo.

nothing
Would you like something else?
—No, nothing more. That's all.

de ninguna manera

De ninguna manera quiso darme
la razón.

in no way; not at all; by no
means
In no way did he want to admit
that I was right.

al revés

on the contrary

poder
¿No puede darnos más información?

be able; can; may
Can't you give us more
information?

dejar

let; allow

prohibir
Te prohíbo que fumes en mi coche.

forbid; prohibit
I forbid you to smoke in my
car.

prohibido, a
Está prohibido que los perros
se bañen en las playas.

forbidden; prohibited
No dogs are allowed in the
water at the beach.

renunciar
Los autores renunciaron a seguir
discutiendo con el editor.

refuse; decline; renounce
The authors refused to
continue arguing with the
publisher.

permitir
¿Me permite pasar?

allow; permit; let
Will you let me through?

permitido, a
En esta casa están permitidas las
visitas después de las doce de
la noche.

allowed; permitted
In this building, visits after
midnight are allowed.

el **permiso**
Con su permiso.

permission
Excuse me!

en contra de
Todos decidieron en contra de tu
propuesta.

against
Everyone decided against your
proposal.

conforme
¿Estás conforme con mis planes?

acquiescent; compliant
Will you go along with my plans?

la aprobación

approval; consent

aprobar
Don Marcelino no aprueba la conducta de sus hijas.

approve (of)
Don Marcelino does not approve of his daughters' conduct.

tolera
No tolero que me traten como a un niño.

tolerate; permit
I don't tolerate their treating me like a child.

reconocer

acknowledge; admit

legalizar

legalize

la prohibición

prohibition; ban

contradecir
No me contradigas porque sabes que tengo razón.

contradict
Don't contradict me, because you know I'm right.

negar
El presidente negó su culpa.

deny
The president denied his guilt.

negarse
Me niego a creer esa historia.

refuse
I refuse to believe this story.

hacer reproches
No le hagas reproches; él es así.

make reproaches; criticize
Don't reproach him. That's just how he is.

ni siquiera
Ni siquiera ha venido a visitarme una sola vez.

not even
Not even once did he come to visit me.

quejarse
¡No te quejes tanto!

complain; grumble
Don't complain so much!

en ningún caso
En ningún caso se devolverá el importe del pasaje.

in no case
In no case will travel costs be refunded.

al contrario

on the contrary

¡Qué va!
Habrá sido muy caro el regalo, ¿no?—¡Qué va!

Nonsense! Not true!
The gift was probably very expensive, wasn't it?—Nonsense!

¡Basta!

That's enough!, Enough!, Stop that!

¡Basta ya de bromas!

Now that's enough joking!

Exhorting and Wishing

pedir
Me ha pedido que vuelva pronto.

request; ask
He asked me to come back soon.

deber
Debimos llamar a tu madre para
decirle que ya es abuela.

ought; must; should
We should have called your
mother to tell her that she's a
grandmother now.

no deber
Manuel no debe tomar dulces
porque se lo ha prohibido el
médico.

ought; must; should not
Manuel should not eat sweets
because the doctor told him
not to.

¡Vamos!; ¡Vámonos!
¡Vámonos a la playa!

Come on!; Let's go!
Let's go to the beach!

¡Fuera!
¡Fuera! ¡Salga inmediatamente
de aquí!

Out!
Out! Get out of here right now!

¡Cuidado!
¡Cuidado! ¡No te quemes
con la vela!

Look out!
Look out! Don't burn
yourself on the candle!

¡Ojo!
¡Ojo con los bolsos! En esta
calle hay muchos ladrones.

Look out!, Pay attention!
Keep an eye on your handbags!
There are a lot of thieves in this
street.

ojalá
Ojalá tengas buen tiempo en Bilbao.

Allí llueve mucho.

I hope
I hope you have nice weather in
Bilbao.
It rains a lot there.

desear
Le deseo mucha suerte.

wish
I wish you lots of luck.

(las) felicidades
Te deseo muchas felicidades
por tu cumpleaños.

congratulations; felicitations
I wish you a very happy birthday.

felicitar
Clara no me ha felicitado todavía.

congratulate
Clara hasn't congratulated
me yet.

querer
¿Qué quieres?

want; desire; wish
What do you want?

necesitar

need; require

119

rogar
Le ruego que baje un poco la tele porque no me deja dormir.

request; beg; entreat
I beg you to turn your TV down a little, because it keeps me awake.

solicitar

solicit; apply for

¡Anda!
¡Anda! ¿Qué haces tú por aquí?

Look at that!, Well, I never!
Well, I never! What are you doing here?

¡Socorro!
¡Socorro! Me ahogo.

Help!
Help, I'm drowning!

el **deseo**

wish; desire

preciso, a

necessary

(la) **enhorabuena**
Enhorabuena por tu éxito en los exámenes.

congratulation
Congratulations on passing your exams.

la **petición**
Hemos presentado una petición al alcalde.

petition; request
We have presented a petition to the mayor.

exigir
Exija siempre el certificado de garantía.

demand; require
Always demand a warranty.

conviene
Conviene que estudies más para ese examen.

it is advisable
It's advisable that you study more for this exam.

pretender

require; (lay) claim

la **felicitación**
Mi más cordial felicitación por su matrimonio.

congratulation; felicitation
Congratulations on your marriage.

Confirming and Qualifying

confirmar
Quiero confirmar mi vuelo de regreso.

confirm
I would like to confirm my return flight.

comprobar

verify; confirm; check

exacto, a
Exacto, aquí está su reserva de asiento.

exact; correct; right
Right, here is your seat reservation.

cierto, a
Te aseguro que todo lo que
te he dicho es cierto.
Las noticias ciertas deberían
salir más en la prensa.

true; certain; sure
I assure you that everything I've
told you is true.
True news ought to appear
more often in the press.

asegurar
El mecánico les aseguró que
arreglaría el camión para el lunes.

assure; affirm
The mechanic assured them that
he would repair the truck by
Monday.

¡Así es!
Cada vez creo menos en los políticos.
—¡Así es!

That's true!, Right!, Same here!
I believe politicians less and less.
—Same here!

desde luego
Hay excepciones, desde luego.

of course; naturally
There are exceptions, of course.

¡Eso es!
Así que nos veremos mañana.—Eso es.

That's right!, Exactly!, Right!
So we'll see each other
tomorrow.—Right!

de todos modos

at any rate, anyway

¿verdad?
Me has comprendido, ¿verdad?—
¡Claro que sí!

Isn't it?, Isn't that so?
You understood me, didn't you?—
Of course!

por cierto
Por cierto, ¿qué tal te ha ido por
Venezuela?

by the way
By the way, how did things go for
you in Venezuela?

quizá(s)
Quizás iré al cine hoy.

perhaps; maybe
Maybe I'll go to the movies
today.

Quizás venga Rafael pronto del
trabajo.

Perhaps Rafael will
come back from work soon.

a propósito
A propósito, ¿cuándo nos vemos?

by the way; incidentally
By the way, when will we see
each other again?

la **afirmación**

affirmation

afirmar
Afirmaron su inocencia.

affirm; declare; assert
They asserted their innocence.

la **confirmación**
Necesitamos una confirmación de
su pedido.

confirmation
We need a confirmation of your
order.

la **regla**

rule; regulation

evidente
Es evidente que cada vez llueve
menos en España.

obvious; clear; evident
It is obvious that it is raining less
and less in Spain.

garantizar
Me garantizaron que terminarían el
trabajo hacia marzo.

guarantee, vouch for; assure
They assured me that they
would finish the work by March.

¡Ya lo creo!
¿Son buenas las pistas de esquí
de Guadarrama?—Ya lo creo.

Of course!, You bet!
Are the Guadarrama ski
courses good?—Of course!

la **excepción**

exception

reservado, a
Reservado para minusválidos.

restricted; reserved
Reserved for the handicapped.

Particles of Speech

igual
¿Quieres café o té?—Me es igual.

equal
Would you like coffee or tea?
—It's all the same to me.

a ver
A ver, ¿quién ha cogido mi cartera?
De todos modos nunca llevo dinero.

let's see
Let's see, who took my billfold?
I never carry money in it anyway.

en fin
En fin, ya veremos cómo
encontramos un piso.
Es que han subido mucho los
alquileres.

finally; in short; well
Well, we'll see about finding an
apartment.
The rents have gone up a lot, you
know.

¡Vaya!

Well!; Indeed!

¡Qué lío!
¡Vaya! ¡Que mala suerte tienes!

What a mess!
Well! What bad luck you have!

es que

you know; for; you see

por decirlo así
Asturias es, por decirlo así, la Suiza
española.
—Pues a mí no me lo parece.

so to speak; as it were
Asturias is, so to speak, the
Switzerland of Spain.—
Well, I don't think so.

o sea

that is (to say); in other words;
then

pues
¿Has terminado el trabajo? ¡Pues,
vámonos!

then; since; because; well
Have you finished work? Then
let's go!

entonces
Entonces no conocéis el Norte de
España.

then
Then you aren't familiar with
northern Spain.

por si acaso
Siempre llevo el dinero en el bolsillo del pantalón por si acaso.

just in case
Just in case, I always carry money in my pants pocket.

total
Total, que te quieres casar con él.—¿Y qué?

in short; to sum up
In short, you want to marry him.—What of it?

¿Y qué?

Well?, So what?, What of it?

¡Ahí va!
¡Ahí va! Nos olvidamos de las llaves del coche.
—O sea, que tendremos que tomar un taxi.

Good Lord!, Oh!, Damn!
Damn! We forgot the car keys.
—Then we'll have to take a taxi.

¡Cielos!

Heavens!

¡Caramba!

Wow! Great guns!

Los españoles conversan y discuten sobre cualquier cosa.
Spaniards discuss and argue over anything.

13 | Making Evaluations

Statements and Positions

estar seguro, a
Estoy segura de que tu marido nos engaña.

be sure; certain
I am sure that your husband is cheating us.

creer
No creo que podamos ayudarles en este asunto.

believe; think
I don't think we can assist you in this matter.

la opinión
En mi opinión, se deberían legalizar las drogas duras.—No soy de tu opinión.

opinion; view
In my opinion, they ought to legalize hard drugs.—I don't share your opinion.

opinar
¿Qué opina usted?

think
What do you think?

juzgar
¿Cómo juzgarías esta obra?

judge
How would you judge this work?

parecer
¿Qué le parece a usted esta traducción?

appear; seem; look like
How does this translation seem to you?

considerar
Considero a Dalí un verdadero genio.

consider
I consider Dali a true genius.

pensar
Roberto pensó que le iban a suspender en el examen.

think
Roberto thought he would not pass the exam.

el hecho

fact

suponer
Supongo que has traído las llaves del coche.

suppose; assume
I assume that you have brought the car keys.

necesario, a

necessary

probable

probable; likely

en cuanto a
En cuanto a su pedido, le enviamos las muestras a vuelta de correo.

as for; as regards
As regards your order, we are sending you the samples by return mail.

corriente

ordinary; common; regular; standard

Empleas telas corrientes para hacer cortinas.

Use ordinary fabrics to make curtains.

exagerar
¡No exageres! Tanto no has bebido.

exaggerate
Don't exaggerate! You haven't
drunk that much.

---

el **juicio**
A nuestro juicio, esta película es
muy mala.

judgement; thinking
In our judgement, this film is very
poor.

el **concepto**

thought; concept; opinion

el **criterio**

criterion; judgement

la **conclusión**
Vicente llegó a la conclusión de que
este proyecto no valía la pena.

end; conclusion
Vicente came to the conclusion that
this project is not worthwhile.

el **resumen**

summary

resumir

summarize

el **parecer**
Me interesa su parecer sobre la
literatura moderna.

opinion; view
Your opinion of modern
literature interests me.

opuesto, a
Sobre la guerra hay
opiniones opuestas.

opposite; opposing
There are opposing
opinions about war.

verdadero, a

true; genuine

relativo, a

relative; respective

correspondiente

corresponding

indispensable
Es indispensable que
paguemos las cuentas.

indispensable; vital; essential
It is essential that
we pay the bills.

la **necesidad**

necessity

hacer falta

be necessary

esencial
Lo esencial no es la cantidad,
sino la calidad.

essential
The essential thing is not the
quantity, but the quality.

la **probabilidad**

probability

■ Positive Evaluations ■

apreciar
Clara no supo apreciar el
regalo de sus padres.

appreciate; value; esteem
Clara was unable to appreciate
her parents' gift.

estimar
Clotilde estima mucho a su profesora.

estimate; esteem; judge
Clotilde holds her teacher in high
esteem.

tener suerte

be lucky

bien
Me parece muy bien que te tomes
vacaciones.

well; nice; very *(adverb)*
I think it's very nice that you're
taking a vacation.

mejor
Como tienes fiebre, será mejor que
te vayas a la cama.

better *(adverb)*
Since you have fever, it will be
better for you to go to bed.

bueno, a
¿Me puedes recomendar un buen libro?
—Bueno, ahora no recuerdo ninguno.
Pero en una buena librería
encontrarás alguno.

good *(adjective)*
Can you recommend a good book
to me?—Well, I can't think of one
at the moment. But you'll find
one in a good bookstore.

mejor
Este piso es mejor que el mío.

better *(adjective)*
This apartment is better than mine.

el, la **mejor**
Por favor, dénos la mejor fruta que
tenga.

best
Please give us the best fruit you
have.

excelente
Tomás es un amigo excelente.

excellent
Tomás is an excellent friend.

extraordinario, a
Don Quijote vivió aventuras
extraordinarias.

extraordinary
Don Quijote experienced
extraordinary adventures.

fantástico, a
El otro día vi una película fantástica
de Saura.

fantastic
The other day I saw a fantastic
film by Saura.

estupendo, a
Tuvieron la ocasión de ver un
partido de fútbol estupendo.

wonderful; stupendous
They had the opportunity to
see a wonderful soccer game.

maravilloso, a
Don Juan es un amante
maravilloso.

wonderful; marvelous
Don Juan is a marvelous
lover.

hermoso, a
pretty

famoso, a
famous; well-known
Guernica es el nombre de un pueblo
vasco y el título del famoso cuadro
de Picasso.
Guernica is the name of a Basque
village and the title of the famous
painting by Picasso.

perfecto, a
perfect

agradable
pleasant; agreeable
Conchita es una mujer muy
agradable.
Conchita is a very pleasant
woman.

posible
possible

la **posibilidad**
possibility

interesante
interesting
La mujer de Paco es una persona
muy interesante.
Paco's wife is a very
interesting person.

importante
important; significant

la **importancia**
importance; significance

valer la pena
be worthwhile
¿Vale la pena ver la obra de teatro?
Is it worthwhile to see the play?

preferir
prefer
¿Prefieres ir al cine en lugar de ir
a la ópera?—Como quieras.
Would you prefer to go to the
movies instead of the opera?—
Whatever you wish.

conveniente
useful; suitable; advantageous
Sería conveniente que discutiéramos
este problema.
It would be useful for us to discuss
this problem.

útil
useful
Estos mapas te van a ser muy
útiles para el viaje.
These maps will be very useful
to you for the trip.

práctico, a
practical
El ordenador es muy práctico.
Computers are very practical.

seguro, a
safe; sure

alabar
praise
Marisa alaba la paella que hizo su
marido.
Marisa praises the paella that her
husband made.

merecer
deserve

magnífico, a
magnificent, excellent
Ayer pasamos un día magnífico en
El Escorial.
Yesterday we spent a magnificent
day in The Escorial.

formidable
terrific; super
Tenéis un yate formidable.
You have a terrific yacht.

la **maravilla**
Es una maravilla bañarse en el Mediterráneo.

wonder, marvel
Swimming in the Mediterranean is marvelous.

ideal

ideal

apreciable
Su actitud es muy apreciable.

estimable; worthy
His attitude is very worthy.

majo, a
Tu hermano es un chico muy majo.

nice
Your brother is a very nice guy.

el **premio**
En 1990 Octavio Paz recibió el premio Nobel de Literatura.

prize, award
In 1990 Octavio Paz received the Nobel Prize for Literature.

el **mérito**

merit; value

el **valor**
Atahualpa es famoso por su valor.

bravery, valor
Atahualpa is famous for his bravery.

sorprendente

surprising, astonishing

preferible
Será preferible terminar este asunto hoy.

preferable
It will be preferable to finish this business today.

preferido, a
¿Cuál es tu plato preferido?

favorite
What is your favorite dish?

positivo, a

positive

la **ventaja**
Es una ventaja saber tantas lenguas.

advantage
It is an advantage to know so many languages.

corresponder
El sueldo no corresponde a su gran rendimiento.

correspond
The salary does not correspond to his great efficiency.

singular

unusual

Negative Evaluations

criticar
En Hispanoamérica se critica mucho la corrupción de los políticos.

criticize
In Spanish America, the corruption of the politicians is criticized greatly.

crítico, a
Su tío está en una situación muy crítica.

critical
His uncle is in a very critical situation.

tener mala suerte

have bad luck

mal

badly; poorly *(adverb)*

Esta casa está mal hecha.

This house is poorly built.

peor

worse *(adverb)*

Bartolo escribe peor que lee.

Bartolo writes worse than he reads.

malo, a

bad; evil *(adjective)*

Lo malo es que el mal café no mejora poniéndole azúcar.

The bad thing is that bad coffee is not improved by adding sugar.

peor

worse *(adjective)*

Mis peores alumnos saben más que tus mejores.

My worse pupils know more than your better ones.

el, la **peor**

worst

Prefiero la peor moto que ir a pie.

I prefer the worst motorcycle to going on foot.

pésimo, a

very bad; very worst

increíble

unbelievable; incredible

¡Es increíble! ¿Cómo has podido permitir que hagan tal cosa?

It's incredible! How could you allow them to do such a thing?

¡Por Dios!

For God's sake!, My God!

¡Por Dios! ¿Cómo has podido comprarte ese abrigo?

For God's sake! How could you buy that coat?

incorrecto, a

wrong; impolite

Es incorrecto saludar a los hombres antes que a las mujeres.

It is impolite to greet men before women.

raro, a

rare; odd

Tu abuelo es una persona bastante rara.

Your grandfather is a rather odd person.

terrible

terrible

Jaimito es un niño terrible.

Jaimito is a terrible boy.

horrible

horrible; awful; terrible

Llevas una corbata horrible.

You're wearing an awful tie.

peligroso, a

dangerous

¡Cuidado con ese tipo! Parece peligroso.

Be careful with that guy! He looks dangerous.

pesado, a

tiresome; annoying

Su madre es muy pesada. Siempre está quejándose.

Your mother is very annoying. She's always complaining.

antipático, a

uncongenial; disagreeable

Oye, ¡eres una tía antipática!

Listen here, you're a disagreeable old bag!

imbécil   imbecile; silly; half-witted

inútil   needless; useless; idiotic
Es inútil que la llames si no está   It's useless to call her if she isn't
en casa.   at home.

---

la **antipatía**   antipathy; dislike;
     unfriendliness
Somos famosos por nuestra antipatía.   We are well known for our
     unfriendliness.

despreciar   despise; scorn

incomprensible   incomprehensible
A Pablo le pareció incomprensible   The motive for the suicide seemed
el motivo del suicidio.   incomprehensible to Pablo.

el **prejuicio**   prejudice

inmoral   immoral
Mucha gente cree que el aborto es   Many people believe that abortion
inmoral.   is immoral.

extraño, a   strange; foreign
En esta casa se oyen ruidos extraños.   Strange noises are heard in this
     house.

reclamar   demand; complain about; send a
     reminder
Llamamos a la fábrica para reclamar   We called the factory to complain
unas piezas.   about some parts.
Me han reclamado el pago de la factura.   They sent me a reminder to pay
     the bill.

la **reclamación**; **reclamo**   complaint; claim
Aquí hay un error. Mandaré una   There's an error here. I will lodge a
reclamación al responsable.   complaint with the person
     responsible.

el **error**   error; mistake

falso, a   false
Los falsos amigos son más peligrosos   False friends are more dangerous
que los enemigos.   than enemies.

absurdo, a   absurd

fatal   fatal; disastrous; fated

odioso, a   odious; hateful
Las mentiras son odiosas.   Lies are hateful.

arbitrario, a   arbitrary
No toleramos decisiones arbitrarias.   We do not tolerate arbitrary
     decisions.

la **queja**	complaint; grumbling
Estoy harto de oír quejas.	I'm fed up with hearing complaints.
harto, a	full; enough; satiated
el **rollo**	tedious nonsense
idiota	idiotic
Eres idiota sin remedio.	You're hopelessly idiotic.
ridículo, a	ridiculous
Nos dieron una tortilla ridícula.	They gave us a ridiculously small omelet.
confuso, a	confused
negativo, a	negative
tremendo, a	tremendous; terrible
Está haciendo un calor tremendo.	It is terribly hot.
la **desventaja**	disadvantage
la **dificultad**	difficulty
monótono, a	monotonous
la **desgracia**	misfortune; disgrace
desagradable	disagreeable; unpleasant

Segun él la situacion es desagradable, idiota y absurda. Segun ella, es estupenda, hermosa y agradable.
According to him, the situation is unpleasant, idiotic, and absurd.
According to her, it is wonderful, beautiful, and pleasant.

la **familia**
Todos los domingos se reúne
la familia a comer.

family
Every Sunday the entire family
gathers for dinner.

el **abuelo**; la **abuela**; los **abuelos**

Su abuela sabía preparar un
gazpacho muy bueno.
Nuestros abuelos viven en Guatemala.

grandfather; grandmother;
grandparents; ancestors
His grandmother knew how to
make a very good gazpacho.
Our grandparents live in
Guatemala.

casarse

marry; get married

el **padre**; los **padres**
Rubén es padre de tres hijos.

Tus padres se casaron hace treinta años.

father; parents; ancestors
Rubén is the father of three
children.
Your parents married 30 years ago.

el **papá**
En aquellos tiempos nos llevaba
papá al fútbol.

papa; daddy; dad
In those days Papa took us to
soccer games.

la **madre**
Es difícil ser una madre soltera.

mother
It is hard to be a single mother.

la **mamá**
Mi mamá me mima mucho.

mama; mommy; mom
My mama spoils me a lot.

el **marido**
Ignacio es un marido muy atento.

husband
Ignacio is a very attentive husband.

la **mujer**
En España las mujeres casadas no
pierden su apellido de solteras.

wife; woman
In Spain, married women do not
forfeit their maiden names.

el **matrimonio**

El matrimonio de mis nietos es
muy feliz.
El matrimonio Vallés celebró sus
bodas de plata.

marriage; matrimony; married
couple
My grandchildren are very happily
married.
Mr. and Mrs. Vallés celebrated
their silver wedding anniversary.

el **novio**; la **novia**; los **novios**

Francisco tiene novia pero
no quiere casarse con ella.

fiance(e); bride; groom;
girl/boyfriend; engaged couple
Francisco has a girlfriend,
but he doesn't want to marry her.

el **hijo**; la **hija**; los **hijos**
¿Ya va tu hija a la escuela?

Tener hijos es más fácil que
mantenerlos.

son; daughter; children; sons
Does your daughter go to school
yet?
Having children is easier than
supporting them.

el, la **mayor** — oldest

Isabel es la mayor y Manuel es el menor de mis hermanos. — Isabel is the oldest and Manuel is the youngest of my siblings.

el, la **menor** — youngest

el **hermano**; la **hermana**; los **hermanos** — brother; sister; siblings; brothers

¿Eres hijo único?—No, tengo dos hermanas y un hermano. — Are you an only child?—No, I have two sisters and one brother.

Mi padre no tiene hermanos. — My father has no siblings.

el **suegro**, la **suegra**; los **suegros** — father-in-law; mother-in-law; parents-in-law

La suegra de Carmelo discute mucho con su madre. — Carmelo's mother-in-law argues a lot with his mother.

Los suegros quieren acompañar a los novios en su viaje de bodas. — The in-laws want to accompany the married couple on their honeymoon.

el **tío**; la **tía**; los **tíos** — uncle; aunt; uncle(s) and aunt(s); uncles

Nuestro tío es pintor y profesor de arte. — Our uncle is a painter and an art teacher.

Su tía nunca me ha caído bien. — I have never liked his aunt.

Todos tus tíos van a venir a la boda. — All your aunts and uncles will come to the wedding.

familiar — familiar; domestic

Las relaciones familiares son a veces muy confusas. — Domestic relations are sometimes very confused.

la **generación** — generation

prometerse — become engaged

Carmela y Roberto se han prometido. — Carmela and Roberto have become engaged.

la **boda** — wedding

Este año he estado en cinco bodas. — This year I attended five weddings.

separarse — separate

divorciarse — get divorced

Antes no se podía divorciar nadie en España. — Previously, no one in Spain could get divorced.

el **divorcio** — divorce

Mi marido ha pedido el divorcio. — My husband has filed for divorce.

el **huérfano**; la **huérfana** — orphan

el, la **pariente**
¿Cuántos parientes tienes en Bilbao?
—Mis tíos viven allí.

relative
How many relatives do you have
in Bilbao?—My uncle and aunt
live there.

el **yerno**
Voy a ser el padrino del primer hijo
de mi yerno.

son-in-law
I'm going to be the godfather of
my son-in-law's first child.

la **nuera**
Mi nuera no se entiende con mi
mujer.

daughter-in-law
My daughter-in-law doesn't get
along with my wife.

el **padrino**; los **padrinos**

godfather; sponsors

la **madrina**
Carlos no sabe quién es su madrina.

godmother
Carlos doesn't know who his
godmother is.

el **cuñado**; la **cuñada**;
los **cuñados**
Tienes una cuñada muy simpática.

brother/sister-in-law(s)

You have a very nice sister-in-law.

el **nieto**; la **nieta**; los **nietos**

grandson; granddaughter;
grandchildren
Sus padres están muy felices
con su primera nieta.
La abuela tiene más nietos que hijos.

Your parents are very happy
about their first granddaughter.
The grandmother has more
grandchildren than children.

el **primo**; la **prima**; los **primos**
Cuando veas a tu prima dale
recuerdos de mi parte.

cousin; cousins
When you see your cousin,
give her my regards.

el **sobrino**; la **sobrina**;
los **sobrinos**
¿Cómo se llamará vuestro sobrino?

nephew; niece; nephew(s) and
niece(s); nephews
What will your nephew be named?

los **gemelos**
Antonio y Vicente no son gemelos
aunque se parecen mucho.

twins
Antonio and Vicente are not twins,
although they look very much
alike.

Social Contacts

el **amigo**; la **amiga**
Jorge tiene pocos, pero buenos
amigos.

male friend; female friend
Jorge has few friends, but good
ones.

la **amistad**
No me gustan tus amistades.
Guardo mi amistad con Tomás
desde nuestra infancia.

friendship; circle of friends
I don't like your circle of friends.
My friendship with Tomás
goes back to our childhood.

el, la **amante**

lover

el **compañero**; la **compañera**
Anoche fuimos con los compañeros
de clase a cenar.

companion; fellow pupil; associate
Last night we went to dinner
with our classmates.

el, la **colega**
Me entiendo muy bien con mis
colegas.

colleague; fellow worker
I get along very well with my
colleagues.

el **conocido**; la **conocida**
Cuando estuve en Ceuta, me encontré
a varios conocidos.

acquaintance
When I was in Ceuta, I ran into
several acquaintances.

el **tío**

fellow; guy

la **cita**
A las diez tengo una cita con mi
corredor.

appointment; date
I have an appointment with my
broker at 10 o'clock.

quedar
Julián ha quedado con Ana para ir
al cine.
Hemos quedado con los colegas en
no trabajar mañana.

agree (to); make a date
Julián made a date with Ana to go
to the movies.
We agreed with our colleagues not
to work tomorrow.

visitar
Esta noche visitaremos a los señores
Ramírez.

visit
This evening we'll visit Mr. and
Mrs. Ramírez.

la **visita**
Voy a tener visita de mis compañeros.

visit
I'm going to get a visit from my
associates.

común
Daniel y tu prima tienen muchos
amigos comunes.

mutual; common
Daniel and your cousin have many
mutual friends.

colectivo, a
En México hay taxis colectivos.

collective; joint; communal
In Mexico there are shared taxis.

la **gente**
La gente de su barrio es muy amable.

people
The people in his part of town are very friendly.

el **grupo**
Todos los martes hacemos una excursión en grupo.

group
Every Tuesday we make a group excursion.

encontrar
Esta tarde encontramos a Teobaldo y sus amigos.

meet
This afternoon we met Teobaldo and his friends.

el **encuentro**
Vamos al encuentro de Julio.

meeting; encounter
We're going to meet Julio.

la **fiesta**
El viernes Roberto nos invitó a su fiesta.

party
On Friday Roberto invited us to his party.

invitar

invite

el **invitado**; la **invitada**
Como alcalde, serás nuestro invitado de honor.

guest
As mayor, you will be our guest of honor.

la **invitación**
El cónsul de Guatemala nos ha enviado una invitación para la recepción.

invitation
The consul of Guatemala has sent us an invitation to the reception.

la **recepción**

reception

la **presencia**

presence

reunirse
El domingo se reúne toda la familia para celebrar el santo del abuelo.

get together; gather
On Sunday the entire family is gathering to celebrate the grandfather's name day.

social
En Uruguay hay muchos problemas sociales.

social
In Uruguay there are many social problems.

la **humanidad**
La humanidad está destruyendo la tierra.

mankind; humanity
Mankind is destroying the earth.

la **relación**
Doña Teresa tiene buenas relaciones en el Ministerio del Interior.

relation; connection
Doña Teresa has good connections to the Ministry of the Interior.

el **contacto**	contact; connection
Marta se ha puesto en contacto con la señora Sánchez para comprar el coche.	Marta got in contact with Mrs. Sánchez in order to buy the car.
la **intimidad**	intimacy; close friendship; fellowship
Parece simpático pero en la intimidad es insoportable.	He seems nice, but in a close relationship he's intolerable.
cercano, a	near; close
lejano, a	far; distant
Paco es un pariente lejano.	Paco is a distant relative.
citarse	make an appointment
Me he citado con el jefe a las cuatro.	I made an appointment with the boss for 4 o'clock.
la **pareja**	pair; couple
la **compañía**	company
Nuestro gato nos hace mucha compañía.	Our cat provides a lot of company for us.
la **comunidad**	community
Hemos formado una comunidad de vecinos para defender nuestros derechos.	We have formed a citizens' group to protect our rights.
la **sociedad**	society; company
el **individuo**	individual
la **reunión**	meeting; gathering; reunion
Ayer se celebró una reunión de vecinos en el ayuntamiento.	Yesterday a citizens' meeting was held at City Hall.
el **club**	club
Mis nietos son socios de un club de golf.	My grandchildren are members of a golf club.
el **socio**, la **socia**	member
el **miembro**	member
Los miembros del Parlamento visitarán los países vecinos.	The members of Parliament will visit the neighboring countries.
la **reputación**	reputation
el **honor**	honor
Es un honor recibirles en mi casa.	It is an honor to receive you in my home.

Forms of Address, Greetings, Making Introductions, and Saying Goodbye

---

saludar
Discúlpenme, voy a saludar a esos señores.

greet
Excuse me, please, I would like to greet these gentlemen.

¡Hola!
¡Hola! ¿Qué tal?—Bien, ¿y tú?

Hello!
Hello! How are you?—Fine, and you?

¡Buenos días!
Buenos días, ¿cómo está usted?
—Muy bien gracias, ¿y usted?

Good morning!, Good day!
Good morning, how are you?
—Fine, thanks, and you?

¡Buenas tardes!
Buenas tardes, vengo a recoger los libros.

Good afternoon!
Good afternoon, I'm coming to pick up the books.

¡Buenas noches!
Buenas noches y que descanses.
Buenas noches. Qué bien verles otra vez.

Good evening!; Good night!
Good night, and sleep well.
Good evening. How nice to see you again.

¡Adelante!
¡Adelante! ¡Pase y tome asiento!

Come in!
Come in! Come in and have a seat!

el, la **siguiente**
Que pase el siguiente.

next one
Let the next person come in.

¡Adiós!
Adiós, hasta mañana.

Goodbye!
Goodbye, see you tomorrow.

¡Hasta luego!

So long! See you later!

¡Hasta pronto!

See you soon!

el **saludo**

greeting

conocer
Me alegro de haberte conocido.
¿Conoces a la novia de José?

know; meet
I'm glad to have met you.
Do you know José's fiancée?

presentar
Le presento a la señora Marco.
—Encantado.

present; introduce
I would like to introduce Mrs. Marco to you.—Delighted.

encantado, a

delighted; pleased to meet you

estimado, a
Estimado señor Valenti,
Estimados señores,

Dear (*opening of letter*)
Dear Mr. Valenti,
Ladies and Gentlemen:

querido, a	Dear *(opening of letter)*
Querida Gabriela,	Dear Gabriela,
Queridos amigos,	Dear Friends,
los **recuerdos**	regards
Recuerdos a tus padres.	Regards to your parents.
un **abrazo**	embrace; hug; warmly; cordially
Un fuerte abrazo de tu amigo.	Warmest regards from your friend.
cordialmente	cordially *(closing of letter)*
dar la bienvenida	welcome; bid welcome

tutearse	use the familiar "tú"
tratarse de usted	use the polite "usted"
despedirse	take leave; say goodbye
La señora López se está despidiendo de su familia.	Mrs. López is saying goodbye to her family.
la **despedida**	farewell; leave-taking
Anoche dimos una fiesta de despedida para José.	Last night we gave a farewell party for José.
hacer señas	wave
¡Oye!	Look here!, Now listen!
¡Oye, niño! ¡No toque eso!	Now listen, boy! Don't touch that!
¡Oiga!	Hey!, Look here!
¡Oiga! Por favor, tráiganos dos cafés.	Hello! Bring us two cups of coffee, please.
de parte de	on behalf of; in the name of; from
muy señor mío; muy señora mía	Dear Sir; Dear Madam *(opening of letter)*
excelentísimo, a	most excellent; Excellence
distinguido, a	Honored; Dear *(opening of letter)*
atentamente	yours faithfully; sincerely yours *(closing of letter)*
En espera de sus noticias, les saludamos atentamente.	Looking forward to your news, we remain yours faithfully.

■■■ Social Behavior and Modes of Conduct ■■■

abrazar
embrace

acompañar
accompany
Si quieres te acompaño al teatro.
If you wish, I'll accompany you to the theater.

con mucho gusto
gladly
¿Me puede prestar el bolígrafo un momento?—Con mucho gusto.
Would you lend me your ballpoint pen for a moment?—Gladly.

dirigirse a
address; speak; go to
Si tienen alguna pregunta, diríjanse a nuestra secretaria.
If you have any questions, please speak to our secretary.

agradecer
be grateful; thank
Agradecemos que estén dispuestos a ayudarnos.
We are grateful that you are ready to help us.

dar las gracias
thank; say thank you
¿Le has dado las gracias a tu tío por el regalo?
Have you thanked your uncle for the gift?

ayudar
help
Nadie quiso ayudarme.
Nobody wanted to help me.

la **ayuda**
help
Doña Clotilde es realmente una ayuda en esta oficina.
Doña Clotilde is really a help in this office.

contar con
count on
Si tenéis algún problema, podéis contar conmigo.
If you have any problem, you can count on me.

entenderse
understand one another; get along
Don José no se entiende con su primo.
Don José doesn't get along with his cousin.

deber
must; ought; should
Deberías cumplir tu promesa.
You ought to keep your promise.

la **promesa**
promise

cumplir
fulfill; perform one's duty
Por hoy hemos cumplido y nos podemos ir a casa.
We've done our duty for today and we can go home.

el **favor**
favor; compliment
¿Me puedes hacer el favor de ir a correos?
Will you do me the favor of going to the post office?

140

regalar
¿Qué te han regalado para tu
cumpleaños?

give as a present
What did they give you for your
birthday?

el **regalo**
Los señores Ramírez nos
hicieron un buen regalo.
En muchas familias españolas se
hacen los regalos el día de Reyes.

gift; present
Mr. and Mrs. Ramírez gave us a
fine gift.
In many Spanish families,
gifts are given at Epiphany.

sorprender

surprise; astonish

la **sorpresa**

surprise

misterioso, a

mysterious

devolver

give back; return

la **culpa**
Se ha roto el disco por tu culpa.

guilt; fault
It's your fault the record
broke.

engañar
Os han engañado con este coche.

deceive; cheat
They cheated you on this car.

molestarse
¡No se moleste usted!

bother; put oneself out
Don't go to any trouble!

la **molestia**

bother; trouble

pegar
¿Por qué has pegado al niño?

hit; beat; slap
Why did you hit the child?

el **golpe**

blow

pelearse
Carmelo y Antonia se pelean
todos los días.

scuffle; come to blows
Carmelo and Antonia come
to blows every day.

el **respeto**
No te mereces nuestro respeto.

respect
You don't deserve our
respect.

cortés
Jacinto es un chico muy cortés.

courteous; polite
Jacinto is a very polite
boy.

presentarse

present oneself; appear

ligar

join; make advances; pick up

estar relacionado, a
Estoy muy bien relacionada.

have good connections
I have very good connections.

excusar
Nos tenéis que excusar esta tarde.

excuse
You will have to excuse us this
afternoon.

prometer

promise

estar dispuesto, a
Paco está dispuesto a cuidar de los niños.

be ready
Paco is ready to take care of the children.

la **influencia**
Don Ramiro tiene mucha influencia política en este pueblo.

influence
Don Ramiro has great political influence in this village.

ocuparse de
No se preocupe. Me ocuparé en seguida de su problema.

worry about; attend to
Don't worry. I will attend to your problem at once.

el **deber**
Pablo cumple muy bien con todos sus deberes.

duty; obligation
Pablo meets all his obligations very well.

la **obligación**
Hombre, no es una obligación, pero lo haré con mucho gusto.

obligation; duty
Look, it's not an obligation, but I'll gladly do it.

obligar
No se sienta obligado a ayudarnos.

force; obligate
Don't feel obligated to help us.

cuidar de
Las enfermeras tienen que cuidar de los enfermos.

take care of
The nurses have to take care of the patients.

mimar

spoil

servir
¿En qué puedo servirle?

serve; be of use
How can I help you?

el **servicio**
Me has hecho un gran servicio trayéndome estos libros.

service
You have done me a great service by bringing me these books.

intolerante
Mucha gente es intolerante frente a minorías.

intolerant
Many people are intolerant of minorities.

tolerante
No todos tus amigos son tan tolerantes como yo.

tolerant
Not all your friends are as tolerant as I.

meterse
Se está metiendo usted en asuntos que no le importan.

meddle; interfere
You're meddling in matters that don't concern you.

mentir
¡No me mientas!

lie
Don't lie to me!

la **mentira**	lie
¡Eso es mentira!	That's a lie!
molestar	bother; annoy; disturb
Espero que no les moleste.	I hope I'm not disturbing you.
mendigar	beg
el **conflicto**	conflict
No quiero entrar en conflicto con su empresa.	I don't want to get into a conflict with your firm.

Social Phenomena

el **fenómeno**	phenomenon
el **machismo**	exaggerated sense of masculinity
el **machista**	man characterized by machismo
la **emancipación**	emancipation; liberation
emancipado, a	emancipated; liberated
la **feminista**	feminist
la **emigración**	emigration
la **integración**	integration
integrar	integrate

la **desigualdad**	inequality
la **soledad**	loneliness; solitude
aislado, a	isolated
el **chulo**	pimp
la **prostitución**	prostitution
discriminar	discriminate
el, la **pasota**	discouraged; apathetic youth
el **pasotismo**	apathetic attitude; indifference of youth
los **marginados (sociales)**	marginal groups of society
el **mendigo**; la **mendiga**	beggar

Relationships of Possession

tener
Ahora tengo mil discos.

possess; own; have
Now I have 1,000 records.

propio, a
Estos apartamentos tienen una
piscina propia.

own
These apartments have their own
swimming pool.

poseer
Don Camilo posee una biblioteca
enorme.

possess
Don Camilo possesses an
enormous library.

disponer
Disponemos de muchas posibilidades
para resolver su asunto.

have at one's disposal
We have at our disposal many
possibilities for settling your
business.

la **fortuna**
Nos ha costado una fortuna arreglar
el coche.

fortune
It cost us a fortune to repair the
car.

rico, a
Estos señores son muy ricos.

rich
These gentlemen are very rich.

pobre
Al final de mes siempre estoy muy
pobre.

poor
At the end of the month I'm
always very poor.

ser de
¿De quién es el libro?—Es mío y
la libreta también es mía.

belong
Whose book is this?—It's
mine, and the notebook is mine
too.

el **mío**; la **mía**; **los míos**;
las **mías**

mine

el **tuyo**; la **tuya**; los **tuyos**;
las **tuyas**
Estas llaves son las tuyas, ¿no?
—Sí, son las mías.

yours

These keys are yours, aren't they?
—Yes, they're mine.

el **suyo**; la **suya**; los **suyos**;
las **suyas**

his; hers; its; one's; yours

el **nuestro**; la **nuestra**; los
nuestros; las **nuestras**

ours

el **vuestro**; la **vuestra**; los
vuestros; las **vuestras**

yours

el **suyo**; la **suya**; los **suyos**;
las **suyas**

yours; theirs

mi; **mis**
Mis padres se van de vacaciones
mañana.

my
My parents are going on vacation
tomorrow.

tu; **tus**
¿Tu nieta también vive en Vigo?

your
Does your granddaughter also live
in Vigo?

su; **sus**

his; her; its; your

nuestro; **a**; **os**; **as**

our

vuestro; **a**; **os**; **as**

your

su; **sus**

your, their

---

pertenecer
¿A quién pertenecen estas tierras?

belong
To whom do these lands belong?

la **posesión**
La posesión de drogas duras está
prohibida en España.

possession
The possession of hard drugs is
prohibited in Spain.

particular

private

la **riqueza**
En este mundo las riquezas
están mal divididas.

riches; richness
In this world the riches are
unjustly divided.

el **lujo**

luxury

la **prosperidad**

prosperity

la **pobreza**
En Latinoamérica hay mucha pobreza.

poverty
In Latin America there is a great
deal of poverty.

la **miseria**

misery

el **testamento**

testament; will

heredar
He heredado una casa de campo.

inherit; deed to another
I have inherited a country house.

el **heredero**; la **heredera**

heir

repartir

divide; distribute

▬▬▬ Kindergarten, School, University ▬▬▬

el jardín de la infancia
Lucas ya va al jardín de la infancia, donde aprende jugando.

kindergarten
Lucas already goes to kindergarten, where he learns through play.

aprender
La señora Vázquez está aprendiendo a leer y a escribir.

learn
Mrs. Vázquez is learning to read and write.

enseñar
Mi prima me enseñará latín.

teach; train; show
My cousin will teach me Latin.

la enseñanza
En España la Enseñanza General Básica (E.G.B.) es gratuita.

teaching; education
In Spain, primary education is free of charge.

gratuito, a

gratis; free (of charge)

el colegio
En España los niños van a los siete años al colegio.

school
In Spain, children start school at the age of seven.

la escuela
¿A qué escuela va tu sobrino?

school
What school does your nephew go to?

la universidad

university

la carrera
Tomás ya ha acabado la carrera.

study; studies; career
Tomás has already concluded his studies.

la academia
Don Eulogio da clase de lengua en una academia.

academy; private school
Don Eulogio teaches languages at a private school.

el maestro; la maestra
¿Cómo era tu primera maestra?

(primary school) teacher
What was your first teacher like?

la clase
Nuestro hijo ya está en la segunda clase.
Esta tarde tenemos clase de historia.

¿Dónde está tu clase?
Mi clase aprende deprisa.

class; grade; classroom
Our son is already in second grade.
This afternoon we have history class.
Where is your classroom?
My class learns quickly.

dar clase
Mañana no daré clase porque es Pentecostés.

teach; give lessons
I won't teach tomorrow, because it is Pentecost.

el, la **estudiante**
Los estudiantes se tienen que
matricular para el próximo año.
Octavio es estudiante de Medicina.

pupil; student
The pupils have to register for the
next year.
Octavio is a medical student.

estudiar
El próximo año estudiaré en la
Universidad de Salamanca.
Enrique empieza a estudiar en
enero para los exámenes de junio.

study
Next year I will study at the
University of Salamanca.
Enrique is starting to study in
January for the exams in June.

el **profesor**; la **profesora**
Me ha dicho tu profesora que
no hiciste las tareas.
¿Conocéis algún profesor de la
Universidad de Alcalá de Henares?
—No, sólo conocemos unos
catedráticos.

teacher; instructor
Your teacher told me that you
didn't do your homework.
Do you know any of the
instructors at the University of
Alcalá de Henares?
—No, we only know some
professors.

la **ciencia**
A Maruja le entusiasma la ciencia.
Lo que habéis hecho no tiene ciencia.

science; knowledge
Maruja is enthusiastic about science.
What you have done is not difficult.

la **biblioteca**
En la biblioteca tienen muchos libros
de autores desconocidos y conocidos.

library
In the library they have many
books by unknown and well-
known authors.

conocido, a

well-known; prominent

desconocido, a

unknown

la **educación**
Ministerio de Educación y Ciencia
(MEC).

education; upbringing
Ministry of Education and
Science.

la **instrucción**

instruction

escolar
En España los alumnos tenían que
llevar uniforme escolar.

scholastic
In Spain, pupils had to
wear a school uniform.

obligatorio, a
Es obligatorio en España ir a la
escuela hasta los catorce años.

obligatory; compulsory
In Spain, school attendance is
compulsory until the age of 14.

el **analfabetismo**

illiteracy

el **instituto**
Hasta los catorce años tuve que ir a la
escuela, luego fui al instituto hasta
terminar el bachillerato para poder
matricularme en la universidad.

high (secondary) school; institute
Until I was 14 I had to go to
primary and middle school. Then
I attended high school until I
graduated, so that I could enroll
in the university.

matricularse · register; matriculate; enroll

la **matrícula** · registration; matriculation (fee)
La matrícula de los colegios puede ser muy cara. · The registration fees of private schools can be very steep.

el **director**; la **directora** · principal; director
La directora del instituto es simpática. · The principal of the high school is nice.

el **académico**; la **académica** · member of an academy
Los académicos forman las Academias. · The academy members form the Academies.

el **licenciado**; la **licenciada** · university graduate
Juana María es licenciada en filosofía y letras. · Juana María has a degree in philosophy and letters.

el **alumno**; la **alumna** · pupil; student
¿Cuántos alumnos sois en vuestra clase? · How many pupils are in your class?

universitario, a · university
La carrera universitaria dura cinco años en España, excepto Medicina. · In Spain, university studies last five years, except for medical school.

los **estudios** · studies
Mi padre se tuvo que pagar sus estudios dando clases particulares. · My father had to finance his studies by giving private lessons.

el **título** · diploma; degree
Cuando termines la carrera, ¿qué título recibirás? · When you finish your studies, what degree will you receive?

el **doctor**; la **doctora** · doctor
A veces el doctor es también un médico. · Sometimes a doctor is also a physician.

el **doctorado** · doctorate

doctorarse · obtain a doctorate

el **catedrático**; la **catedrática** · (full) professor

la **cátedra** · (professorial) chair; professorship
¿Quién va a ocupar la cátedra de Biología? · Who will hold the biology chair?

las **oposiciones** · competitive exams for professorships, etc.
Tomasa va a hacer oposiciones a la cátedra de Español. · Tomasa will take the competitive exams for the Spanish professorship.

el **lector**; la **lectora** · lecturer; instructor
Nuestra lectora de portugués es muy competente. · Our Portuguese instructor is very competent.

la **beca**	scholarship; fellowship
Voy a solicitar una beca para Estados Unidos.	I'm going to apply for a fellowship to study in the United States.
la **aula**	lecture room

Classroom Instruction

la **aula**
lecture room

asistir
Ayer no asistí a clase de chino

attend; be present
I didn't attend Chinese class yesterday.

el **dibujo**
¿Qué dibujaron los niños en la clase de dibujo?

drawing; sketch
What did the children draw in drawing class?

la **lección**
Como no se sabía la lección de memoria, el maestro le puso una mala nota.

lesson; lecture; reading
Since he didn't know the lesson by heart, the teacher gave him a bad grade.

de **memoria**
by heart

contar
¡A ver! ¿Quién sabe contar un cuento?

count; tell
Let's see! Who can tell a story?

la **letra**
letter

el **dictado**
La maestra nos hizo un dictado muy gracioso.

dictation
The teacher gave us a very funny dictation.

dictar
dictate

traducir
En clase no hemos traducido nada al latín.

translate
In class we didn't translate anything into Latin.

significar
¿Qué significa esta palabra?

mean
What does this word mean?

la **traducción**
Las traducciones al inglés me parecen muy fáciles.

translation
I think translations into English are very easy.

fácil
easy

difícil
hard; difficult

el **examen**
Al final de cada curso hay que presentarse a exámenes.

exam; test
At the end of each school year, one has to take exams.

examinarse
No me examiné de geografía porque estaba seguro de que me iban a suspender.

be tested; take an exam
I didn't take the geography exam, because I was certain that I would fail.

suspender

fail (an exam)

el **desconocimiento**
Suspendí el examen por desconocimiento del tema.

ignorance
I failed the exam through ignorance of the subject.

aprobar
Mi nieto aprobó todo el curso con matrícula de honor.

pass (an exam)
My grandson passed all his final exams with honor.

escrito, a

written

oral
¿Cuándo es su examen oral?
—El día dos será el examen escrito y el cinco el oral.

oral
When is your oral exam?
—The written exam will be on the 2nd and the oral on the 5th.

el **horario**
¡Mira en tu horario cuándo tienes clase de Español!

schedule
Look at your schedule to see when you have Spanish class!

el **bachillerato**

high school graduation; diploma

el **B.U.P.**
El B.U.P. es el Bachillerato Unificado Polivalente.

The B.U.P. is the Spanish high school degree.

la **evaluación**
El año pasado saqué malas notas en las evaluaciones de matemáticas.

evaluation; classroom test
Last year I got bad grades on my math tests.

la **nota**
En España la mejor nota es 10 y la peor 0.

grade; mark
In Spain, the best grade is 10 and the worst is 0.

corregir
Esta noche tengo que corregir estos cuadernos.

correct
Tonight I have to correct these notebooks.

el **cuaderno**

notebook; exercise book

la **libreta**

notebook; copybook

subrayar

underline

el **signo**

sign; symbol

la **pizarra**	blackboard
Puri: escribe en la pizarra lo que te dicte Antonio.	Puri, write on the blackboard what Antonio dictates to you.
la **tiza**	chalk
la **esponja**	sponge
la **tarea**	homework
el **recreo**	break; recess
Durante el recreo jugábamos al fútbol.	During recess we played soccer.

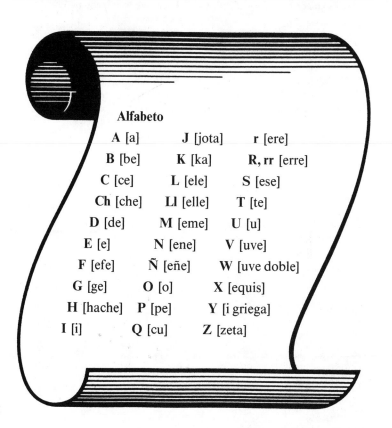

Alfabeto

A [a]	J [jota]	r [ere]
B [be]	K [ka]	R, rr [erre]
C [ce]	L [ele]	S [ese]
Ch [che]	Ll [elle]	T [te]
D [de]	M [eme]	U [u]
E [e]	N [ene]	V [uve]
F [efe]	Ñ [eñe]	W [uve doble]
G [ge]	O [o]	X [equis]
H [hache]	P [pe]	Y [i griega]
I [i]	Q [cu]	Z [zeta]

Teaching and Research

el **curso**
Quiero hacer un curso de español
para extranjeros en España.
Este año terminarás el
segundo curso de B.U.P.

course; course of study
I would like to take a Spanish
course for foreigners in Spain.
This year you will finish the
12th grade of high school.

el **certificado**
Necesito un certificado académico.

certificate
I need an examination
certificate.

el **tema**
¿Qué tema has escogido para el
ensayo?

topic; subject; theme
What topic have you chosen for
the essay?

el **ensayo**

essay

el **ejercicio**
Para mañana tenemos que
preparar estos ejercicios.

exercise; practice
For tomorrow we have to
prepare these exercises.

el **problema**

problem

la **gramática**

grammar

el **ejemplo**
No entendimos el ejemplo del
profesor.
España tiene grandes autores,
por ejemplo Cervantes y Larra.

example
We didn't understand the
teacher's example.
Spain has great writers,
for example, Cervantes and
Larra.

la **investigación**

research

la **falta**

mistake

apuntar

write down; make a
note of

Juan apunta en un cuaderno
las tareas.

Juan writes down the
homework assignments
in a notebook.

el **globo**
El primer globo de la tierra es del
siglo I a. C..

globe
The first globe dates from the first
century B.C.

la **solución**
A este problema no le encuentro
solución científica.

solution
I find no scientific
solution to this problem.

científico, a

scientific

el **método**	method
didáctico, a	didactic
sencillo, a	simple
Este problema matemático es muy sencillo pero nada simple.	This math problem is very simple, but not at all easy.
simple	easy; simple
investigar	do research on; investigate
El profesor García investiga problemas químicos.	Professor García does research on chemical problems.
el **laboratorio**	lab(oratory)
la **fórmula**	formula
la **estadística**	statistics

▬▬ Subjects of Instruction and Fields of Study ▬▬

la **asignatura**
¿Qué asignatura enseña usted?

subject (in curriculum)
What subject do you teach?

las **ciencias**

natural sciences (and mathematics)

En clase de ciencias siempre me duermo.

In science class I always fall asleep.

la **biología**
Marta es profesora de biología.

biology
Marta is a biology teacher.

las **matemáticas**
Don Jorge da clases de matemáticas.

mathematics
Don Jorge teaches mathematics.

la **química**
No soy bueno en química.

chemistry
I am not good in chemistry.

la **física**

physics

la **geografía**
¿Qué asignaturas tienes hoy?
—Tengo matemáticas, física, geografía y filosofía.

geography
What subjects do you have today?
—I have math, physics, geography, and philosophy.

las **letras**

letters; liberal arts; humanities

la **filosofía**
En la filosofía se piensa también sobre la creación del mundo.

philosophy
In philosophy one also thinks about the creation of the world.

la **historia**	history
la **lengua**	language; tongue
He aprobado el examen de lengua española.	I passed the Spanish language exam.
el **latín**	Latin
el **derecho**	law

la **especialidad**	major (subject of study)
la **facultad**	faculty; school
la **gimnasia**	gymnastics
La gimnasia es la asignatura preferida de Clara.	Gymnastics is Clara's favorite subject.
la **arqueología**	archeology
matemático, a	mathematical
la **teología**	theology
las **bellas artes**	art; fine arts
Alfonso ha estudiado pintura en bellas artes.	Alfonso studied painting at the Art Academy.
la **pedagogía**	pedagogy
la **psicología**	psychology

Vocational Training

la **formación**	training
En España la formación profesional son cuatro años.	In Spain, vocational training lasts for four years.
la **escuela de formación**	vocational (trade, technical) school
la **experiencia**	experience
Buscamos aprendices con experiencia práctica.	We are looking for trainees with practical experience.
la **práctica**	practice
¿Se necesita mucha práctica para arreglar un televisor?	Do you need much practice to repair a TV set?
el **conocimiento**	knowledge
Esta chica tiene conocimientos sorprendentes de medicina.	This girl has a surprising knowledge of medicine.
profesional	professional
Charo es una peluquera profesional.	Charo is a professional hairdresser.

dedicarse
¿A qué te vas a dedicar cuando termines el aprendizaje?

do professionally; devote oneself to
What will you do professionally when you finish your training?

especializarse
Rafael se especializó en la arquitectura de mezquitas.

specialize in
Rafael specialized in the architecture of mosques.

especializado, a
Este programa está especializado en problemas matemáticos.

specialized
This program specializes in math problems.

---

el **aprendiz**; la **aprendiza**
En esta empresa han hecho su aprendizaje dos aprendices.

trainee; apprentice
Two trainees have done their training in this company.

el **aprendizaje**

vocational training; apprenticeship

el **oficial**; la **oficiala**
El oficial todavía no es maestro.

journeyman
The journeyman is not yet a master craftsman.

el **maestro**; la **maestra**
Joaquín es maestro de mecánica.

master (craftsman)
Joaquín is a master mechanic.

teórico, a
Algunos camareros españoles no reciben formación teórica.

theoretical; academic
Some Spanish waiters receive no academic training.

la **teoría**
Las clases de teoría son bastante aburridas.

theory
The classes in theory are rather boring.

las **prácticas**
Arturo está haciendo unas prácticas de óptico.

practical training
Arturo is doing practical training to become an optician.

En el presente quedan muy pocas profesiones determinadas por sexo.
Currently, very few sex-determined professions remain.

17 | Professional Life

Professions

el, la **agente**
Tomás es agente de seguros.

representative; agent
Tomás is an insurance agent.

el **carnicero**; la **carnicera**
Muchas veces la carnicera es sólo
la mujer del carnicero.

butcher; meat vendor
Often the "carnicera" is only
the butcher's wife.

el **cocinero**; la **cocinera**

cook; chef

el **dependiente**; la **dependienta**
En los almacenes siempre encontramos
dependientas muy amables.

salesman; saleswoman; clerk
In department stores we always
come across very friendly
saleswomen.

el **empleado**; la **empleada**
Los empleados de oficina toman
un café antes de entrar a trabajar.

employee
The office employees drink
coffee before starting work.

el **funcionario**; la **funcionaria**
Tomás es funcionario porque le
gusta trabajar en la Administración.

public official
Tomás is a public official because
he likes working in the Civil Service.

el **inventor**; la **inventora**
El inventor Juan de la Cierva
murió en un accidente aéreo.

inventor
The inventor Juan de la Cierva
died in an aircraft crash.

el **jardinero**; la **jardinera**
El jardinero está regando las flores.

gardener
The gardener is watering the
flowers.

el **limpiabotas**
En Bogotá muchos niños son
limpiabotas.

bootblack
In Bogotá many children are
bootblacks.

el **mecánico**; la **mecánica**
El mecánico arregló el camión en
un momento.

mechanic
The mechanic repaired the truck
very quickly.

el **notario**; la **notaria**
El notario nos entregó la escritura.

notary public
The notary public handed us the
contract.

el **obrero**; la **obrera**
Muchos obreros españoles
emigraron en los años 60.

worker; laborer
Many Spanish workers
emigrated in the sixties.

el **panadero**; la **panadera**
En España los panaderos y los
pasteleros trabajan también los
domingos.

baker
In Spain, bakers and pastry
cooks also work on Sunday.

| el **pastelero**; la **pastelera** | pastry cook |

el **pastor**; la **pastora**
El pastor cuida el rebaño con
ayuda de su perro.

shepherd(ess); pastor; clergyman
The shepherd guards the flock
with the help of his dog.

el **peluquero**; la **peluquera**
La peluquera no me ha cortado el pelo.

hairdresser
The hairdresser didn't cut my
hair.

el **piloto**
Mi padre quiso ser piloto pero
no daba la talla.

pilot
My father wanted to be a pilot,
but he wasn't tall enough.

el **secretario**; la **secretaria**
Mi secretaria sabe muy bien español.

secretary
My secretary knows Spanish very
well.

el **trabajador**; la **trabajadora**

worker; laborer

el **zapatero**; la **zapatera**
El zapatero tendrá las botas para
el martes.

shoemaker
The shoemaker will have the boots
ready on Tuesday.

---

el, la **asistente**

assistant

el **bibliotecario**; la **bibliotecaria**
Como la biliotecaria está enferma
no puedo devolver los libros.

librarian
Since the librarian is ill,
I can't return the books.

el **chofer**; el **chófer**

chauffeur; driver

el, la **detective**
Pepe Carvalmo es un detective de
Barcelona.

detective
Pepe Carvalmo is a detective from
Barcelona.

el **farmacéutico**; la **farmacéutica**
El farmacéutico me dio unas
pastillas contra el dolor de cabeza.

pharmacist
The pharmacist gave me some
tablets for my headache.

el **fotógrafo**; la **fotógrafa**
El novio de mi hermana era
fotógrafo de publicidad.

photographer
My sister's fiance was a
commercial photographer.

el **ginecólogo**; la **ginecóloga**
¿Conoces una buena ginecóloga?

gynecologist
Do you know a good
gynecologist?

el **ingeniero**; la **ingeniera**
Los ingenieros no saben por
qué se rompió el muro del pantano.

engineer
The engineers don't know why
the wall of the dam broke.

el **inspector**; la **inspectora**
Los inspectores de Hacienda son
temidos.

inspector
Tax inspectors are feared.

el, la **intérprete** Mi hermana fue intérprete del presidente.	interpreter My sister was the president's interpreter.
el **joyero**; la **joyera** Ayer atacaron al joyero de la esquina.	jeweler; jewelry dealer Yesterday the jeweler on the corner was attacked.
el **labrador**; la **labradora** Los labradores no están contentos con la cosecha.	farmer; peasant The farmers are not satisfied with the harvest.
el **locutor**; la **locutora** La locutora de las noticias se equivoca mucho.	(radio) announcer The woman newscaster makes mistakes frequently.
el **óptico**; la **óptica** ¿Es muy difícil ser óptico?	optician Is it very difficult to become an optician?
el **peón**	day laborer
el **psicólogo**; la **psicóloga** Muchos psicólogos argentinos vinieron a España.	psychologist Many Argentine psychologists came to Spain.
el **relojero**; la **relojera** El relojero nos recomendó que compráramos un reloj nuevo.	watchmaker The watchmaker recommended that we buy a new watch.
el **traductor**; la **traductora** Los traductores se tienen que defender contra muchos ignorantes.	translator Translators have to defend themselves against many uninformed people.
el (**vendedor**) **ambulante**; la (**vendedora**) **ambulante**	street salesman; peddler
el **veterinario**; la **veterinaria** Como el gato se ha comido una serpiente, lo llevamos al veterinario.	veterinarian Because the cat ate a snake, we took it to the veterinarian.

Working World

el **oficio** ¿Qué oficio os gustaría aprender?	occupation; trade; business What trade would you like to learn?
el **trabajo**	work

ganar
Trabajamos mucho pero ganamos poco.

earn
We work a lot, but we earn little.

el jornal
Los campesinos que trabajan en la vendimia reciben un jornal.

salary; daily wage
The farm workers who help with the grape harvest receive a daily wage.

trabajar

work

la oficina
El trabajo de oficina puede ser muy aburrido.

office
Office work can be very tedious.

el personal
Todo el personal de esta empresa está asegurado.

personnel; staff
All the personnel of this firm are insured.

el puesto de trabajo
Cuando se pierde el puesto de trabajo a veces se recibe el subsidio de paro.

employment; job; workplace
If you lose your job, sometimes you get unemployment benefits.

fijo, a
¿Cuántos empleados fijos sois en la fábrica?

permanent
How many permanent employees are in your factory?

el subsidio de paro

unemployment benefits

el paro
El paro juvenil es un problema actual.

unemployment
Unemployment among young people is a current problem.

el parado; la **parada**
En España los parados sólo reciben seis meses el subsidio de paro.

unemployed person
In Spain, the unemployed receive unemployment benefits for only six months.

emigrar

emigrate

el salario
Los precios suben más que los salarios.

wages; salary
Prices are rising more than wages.

el sueldo
¿Cuánto cobras de sueldo?

salary; wages
How high is your salary?

jubilado, a
Don José tiene sesenta y cinco años y está jubilado.

retired; pensioned off
Don José is 65 years old and retired.

la pensión

pension

despedir
¿Quién os ha despedido?

dismiss; let go; fire
Who dismissed you?

el **despido**
El despido puede significar la
ruina de una familia.

dismissal; layoff
Dismissal can mean the ruin of a
family.

la **jornada**
En verano hacemos jornada única
de 7 a 2 de la tarde.

working day; workday
In summer we have a
continuous workday from
7 A.M. until 2 P.M.

el **trabajo temporero**

seasonal work

el **temporero**; la **temporera**

seasonal worker

manual
El trabajo manual puede ser muy caro.

manual; handy
Handiwork can be very
expensive.

pendiente

pending; due

el **pago**
El patrono no ha realizado
los pagos pendientes.

payment
The employer has not made
the payments due.

el **empleador**; la **empleadora**

employer

el **patrón**; el **patrono**; la **patrona**

employer; boss

la **huelga**
Los sindicatos han organizado
para mañana una huelga general.

strike
The unions have organized a
general strike for tomorrow.

el **sindicato**

union

organizar

organize; arrange

la **solidaridad**

solidarity

el **empleo**
Estamos buscando un empleo
desde hace dos años.

employment, job
We've been looking for a
job for two years.

el **enchufe**
Miguel está trabajando en
el banco por enchufe.

good connection
Miguel is working at the
bank because he has good
connections.

la **Oficina de Empleo**

employment office

solicitar
Ana ha solicitado un aumento de
sueldo.
He solicitado trabajo en la Seat.

apply for; solicit
Ana has asked for a raise in salary.

I have applied for work at
SEAT.

el **porvenir**
Esta actriz tiene un gran porvenir.

future
This actress has a great
future.

el **cargo**
¿Desde cuándo tiene usted el
cargo de diputado?

post; position; duty
How long have you held
the post of deputy?

la **función**

function; duty

laborable
Los días laborables se me hacen muy
largos.

workable; working
The working days seem very long
to me.

laboral
El abogado se especializó en derecho
laboral.

labor
The lawyer specialized in labor
law.

nombrar
Nicolás ha sido nombrado Secretario
General del Ministerio.

name
Nicolás has been named secretary-
general of the ministry.

el, la **especialista**
Los especialistas siguen investigando
el origen del Sida.

specialist; expert
The experts are continuing to
investigate the cause of AIDS.

el **campo**
En el campo de la informática hay
muchas posibilidades.

field
In the field of information
technology there are many
opportunities.

el **turno**
El turno de noche me es más
agradable que el turno de mañana.

shift
I prefer the night shift to the
morning shift.

la **seguridad social**
La seguridad social incluye el
seguro de enfermedad.

social security
Social security includes health
insurance.

el **seguro de desempleo**
El seguro de desempleo ha vuelto
a subir.

unemployment insurance
Unemployment insurance has
risen again.

¡Cuán grande es la variedad de trabajos en el mundo!
How large is the variety of jobs in the world!

■■■■ Business ■■■■

la **empresa**	company; firm; enterprise
el **jefe**; la **jefa** Cuando el jefe no está, aquí nadie trabaja.	boss When the boss is away, nobody here does any work.
dirigir Como no sabían dirigir la compañía acabaron vendiéndola.	manage; direct Because they weren't able to manage the company, they finally sold it.
la **compañía**	company
la **cooperativa** En España hay muchas cooperativas agrícolas.	cooperative In Spain there are many agricultural cooperatives.
el **departamento** En esta sucursal no hay un departamento de créditos.	department This branch has no credit department.
la **sucursal**	branch
fundar	found

el **empresario**; la **empresaria** Muchos empresarios están en la ruina.	entrepreneur Many entrepreneurs face bankruptcy.
el, la **contable** La contable se olvidó de pagar los impuestos.	bookkeeper; accountant The bookkeeper forgot to pay the taxes.
la **contabilidad** En esta empresa la contabilidad es llevada por computadora.	bookkeeping; accounting In this company, the bookkeeping is done by computer.
el, la **gerente** El gerente no sabía nada de su pedido.	manager The manager knew nothing about your order.
la **gestión**	management
la **secretaría** Puede recoger sus papeles en la secretaría.	secretary's office; secretariate You can pick up your papers in the secretary's office.
interno, a	internal

la **asociación**	association; partnership; union
Esta asociación tiene muchos problemas internos, por eso está en quiebra.	This association has many internal problems; that is why it is in bankruptcy.
la **quiebra**	bankruptcy; failure
la **sociedad anónima**	stock company

Trade and Services

la **economía**
La economía española ya no está en crisis.

economy
The Spanish economy is no longer in crisis.

económico, a
El señor Muñoz ha comprado un coche muy económico.
Según los estudios económicos se espera un aumento de la inflación.

economic(al); thrifty
Mr. Muñoz has bought a very economical car.
According to economic studies, inflation is expected to increase.

la **exportación**
Al principio nos dedicamos a la exportación de aceite de oliva.

export
Initially we engaged in the export of olive oil.

exportar
Colombia no sólo exporta café sino también plátanos.

export
Colombia exports not only coffee, but also bananas.

importar
¿Qué productos no se pueden importar en Chile?

import
What products may not be imported to Chile?

la **importación**
Luis lleva un negocio de importación de textiles.

import
Luis manages a clothing import business.

la **mercancía**
En la aduana retuvieron la mercancía.

merchandise; goods; wares
The goods were retained at customs.

el **comercio**
El comercio se queja por la introducción del I.V.A. (Impuesto sobre el Valor Añadido).

commerce; business; trade
Business complains about the introduction of the V.A.T. (Value Added Tax).

comercial
La secretaria lleva la correspondencia comercial de la empresa.

commercial; business
The secretary does the business correspondence of the firm.

el **negocio**

business; store

la **venta**
Este año la venta de aceite de
oliva no ha mejorado.

sale(s)
This year, sales of olive
oil did not improve.

la **condición**
No puedo aceptar sus condiciones
de compra.

condition
I can't accept your purchase
conditions.

la **compra**
La compra de esta casa ha
sido un buen negocio.

purchase; buying; shopping
The purchase of this house
was a good deal.

encargar
La secretaria me ha encargado de
este asunto.

entrust
The secretary entrusted this matter
to me.

consumir
En Navidades la gente consume más
que durante el resto del año.

consume; use
At the Christmas season,
people consume more than
during the remainder of the
year.

suministrar
¿Cuándo nos suministrarán el pedido
que les hicimos hace un mes?

supply; furnish; provide
When will you supply us with
the order that we placed a month
ago?

el **pedido**

order

la **factura**
En cuanto recibamos la factura
les enviaremos un cheque.

invoice; bill
As soon as we receive the
invoice, we will send you
a check.

el **contrato**
Aún no hemos firmado el
contrato.

contract
We haven't signed the contract
yet.

firmar

sign

la **firma**
La firma de este talón no es
válida.

signature
The signature on this check is not
valid.

la **agencia**
La agencia de seguros está
cerrada por vacaciones.

agency
The insurance agency is
closed for vacation.

el **seguro**

insurance

la **crisis**	crisis
la **inflación**	inflation
el, la **economista**	economist
Los economistas también se equivocan.	Economists also make mistakes.
la **empresa exportadora**	export company
Algunas empresas exportadoras tienen problemas con la aduana.	Some export companies have problems with customs.
comerciar	trade; engage in commerce
Comerciar al por menor estos productos no es buen negocio.	Selling these products at retail is not good business.
el, la **comerciante**	trader; merchant; dealer
Benito es un buen comerciante al por mayor.	Benito is a good wholesale dealer.
Vicente es uncomerciante muy formal.	Vicente is a very reliable businessman.
el, la **representante**	representative
Vicente trabajó muchos años de representante.	Vicente has worked for many years as a representative.
la **competencia**	competition; rivalry
En el mercado nacional hay mucha competencia entre los viajantes.	In the national market, there is a lot of competition among traveling salesmen.
competir	compete
Pronto van a competir muchas empresas en el mercado europeo.	Soon many firms will be competing in the European market.
la **colaboración**	collaboration
el, la **viajante**	traveling salesman
La vida de viajante debe ser muy dura.	The life of a traveling salesman must be very hard.
regular	regulate; govern; control
la **oferta**	offer; offering
La oferta y demanda regulan los precios.	Supply and demand govern prices.
la **demanda**	demand
la **muestra**	sample; specimen
el **surtido**	assortment; stock
Su surtido de muestras es muy interesante.	Your assortment of samples is very interesting.

el **costo**
El costo de la vida ha subido mucho.

cost; price; expense
The cost of living has risen greatly.

el **encargo**
Todavía no hemos podido realizar su encargo.

request; order
We have not yet been able to carry out your request.

la **carga**
La mula es un animal de carga.

burden
The mule is a beast of burden.

descargar
Hay que descargar los camione santes de que vengan más.

unload
The trucks have to be unloaded before more arrive.

el **consumidor**; la **consumidora**
Me parece que la protección al consumidor no ha mejorado mucho.

consumer
It seems to me that consumer protection has not improved much.

el **consumo**
El consumo de tabaco perjudica la salud.

consumption
The consumption of tobacco endangers health.

la **marca**
¿Qué marca de jerez prefieres?

brand
Which brand of sherry do you prefer?

la **garantía**
Algunos coches ya tienen tres años de garantía.

guarantee; warranty
Some cars now have a three-year warranty.

el **suministro**
El suministro se realizará por barco dentro de 15 días.

delivery; supply
Delivery will be made by ship within 15 days.

Industry and Handicraft

la **industria**
La industria española de automóviles ya no es nacional.

industry
The Spanish automobile industry is no longer state-owned.

industrial
Manuel vive en la zona industrial del puerto.

industrial
Manuel lives in the industrial area of the port.

la **fábrica**
En Cataluña hay fábricas textiles.

factory; mill
In Catalonia there are textile mills.

el **artículo**
Ya no fabricamos estos artículos.

article; product
We no longer make these products.

fabricar

make; manufacture

el **producto**

product; article

producir
En España se producen muchos artículos de alta calidad.

produce; make
In Spain, many high-quality products are made.

montar
En esta fábrica se montan coches.

assemble; put together
In this factory, cars are assembled.

la **artesanía**
En Perú los indios conservan su artesanía.

craftmanship; artisan work
In Perú the Indians maintain their craftmanship.

el **artesano**; la **artesana**
Algunos artesanos sólo trabajan con barro.

artisan; craftsman
Some craftsmen work only with clay.

industrializado, a
Algunos países hispanoamericanos no están bastante industrializados.

developed; industrialized
Some Spanish American countries are not sufficiently developed.

industrializar
Extremadura está por industrializar.

industrialize
Estremadura is not yet industrialized.

fundir

fuse; melt; blend

la **fundición**

La fundición de hierro es una industria principal en el norte de España.

smelting; casting; founding; foundry
Iron founding is a major industry in northern Spain.

la **cerámica**

ceramic art; ceramics

la **orfebrería**

gold or silver work

Agriculture, Fishing, and Mining

el **agricultor**; la **agricultora**
Los agricultores están preocupados
por el cambio de clima.

agriculturist; farmer
The farmers are worried
about the change in the
climate.

la **agricultura**
La agricultura tiene mucha
importancia en Latinoamérica.

agriculture; farming
Agriculture is very important
in Latin America.

la **producción**
La producción agrícola no disminuyó
en los últimos años.

production
Agricultural production did not
decline in the past few years.

agrícola

agricultural

el **latifundio**

large estate

el **campesino**; la **campesina**
Muchos campesinos son muy pobres.

farmer
Many farmers are very poor.

el **campo**
Los campos regados de Murcia y
Valencia se llaman huertas porque
se cultiva fruta y verdura.

field
The irrigated fields of Murcia and
Valencia are called "huertas"
because fruits and vegetables
are grown there.

el **cultivo**
El cultivo de arroz en España se
realiza principalmente en Valencia
y Murcia.

cultivation; growing
In Spain, rice is cultivated
primarily in Valencia and Murcia.

cultivar

cultivate; grow

la **tierra**
La tierra de Castellón es muy fértil.

soil
The soil of Castellón is very
fertile.

el **tractor**
El tractor es la máquina más
importante para el agricultor.

tractor
The tractor is the most important
machine for a farmer.

criar
En Andalucía se crían toros.

breed; bring up
In Andalusia, bulls are bred.

la **época de recogida**
Durante la época de recogida los
campesinos tienen mucho trabajo.

harvest season
During the harvest season, the
farmers have a lot of work.

recoger
Lucía siempre ayuda a recoger las
olivas.

pick; gather
Lucía always helps pick the olives.

el **ganado**	cattle
En esta finca tienen mucho ganado.	A lot of cattle are kept on this ranch.
el **pescador**; la **pescadora**	fisherman; fisher
la **pesca**	fishing; fishery; catch
Las catástrofes marítimas dañan la pesca.	Maritime disasters are harmful to fishing.
pescar	fish
la **mina**	mine

el **terrateniente**	landowner; landholder
la **cosecha**	harvest
Muchos andaluces emigran durante la época de la cosecha.	Many Andalusians emigrate during harvest season.
cosechar	harvest
¿Cuándo se cosechan las primeras naranjas?	When are the first oranges harvested?
fértil	fertile
La tierra en la región de Murcia es muy fértil.	The soil in the Murcia region is very fertile.
el **abono**	fertilizer
El abono natural es mejor que el químico.	Natural fertilizer is better than chemical.
la **viña**	vineyard
Las viñas necesitan un cuidado especial.	Vineyards need special care.
la **vendimia**	grape harvest; vintage
sembrar	sow
¿Cuándo se siembra el trigo?	When is wheat sown?
el **insecticida**	insecticide; pesticide
Los insecticidas acaban con los insectos y dañan a las personas.	Insecticides kill insects and harm people.
regar	water; irrigate; sprinkle
En Canarias se gasta el agua para regar los campos de golf y piscinas.	In the Canary Islands, the water is used to water the golf courses and fill the swimming pools.
la **huerta**	orchard; vegetable garden; irrigated land
La huerta murciana es muy productiva.	The irrigated land in Murcia is very productive.
productivo, a	productive

el **riego**
Valencia tiene un inteligente
sistema de riego muy antiguo.

irrigation
Valencia has a well-thought-out,
very old system of irrigation.

el **vaquero**

cowboy; cowherd

el **invernadero**

hothouse

ordeñar
Poca gente sabe ordeñar vacas o
cabras.

milk
Few people know how to milk
cows or goats.

el **establo**
Por la noche las vacas están en el
establo.

stable
At night the cows are in the stable.

la **granja**

farm; farmhouse; grange

explotar
Las campañías inglesas explotan las
minas en el sur de España.

work (a mine); exploit; run (a farm)
English companies work
the mines in southern Spain.

el **rendimiento**
El rendimiento de la cosecha
en esta región es bueno.

yield; output
The yield of the harvest is
good in this region.

la **minería**

mining

minero, a
La industria minera está en crisis.

mining
The mining industry is in a crisis.

la **explotación**
La explotación del estaño
es muy importante en Bolivia.
La explotación de los bosques
crea problemas ecológicos.

working (of a mine); exploitation
Tin mining is very important in
Bolivia.
The exploitation of the forests
creates ecological problems.

El verano es muy caluroso en el centro de España.
Summer is very hot in the center of Spain.

Banking

el **banco**
A Eduardo le gustaría trabajar en un
banco o en una caja de ahorros.

bank
Eduardo would like to work in a
bank or in a savings bank.

la **caja de ahorros**

savings bank

ahorrar
Felipe está ahorrando para
comprarse una bicicleta.

save
Felipe is saving for a bike.

abonar
¿Me pueden abonar este cheque en
mi cuenta corriente?—Por supuesto,
pero tendremos que cargar los gastos
en su cuenta.

credit with; pay in; deposit
Can you deposit this check in my
current account?—Of course, but
we have to charge the expenses to
your account.

el **cheque**

check

el **eurocheque**

Eurocheque

la **cuenta**

account

el **gasto**
Cargaremos los gastos de transferencia
en su cuenta.

expense; cost; outlay
We will charge the transfer
expenses to your account.

gastar
Mucha gente gasta más de lo que
gana.

spend
Many people spend more than
they earn.

retirar
¿Qué cantidad desea retirar de
su cuenta corriente?

withdraw
What amount would you like to
withdraw from your current
account?

la **cantidad**

amount; sum of money; quantity

cobrar
¿En qué banco puedo cobrar el
cheque?
Por favor, cóbrese.

cash (check); collect
At what bank can I cash the
check?
Please, take the cash.

cambiar
¿Me puede cambiar mil pesetas en
monedas?

change
Can you change into coins these
1,000 pesetas for me?

el **cajero**; la **cajera**
El cajero del banco robó dos millones.
Este cajero automático no acepta su
tarjeta de crédito.

cashier; teller
The bank teller stole two million.
This automated teller does not
accept your credit card.

la **tarjeta de crédito**

credit card

en **efectivo**
¿Paga con tarjeta?—No, en efectivo.

in cash
Are you paying with a credit card?
—No, in cash.

la **caja fuerte**
Mi madre guarda las joyas en la caja
fuerte.

safe; strongbox
My mother keeps her jewelry in
the safe.

el **crédito**
La señora Vázquez ha comprado
la casa con un crédito.

credit; loan
Mrs. Vázquez bought the house
with a loan.

la **deuda**
Muchos países latinoamericanos no
pueden pagar los intereses de su
deuda externa.

debt
Many Latin American countries
cannot pay the interest on their
foreign debt.

prestar
A ver cuándo me devuelves
el disco que te presté.

lend; loan
Let's see when you give me
back the record that I loaned you.

el **beneficio**
Los bancos trabajan con un beneficio
enorme.

profit
Banks operate with an enormous
profit.

ahorrador(a)
No soy muy ahorrador, pero
quiero comprar un piso.

thrifty; frugal
I'm not very frugal, but I
would like to buy an apartment.

la **cartilla de ahorro**; la **libreta
de ahorro**

savings book

el, la **titular**
El titular de esta cuenta quiere
retirar dos millones de pesetas.

holder (of an account); depositor
The holder of this account wants
to withdraw two million pesetas.

la **cuenta corriente**

current account

el **extracto de cuenta**

statement of account

ingresar
Por favor, ingrese el importe
total en nuestra cuenta.

deposit; pay in
Please deposit the entire
amount in our account.

el **importe**
Le he ingresado el importe de la
factura en su cuenta.

amount
I have deposited the amount of the
invoice in your account.

la **transferencia**

transfer

los **ingresos**
El año pasado nuestros ingresos
fueron bajos.

receipts; earnings; income
Last year our earnings were low.

el **cheque de viaje**
¿Aceptan ustedes cheques de viaje?

traveler's check
Do you accept traveler's checks?

el **talón**	check
el **talonario de cheques**	checkbook
cancelar	cancel; stop payment
el **fondo** No podemos cobrar este cheque porque no hay fondos en la cuenta.	funds; means; money We can't honor this check, because there are no funds in the account.
el **interés**	interest
la **bolsa** Don Ignacio es un corredor de bolsa muy astuto.	stock exchange Don Ignacio is a very astute stockbroker.
el, la **accionista** Los accionistas en conjunto son propietarios de una sociedad anónima (S.A.).	stockholder; shareholder The shareholders as a whole are the owners of a stock corporation.
la **acción**	stock; share
el **valor** Estas acciones subirán de valor cuando termine la crisis. Este anillo es de gran valor.	worth; value These stocks will rise when the crisis ends. This ring is very valuable.
el **deudor**; la **deudora** El deudor debe pagar el préstamo.	debtor; obligor; liable The obligor has to repay the loan.
el **préstamo**	loan
el **plazo** En enero se acaba el plazo para pagar el crédito.	term; time of payment In January the period for repaying the loan expires.
calcular Hemos de calcular los gastos de viaje.	calculate; compute; estimate We have to calculate the travel costs.

Money

el **dinero** Los billetes y las monedas son dinero en metálico.	money Bills and coins are cash.
el **billete**	bill; bank note
la **moneda** ¿Tienes monedas de cinco pesetas para llamar por teléfono?	coin; currency Do you have 5 peseta coins for making a phone call?

la **peseta**
¿Cuántas pesetas son un duro?
—Cinco pesetas.

peseta
How many pesetas make a
"duro?"—Five pesetas.

el **duro**

five pesetas

el **cambio**

change; exchange; rate of
exchange

Perdone, ¿tiene cambio de mil
dólares?
¿Cómo está el cambio del peso
mejicano?

Excuse me, do you have change
for $1,000?
What is the exchange rate for the
Mexican peso?

la **vuelta**
¡No te olvides de la vuelta!

change
Don't forget your change!

el **resto**

rest; remainder

a **plazos**
Pablo pagó el piso a plazos porque
no pudo pagarlo al contado.

in installlments
Pablo paid for the apartment in
installments because he couldn't
pay cash for it.

al **contado**
¿Paga usted al contado o con tarjeta?

cash
Are you paying in cash or with a
credit card?

el **descuento**
¿Cuánto descuento nos da si
pagamos al contado?
¿Hay un descuento para estudiantes?

discount; deduction
How much of a discount do
you give us if we pay cash?
Is there a student discount?

la **rebaja**
Si se llevan cuatro bicicletas les hago
una rebaja.

reduction; discount
If you take four bikes, I'll give you
a discount.

valer
¿Cuánto vale este libro?

cost
How much does this book cost?

por
He comprado este piso por dos
millones.

for
I bought this apartment for two
million.

las **divisas**
Todas las monedas extranjeras son
divisas.

foreign exchange
All foreign currencies are foreign
exchange.

el **dólar**
El dólar panameño y el balboa son las
monedas aceptadas en Panamá.

dollar
The Panamanian dollar and the
balboa are the accepted currencies
in Panama.

el **franco**
el franco suizo

franc
the Swiss franc

el **marco alemán**	German mark
el **peso** El peso es la moneda de Bolivia, Colombia, Cuba, Chile, la República Dominicana y México.	peso The peso is the unit of currency in Bolivia, Colombia, Cuba, Chile the Dominican Republic, and Mexico.
el **quetzal** En Guatemala la gente paga con quetzales.	quetzal In Guatemala people pay with quetzales.
el **colón** El colón es la moneda de El Salvador y Costa Rica.	colon The colon is the currency of El Salvador and Costa Rica.
el **córdoba** En Nicaragua se llama la moneda córdoba.	cordoba In Nicaragua the currency is the cordoba.
el **lempira** La moneda hondureña es el lempira.	lempira The Honduran currency is the lempira.
el **sucre**	sucre (*currency of Ecuador*)
el **bolívar**	bolivar (*currency of Venezuela*)
el **guaraní**	guarani (*currency of Paraguay*)
el **inti**	inti (*currency of Peru*)
el **austral**	austral (*currency of Argentina*)
suelto, a ¿Llevas dinero suelto para llamar por teléfono?	loose; single; (small) change Do you have small change for making a phone call?
invertir El señor Durruti ha invertido su capital en una fábrica de armas.	invest Mr. Durruti has invested his capital in an arms factory.
el **impuesto** Mañana tengo que presentar mi declaración de impuestos, por eso he de calcular mi renta.	tax Tomorrow I have to turn in my tax declaration, and therefore I have to figure out my income.
la **renta**	income
la **suma**	sum; total; amount
el **recibo** Aquí tiene su recibo.	receipt Here's your receipt.

20 | Professional Tools and Office Items

Professional Tools

el **aparato**
El ventilador es un aparato muy práctico en verano.

device; appliance; machine
The fan is a very practical appliance in summer.

funcionar
¿Ya funciona la máquina de escribir?

function; work; run
Is the typewriter working again?

la **máquina**
En esta fábrica las máquinas hacen el trabajo pesado.

machine
In this factory, machines do the heavy work.

técnico, a
No es necesario ser un especialista técnico para arreglar la bicicleta.

technical
It's not necessary to be a technical expert to repair the bicycle.

la **pila**
Necesito una pila nueva para mi linterna.

battery
I need a new battery for my flashlight.

el **pico**
En las minas se trabaja con pico y pala.

pick; pickaxe
In the mines, they work with pick and shovel.

el **saco**
Nos trajeron el carbón en sacos de cincuenta kilos.

sack; bag
They brought us the coal in 50-kilo sacks.

la **red**
El pescador no puede ir a pescar porque tiene que coser la red.

net
The fisherman can't go out to fish because he has to sew the net.

la **herramienta**
El mecánico no puede trabajar sin herramientas.

tool
The mechanic can't work without tools.

la **ferretería**

hardware store

el **destornillador**
Sólo tengo un destornillador.

screwdriver
I have only a screwdriver.

la **llave**
Esta llave no sirve para montar el aparato.

key; wrench
This wrench is of no use for assembling the device.

las **tenazas**
¿Tiene unas tenazas para cortar cables?

pliers
Do you have pliers for cutting cables?

la **cola**
La madera se pega con cola.

glue
Wood is bonded with glue.

pegar

glue; bond; stick

lijar
Antes de pintar las puertas tienes
que lijarlas con papel de lija.

sand(paper); smooth; rub
Before painting the doors, you
have to sand them with sandpaper.

el **papel de lija**

sandpaper

la **cuerda**
Hay que atar este paquete con una
cuerda para que no se abra.

cord; rope; string
You have to tie this package with
string, so that it doesn't come
open.

el **machete**

machete; cane knife

la **navaja**

pocket knife

la **linterna**

flashlight

la **cinta continua**
El trabajo en una cinta continua es
muy monótono.

conveyor belt; assembly line
Working on an assembly line
is very monotonous.

automático, a

automatic

la **tecnología**

technology

la **instalación**

installation

electrónico, a
Los aparatos electrónicos son muy
caros.

electronic
Electronic equipment is very
expensive.

Office Items

la **máquina de escribir**
Hay que cambiar la cinta de la
máquina de escribir.

typewriter
The typewriter ribbon has
to be changed.

la **computadora**
En la universidad hay una
computadora para los estudiantes de
matemáticas.

computer; calculator
At the university there is a
computer for the math students.

la **fotocopiadora**

photocopier

la **fotocopia**

photocopy

copiar
Como la secretaria hizo muchas
faltas, tuve que copiar la carta
otra vez.

copy
Since the secretary made a lot of
mistakes, I had to copy the letter
again.

179

la **copia**

copy

el **lápiz**
Rosalia escribe sólo con lápiz.

pencil
Rosalia writes only with a
pencil.

el **bolígrafo**; el **boli**
Isabel tiene un boli de cuatro colores.

ballpoint pen
Isabel has a four-color ballpoint
pen.

la **lapicera**; la **pluma**
Marisa firmó el contrato con
la pluma de su marido.

fountain pen
Marisa signed the contract with
her husband's fountain pen.

la **tinta**
No me gusta escribir con tinta azul.

ink
I don't like to write with blue
ink.

el **papel**
Ya no quedan ni sobres ni papel de
cartas.
Tendré que ir a la papelería.

Haz copias con el papel carbón
sobre papel cebolla.

paper
There are no envelopes or writing
paper left.
I have to go to the stationery
store.
Make copies with carbon
paper on onionskin paper.

el **sobre**

envelope

la **papelería**

stationery store

el **bloc**
¿Me das una hoja de tu bloc?

block; pad (of paper)
Will you give me a sheet from
your pad?

la **hoja (de papel)**

sheet (of paper)

la **cinta adhesiva**

adhesive tape; Scotch® tape

la **cinta**

typewriter ribbon; ink ribbon

la **computadora**; el **ordenador**
Alejandro trabaja con la computadora
en casa.

computer; personal computer (PC)
Alejandro works at home on a PC.

el **programa**
¿Me puede recomendar un buen
programa de texto para mi
ordenador?

program
Can you recommend a good word
processing program for my
computer?

borrar
El lápiz se puede borrar con una
goma pero la mancha de
bolígrafo no.

erase; remove; eradicate
Pencil can be erased with a rubber
eraser, but ballpoint pen stains
can't be.

la **goma de borrar**

rubber eraser

el **rotulador**
Mi sobrino está dibujando con
los rotuladores.

felt-tip pen; felt pen
My nephew is drawing
with felt-tip pens.

el **compás**

compass

la **agenda**
Remedios se apunta todo en la
agenda para no olvidarse de nada.

appointment book; memo book
Remedios writes down everything
in her memo book, so that she
doesn't forget anything.

la **carpeta**

folder; desk pad

el **archivador**

file; binder; filing cabinet

el **archivo**
Juan ha estado todo el día en el
archivo pero no ha encontrado ni la
carpeta ni el archivador que se dejó
allí.

filing room
Juan has been in the filing room
all day, but he has found neither
the folder nor the file that he had
there.

el **tampón**

stamp pad; ink pad; tampon

el **sello**
Como no hay tinta en el tampón,
no te puedo poner un sello.

seal; stamp; impression
Since there is no ink in the stamp
pad, I can't stamp anything for you.

la **calculadora**
En el colegio ya permiten que
utilicemos calculadoras.

pocket calculator
In school they now allow
us to use pocket calculators.

Tiralíneas

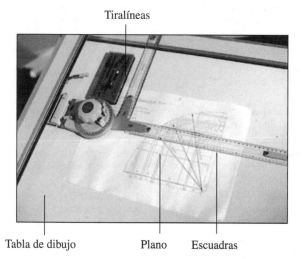

Tabla de dibujo   Plano   Escuadras

21 | Use of Leisure Time

■■■■■ Recreational Activities ■■■■■

el **movimiento**
En Madrid hay siempre mucho movimiento.

movement; activity
In Madrid there's always a lot going on.

la **diversión**
Es una diversión gastar bromas.

entertainment; amusement
It's amusing to crack jokes.

la **broma**

joke; prank

divertido, a
¿Cómo fue la fiesta?—Muy divertida.

amusing; entertaining
How was the party?—Very entertaining.

divertirse
¡Que te diviertas!
Raúl no se sabe divertir sin los amigos.

have a good time
Have fun!
Raúl doesn't know how to have a good time without his friends.

la **distracción**
La mejor distracción para ti es salir con los amigos.

pastime; diversion; distraction
The best diversion for you is to go out with friends.

salir

go out

entretenerse
Me entretengo con la colección de sellos.

amuse oneself; pass time
I amuse myself by collecting stamps.

la **discoteca**

discotheque

bailar
¿Quieres ir a bailar?

dance
Would you like to go dancing?

el **baile**
Durante las fiestas habrá todas las noches baile en la plaza del pueblo.

dance
During the holidays, there will be dancing every night on the village square.

pasear
Como hace buen tiempo hemos venido paseando.

walk; take out to walk
Since the weather is nice, we walked here.

pasearse
En verano mucha gente se pasea por la playa.

(take a) walk
In summer, many people walk on the beach.

la **feria**
La feria de abril de Sevilla es famosa.

fair
The April Fair in Seville is famous.

el **tiempo libre**
¿Qué hace en su tiempo libre?

free time
What do you do in your free time?

la **pausa**

pause; break; rest

distraerse

Muchos niños se distraen viendo la tele.

spend one's time; amuse oneself
Many children spend their time watching TV.

animado, a
La discoteca está muy animada esta noche.

lively; animated
The discotheque is very lively this evening.

el **chiste**

joke

la **lotería**

lottery

el **cupón**

coupon

el **casino**

(gambling) casino

el **pub**
¿Te vienes al pub a tomar una copa?

bar; pub
Are you coming to the bar for a drink?

la **danza**
Esta noche vamos a ver danzas populares.

(folk) dance
Tonight we're going to see folk dances.

el **paseo**
¿Vamos a dar un paseo?

walk
Shall we take a walk?

la **vuelta**
Fui a dar una vuelta por el centro y me encontré a Ramona.

turn; stroll; walk
I took a stroll through the center of town and ran into Ramona.

el **parque de atracciones**
En Barcelona hay un parque de atracciones en Montjuïc.

amusement park
In Barcelona, there is an amusement park on Montjuïc.

el **circo**
Hace muchos años que fuimos al circo, para ver a los payasos.

circus
It's many years since we went to the circus to see the clowns.

el **payaso**; la **payasa**

clown

la **corrida de toros**
Hoy en día a muchos españoles no les gustan las corridas de toros.

bullfight
These days, many Spaniards dislike bullfights.

Theater

el **teatro** Ya he sacado las entradas para el teatro para que luego no tengamos que hacer cola.	theater I have already picked up the theater tickets, so that we don't have to stand in line later.
la **cola**	(waiting) line
la **entrada**	admission ticket
la **obra**	(artistic) work
el **espectáculo** ¿A qué hora empieza el espectáculo?	performance; show; spectacle What time does the performance begin?
el **programa** ¿Tiene el programa de teatro y ópera del mes que viene?	program; schedule Do you have the theater and opera schedule for the coming month?
el **público** El público aplaudió mucho en el estreno.	audience; public The audience applauded wildly at the premiere.
aplaudir	applaud; clap; praise
silbar	whistle; hiss; boo
la **pieza** A Mercedes le encantó la representación de esta pieza.	play Mercedes was enthusiastic about the production of this play.
el **escenario** La decoración del escenario era sorprendente.	stage The stage set was surprising.
la **butaca** Déme dos butacas.	orchestra seat Please give me two orchestra seats.
el **palco**	box; loge
la **comedia** Lope de Vega escribió muchísimas comedias.	comedy Lope de Vega wrote a great many comedies.
la **tragedia**	tragedy
trágico, a	tragic

el **director**; la **directora**	director
No nos gustó la interpretación de la obra que ofreció el director.	We didn't like the interpretation of the work that the director offered.
interpretar	interpret
el **estreno**	premiere; debut; first performance
la **representación**	performance; presentation
silencioso, a	silent; quiet
el **aplauso**	applause
Al final del tercer acto hubo muchos aplausos para la compañía.	At the end of the third act there was a lot of applause for the cast.
el **acto**	act
la **compañía (de teatro)**	cast; company; ensemble
representar	represent; perform; act
¿Quién representa el papel de Don Juan Tenorio?	Who performs the role of Don Juan Tenorio?
el **papel**	role
el **productor**; la **productora**	producer
Los productores corren a veces con todo el riesgo.	Producers sometimes assume the entire risk.
el **ensayo**	rehearsal
Como los actores están de vacaciones no habrá ensayos hasta septiembre.	Since the actors are on vacation, there will be no rehearsals until September.

Movies

el **cine**	movie theater; movies
¿Qué película ponen en el cine?	What film is playing at the movies?
la **película**	(movie, TV) film
Antes nos gustaban mucho las películas de vaqueros.	We used to like westerns a lot.
el **actor**; la **actriz**	actor; actress
¿Cuál es tu actor preferido?	Who is your favorite actor?
actuar	appear; play; act
¿Te acuerdas del chico que actuó en la película de malo?	Do you remember the boy who played the villain in the film?

cómico, a
A Tomás le encantan las películas cómicas de los hermanos Marx.

funny; comic(al); witty
Tomás really likes the Marx Brothers' comedies.

la taquilla
Tenemos que estar a tiempo en el cine porque habrá cola en la taquilla como siempre.

(movie, theater) ticket (box) office
We have to be at the movies on time because, as always, there will be a line at the box office.

la pantalla
En los cines de verano un muro blanco hace de pantalla.

(movie) screen
At summer movie theaters, a white wall serves as the screen.

la sesión
En los cines de barrio hay sesión continua.

showing; session
In the neighborhood movie theaters there are continuous showings.

la escena
La última escena de la película fue muy emocionante.

scene
The last scene of the film was very thrilling.

la estrella
¿Conoces alguna estrella del cine español?

star
Do you know any Spanish movie stars?

la fama
La fama es para quien la gana.

fame
Fame is for the person who earns it.

la función
Esta tarde habrá una función para niños.

(theater, movie) performance
This afternoon there will be a performance for children.

el festival
En San Sebastián se celebra un festival de cine.

festival
In San Sebastián, a film festival is held.

el descanso
En el descanso te compraré caramelos.

break; rest
During the intermission I'll buy you candy.

Hobbies and Games

el aficionado; la **aficionada**
La próxima semana habrá un concurso para aficionados.

amateur; fan
Next week there will be a competition for amateurs.

la fotografía
La gran afición de mi madre es la fotografía, especialmente sacarles fotos a los gatos.

photography
My mother's great hobby is photography, especially taking photos of cats.

la **afición**

hobby; fondness

la **foto**

photo; picture

la **cámara (fotográfica)**

camera

Me robaron la cámara con los
carretes que no habíamos revelado
todavía.

They stole my camera with the
films that we hadn't developed
yet.

la **colección**

collection

Mi abuela tenía una colección
de joyas muy valiosas.

My grandmother had a very
valuable collection of jewelry.

coleccionar

collect

¿Qué colecciona usted?

What do you collect?

jugar

play

¿A qué vamos a jugar?—Pues, al
ajedrez, ¿no?

What are we going to play?—
Chess, all right?

el **juego**

game

¿Conocéis un juego de cartas
divertido?

Do you know an enjoyable card
game?

la **carta**

(playing) card

ganar

win

el **juguete**

toy

Para Reyes queremos muchos
juguetes y muñecas.

For Epiphany we would like
a lot of toys and dolls.

la **muñeca**

doll

el **palo**

suit of cards

la **caza**

hunting

A veces vamos de caza o de pesca
para distraernos.

For amusement we sometimes
go hunting or fishing.

En las reservas naturales está
prohibida la caza.

Hunting is prohibited in nature
preserves.

el **cazador**; la **cazadora**

hunter

cazar

hunt; catch

Roberto ha cazado una mosca.

Roberto has caught a fly.

la **riña de gallos**

cockfight

el **ocio**
En muchas revistas y periódicos hay unas páginas de ocio con crucigramas etc.

pastime; diversion
In many magazines and newspapers there are some pages with pastimes such as crossword puzzles.

el **crucigrama**

crossword puzzle

el **concurso**

contest; competition

el **carrete**

film cartridge

revelar

develop (*photo*)

la **diapositiva**

slide

el **flash**

flash

la **copia**
En cuanto podamos te mandaremos las copias que nos pediste.

copy
As soon as we can, we'll send you the copies you asked us for.

el, la **coleccionista**
Mi cuñado es un coleccionista profesional de sellos.

collector
My brother-in-law is a professional stamp collector.

el **ajedrez**

chess

la **partida**
¿Jugamos una partida de dominó?

game; match
Shall we play a game of dominoes?

el **dominó**

dominoes

el **globo**

balloon

apostar
Mucha gente juega a las cartas apostando mucho dinero.

bet; lay a wager
Many people bet a lot of money when they play cards.

el **dado**
Ya los romanos jugaban a los dados.

die
Even the Romans used to play dice.

la **apuesta**
¡Has ganado la apuesta!

bet
You've won the bet!

la **trampa**
¡No vale hacer trampas!

trap; cheat
Cheating doesn't count!

hacer labores

do needlework; handwork

hacer punto

knit

━━━━━━━━━ **Miscellaneous** ━━━━━━━━━

el, la **deportista**
Mi abuela era una gran deportista.

athlete; sportsman or -woman
My grandmother was a great
sportswoman.

deportivo, a
Durante mis vacaciones me dedico
a actividades deportivas.

relating to sport; athletic
During my vacations I engage
in athletic activities.

el **deporte**
¿Practicas algún deporte?
—Sí, juego al tenis, corro y nado.

sport
Do you go in for sports?
—Yes, I play tennis, run, and
swim.

el **jugador**; la **jugadora**
Los jugadores forman un equipo.

player
The players form a team.

el **equipo**
Nuestro equipo no ganó el partido
por culpa del árbitro.
Miguel no participa en el
entrenamiento porque se ha olvidado
del equipo.

team; sporting equipment
Our team didn't win the game on
account of the referee.
Miguel isn't taking part in the
training because he forgot his
sporting equipment.

el **entrenamiento**

training

participar

take part; participate

el **partido**

game

la **competición**
Las competiciones de motos se
realizan en Jerez de la Frontera.

competition; match; race
Motorcycle races are held in
Jerez de la Frontera.

el **campeonato**
¿Cuándo son los próximos
campeonatos de fórmula uno?

championship
When are the next Formula 1
championships?

el **campeón**; la **campeona**
¿Quién es el actual campeón del
mundo de baloncesto?

champion
Who is the current world
champion in basketball?

el **récord**
El nuevo campeón del mundo ha
batido el récord por dos segundos.

record
The new world champion has
beaten the record by two
seconds.

ganar

win

perder
Si no hubiésemos perdido este partido
hubiéramos ganado la copa.

lose
If we hadn't lost this game,
we would have won the cup.

vencer
El entrenador no se explica cómo pudieron vencer a su equipo.

defeat
The trainer doesn't understand how they were able to defeat his team.

la pelota
Para jugar al tenis necesitas bastantes pelotas.
No sólo en el País Vasco se juega a la pelota sino también se practica una forma de este juego en Estados Unidos.

ball; Basque ball game
To play tennis, you need enough balls.
Pelota is played not only in the Basque Provinces; a form of this game is also practiced in the United States.

---

entrenarse
Los buenos deportistas se entrenan casi todos los días.

train
Good athletes train almost daily.

el **entrenador**; la **entrenadora**

trainer

el **árbitro**

umpire; referee

el **pito**
El árbitro señala el final de un partido con el pito.

whistle
The referee signals the end of a game with the whistle.

la **carrera**

race

marcar
¿Cuántos goles habéis marcado?

score
How many goals have you scored?

la **meta**
Pablo no estaba en forma y por eso no llegó a la meta.

goal; finish line
Pablo was not in shape, and that is why he didn't reach the finish line.

empatar
El Real Madrid y el Barcelona empataron a 2.

tie (in games or voting)
Real Madrid and Barcelona tied, 2:2.

la **Olimpiada**

Olympics

olímpico, a

Olympic

el **gimnasio**

gymnasium

el **estadio**

stadium

el **campo (deportivo)**

playing field

la **pista**
En enero se llenan las pistas de esquí en los Pirineos.

track; run; course
In January the ski runs in the Pyrenees get crowded.

el **telesquí**

ski lift

Types of Sports

practicar	practice; take part in
nadar	swim
la **natación** El médico me ha recomendado que vaya a la piscina y practique la natación.	swimming The doctor has recommended that I go to the pool and swim.
la **piscina**	swimming pool
el, la **atleta** Los atletas no deben fumar.	athlete Athletes should not smoke.
correr Juan corrió dos vueltas. Carlos corre muy deprisa.	run; race Juan ran two laps. Carlos runs very fast.
saltar Jamás creí que pudieras saltar tal altura.	jump I never would have believed that you could jump so high.
el **fútbol** Un partido de fútbol se juega en un estadio y para ganar hay que marcar más goles que el equipo contrario.	soccer A soccer game is played in a stadium, and in order to win you have to score more goals than the opposing team.
el **balón** Cuando el balón entra en la portería y el portero no lo puede parar se ha marcado un gol.	(soccer) ball; balloon When the ball enters the goal box and the goalkeeper can't stop it, a goal has been scored.
montar ¿Sabes dónde se puede montar a caballo por aquí?	ride horseback Do you know where one can ride horseback around here?
boxear Para boxear se necesitan unos guantes especiales.	box For boxing you need special gloves.
esquiar En la Sierra Nevada se puede esquiar todo el año.	ski In the Sierra Nevada you can ski all year round.
remar ¿Cómo quieres remar si no tienes remos?	row; paddle How do you intend to row if you have no oars?
el **tenis**	tennis
la **raqueta**	racket

la **disciplina** ¿Qué disciplinas de atletismo practicas?	discipline; kind of sport What kinds of track-and-field events do you go in for?
el **nadador**; la **nadadora** En los próximos campeonatos van a participar muchos nadadores españoles.	swimmer Many Spanish swimmers are going to participate in the next championships.
el **atletismo**	track-and-field events
el **salto**	jump; leap
el **ciclismo** La carrera de ciclismo española más importante es la Vuelta a España.	bicycling The most important Spanish bicycle race is the Vuelta a España.
el, la **ciclista**	cyclist
el **baloncesto**	basketball
el **balonmano**	handball
el, la **futbolista**	soccer player
el **gol**	goal (*soccer; handball*)
el **portero**; la **portera**	goalkeeper
la **portería**	goal (*box*)
el **hockey**	hockey
el **boxeo** El boxeo es un deporte muy duro.	boxing Boxing is a very rough sport.
el **boxeador**	boxer
el **esquí** Antes de irnos a la montaña tienes que comprarte unos esquíes.	ski Before we go to the mountains, you have to buy yourself some skis.
patinar	skate
el **remo**	oar; paddle
el **golf** En España se juega mucho al golf.	golf In Spain, a lot of golf is played.
navegar a vela En verano navegamos a vela en el velero de mi tío.	sail In summer we sail on my uncle's sailboat.
el **velero**	sailboat
el **surf** Angel tiene un surf desde hace dos años pero no sabe llevarlo.	surfboard Angel has had a surfboard for two years, but he doesn't know how to surf.
bucear	dive

la **equitación**
La equitación tiene mucha tradición en España.

riding; horsemanship
Riding has a long tradition in Spain.

la **gimnasia**
Mi mujer va todas las semanas a hacer gimnasia a un gimnasio.

gymnastics
My wife goes to a gym to do gymnastics every week.

El ciclismo continúa siendo popular para un enorme número de personas en Latinoamérica.
Cycling continues to be popular with an enormous number of people in Latin America.

Traveling

las **vacaciones**
vacation; holidays

la **agencia de viajes**
travel agency
Mientras haces las maletas voy a recoger los billetes a la agencia de viajes.
While you pack the bags, I'll pick up the tickets at the travel agency.

el **prospecto**
brochure; prospectus
¿Tienen nuevos prospectos sobre viajes a la Isla Margarita?
Do you have new brochures on trips to Margarita Island?

el **viaje**
trip
¿Adónde nos vamos de viaje este invierno?
Where shall we go on our trip this winter?
¡Buen viaje!
Have a good trip!

viajar
travel; go on a trip
Beatriz ha viajado para conocer otros países.
Beatriz has traveled to become familiar with other countries.

el **viajero**; la **viajera**
traveler; passenger
Señores viajeros del vuelo con destino a Cartagena, diríjanse a la salida B.
Passengers on the flight to Cartagena, please go to Gate B.

reservar
reserve; book
Quisiéramos reservar dos habitaciones individuales.
We would like to reserve two single rooms.

la **oficina de turismo**
tourist (information) office
En las oficinas de turismo se podrá informar sobre excursiones interesantes.
In tourist offices one can get information about interesting tours.

visitar
visit
Me gustaría visitar Panamá.
I would like to visit Panama.

el, la **guía**
(travel or tourist) guide
En el Prado una guía nos explicó los cuadros de Velázquez.
In the Prado the guide explained the paintings of Velázquez to us.

la **guía**
guide (book); city map
En esta guía no se dice nada sobre el origen de la Alhambra.
In this guide nothing is said about the origin of the Alhambra.
Juan se ha comprado una guía de Sevilla para no perderse.
Juan has bought a city map of Seville to keep from getting lost.

mostrar
show
Mis amigos chilenos nos mostraron Valparaíso.
My Chilean friends showed us Valparaíso.

la **excursión** — excursion; outing; tour; trip

impresionante — impressive

el **equipaje** — baggage; luggage
Cuando vamos de vacaciones siempre llevamos demasiado equipaje. — When we go on vacation, we always take too much baggage.

la **maleta** — suitcase

la **frontera** — border

el **control** — check; control; checkpoint

la **llegada** — arrival
¿A qué hora esperan la llegada del vuelo de Vigo? — What time is the flight from Vigo scheduled for arrival?

el **recuerdo** — memento; souvenir
Miguel nos trajo un recuerdo de Guatemala. — Miguel brought us a souvenir from Guatemala.

el, la **turista** — tourist
Hay turistas que no saben comportarse en el extranjero. — There are tourists who don't know how to behave in a foreign country.

turístico, a — tourist(ic)
Las Islas Canarias son un centro turístico muy importante. — The Canary Islands are a major tourist center.

el **turismo** — tourism
El turismo ha creado muchos problemas en España. — Tourism has created many problems in Spain.

el, la **visitante** — visitor

la **visita** — visit; inspection
Una visita al museo de Dalí en Figueras es recomendable. — A visit to the Dali Museum in Figueras is recommended.

recomendable — recommended; advisable

disfrutar — enjoy
Los señores Cornello disfrutaron de sus vacaciones. — Mr. and Mrs. Cornello enjoyed their vacation.

perderse — get lost

el **folleto** — pamphlet; booklet; brochure
En este folleto se anuncian viajes muy económicos. — Very economical trips are advertised in this pamphlet.

el **servicio** — toilet; service; servants
¿Dónde está el servicio para caballeros? — Where is the men's room?

Caballeros — Men

satisfecho, a — satisfied

el **preparativo** — preparation

ocupado, a — occupied; busy
El guía está muy ocupado con los preparativos para la excursión. — The guide is very busy with the preparations for the excursion.
Este servicio está ocupado. — This toilet is occupied.

el **documento** — document

el **visado** — visa
Para algunos países latinoamericanos es necesario tener un visado. — For some Latin American countries it is necessary to have a visa.

la **aduana** — customs

declarar — declare
¿Tiene algo que declarar? — Do you have anything to declare?

la **ficha** — form

controlar — check; inspect; control

el **aduanero**; la **aduanera** — customs official
El aduanero registró las maletas para ver si llevábamos armas. — The customs officer searched the suitcases to see whether we were carrying weapons.

el **mapa** — map
¿Nos puede indicar en el mapa si vamos bien para Toledo? — Can you show us on the map whether we are going the right way to Toledo?

la **carta verde** — green insurance card

la **mochila** — backpack
Franco viaja sólo con una mochila. — Franco travels with only a backpack.

partir — leave; depart
Antes de partir, no se olviden de despedirse. — Don't forget to say goodbye before leaving.

recorrer — travel in or over

el **autostop** — hitchhiking
Viajar en autostop puede ser peligroso. — Hitchhiking can be dangerous.

el **área de servicio** *f* — service area

la **ruta** — route

el **retraso** — delay
El tren llegó con dos horas de retraso. — The train arrived two hours late.

anular	cancel
He anulado el viaje a Quito.	I have canceled the trip to Quito.
la **aventura**	adventure
Nuestro viaje a Cuba fue realmente una aventura.	Our trip to Cuba was really an adventure.
forastero, a	foreigner; stranger; foreign
Como soy forastero no encuentro el camino al hotel.	Since I'm a stranger, I can't find the way to the hotel.
el **panorama**	panorama
exótico, a	exotic
contemplar	view; look at; contemplate
la **temporada**	season
La última temporada turística ha sido fatal.	The last tourist season was miserable.
el **regreso**	return
Al regreso de Cuba me encontré a Ricardo en el aeropuerto.	On the return trip from Cuba, I ran into Ricardo at the airport.

Accommodations

encontrar	find
el **hotel**	hotel
la **pensión**	small private hotel
Las pensiones son más baratas que los hoteles y los hostales.	Small private hotels are cheaper than hotels and inns.
el **camping**	camp(ing) ground; site
el **hostal**	inn; moderately priced hotel
la **recepción**	reception (desk)
la **habitación**	room
completo, a	full
La recepcionista nos dijo que el hotel estaba completo.	The reception clerk told us that the hotel was full.
¿Cuánto cuesta una habitación doble con pensión completa?	How much does a double room with full board cost?
libre	vacant; free
la **reserva**	(hotel) reservation
¿Los señores tienen reserva?	Do you have a reservation?

el **formulario**	form
deletrear	spell

el **alojamiento**	accommodations; lodgings
alojar	accommodate; put up
La oficina de turismo alojó muy bien a los turistas.	The tourist office found good accommodations for the tourists.
alojarse	lodge; put up at; stay
¿En qué hotel se aloja usted?	What hotel are you staying in?
la **categoría**	category; class
Según cuántas estrellas tiene un hotel es de mejor o de peor categoría.	Depending on how many stars a hotel has, it ranks in a higher or lower category.
el **confort**	comfort
el **Parador Nacional**	state-run Spanish hotel
la **fonda**	inn; modest hotel
el **albergue juvenil**	youth hostel
¿Sabes dónde hay un albergue juvenil aquí?	Do you know where there's a youth hostel here?
acampar	camp out; go camping
Todas las primaveras acampamos un fin de semana en la costa.	Every spring we go camping on the coast one weekend.
la **tienda de campaña**	tent
En este camping podemos alquilar tiendas de campaña.	At this campsite we can rent tents.
la **caravana**	camper; camping van
el **saco de dormir**	sleeping bag
el, la **recepcionista**	receptionist; desk clerk
reservado, a	reserved; booked
Lo sentimos mucho pero todos los apartamentos están reservados.	We're very sorry, but all the apartments are booked.
la **estancia**	stay
¿Cuánto tiempo va a durar su estancia aquí?	How long will you be staying here?
rellenar	fill out; complete
Por favor, rellene el formulario.	Please fill out the form.
el **mozo**	porter; manservant; waiter
Le he dado una propina al mozo por haberme subido el equipaje a la habitación.	I gave the porter a tip because he brought the bags to my room.

llamar	call; wake
¿A qué hora desean que les llame?	What time would you like us to wake you?
el **huésped**	guest
hospitalitario, a	hospitable

Paradores, hoteles, moteles y albergues, impresionantes o modestos, todos se desviven por el turista.
Impressive or modest inns, hotels, motels and hostels, all vie for tourists.

199

Mail, Telex, Fax

correos

Tengo que ir a correos a comprar sellos.
En correos no se puede hablar por teléfono.

post office *(institution when used without article)*
I have to go to the post office to buy stamps.
You can't make telephone calls at the post office.

el **sello**; **estampilla**

stamp

el **correo**
¿Ya ha llegado el correo?
En la estafeta de correos he recogido las cartas de lista de correos.

mail
Has the mail come yet?
At the post office I picked up the general delivery letters.

recibir
Hace una semana que no recibo correo.

receive; get
I haven't received any mail for a week.

mandar

send

la **carta**
Le he escrito una carta a Felisa.

letter
I have written Felisa a letter.

certificado, a
Carlos ha recibido una carta certificada del ayuntamiento.

registered
Carlos got a registered letter from City Hall.

la **(tarjeta) postal**
¿Cuánto cuesta enviar una postal a Uruguay?

postcard
How much does it cost to send a postcard to Uruguay?

urgente
¿Cuánto vale esta carta urgente y por avión?

express; special delivery
How much does this letter cost by special delivery and air mail?

por avión

air mail

el **paquete**
Mis abuelos me enviaban paquetes para Navidad.

package; parcel
My grandparents sent me packages at Christmas.

enviar

send

el **telegrama**
¿Dónde puedo poner un telegrama?
—En Telégrafos.

telegram
Where can I send a telegram?
—At the telegraph office.

la **dirección**
¿Has escrito bien la dirección y el código postal?

address
Did you write the address and the zip code correctly?

el **buzón**	mailbox
¿A qué hora recogen el buzón?	What time is the mail collected?
Voy a echar estas cartas al buzón.	I'm going to put these letters in the mailbox.
el **cartero**; la **cartera**	postman; mail carrier
Nuestra cartera es un poco despistada porque confunde el número de casa con el número de piso.	Our mail carrier is a little absent-minded, because she gets the house number and the apartment number mixed up.

el **franqueo**	postage
Esta carta no lleva suficiente franqueo.	This letter does not have sufficient postage.
la **lista de correos**	general delivery
la **estafeta de correos**	post office
el **apartado (postal)**	post office (P.O.) box
Cuando vivíamos en Valladolid teníamos un apartado postal.	When we lived in Valladolid, we had a P.O. box.
el **envío**	shipment; transport
Los gastos del envío aéreo son aparte.	The airmail charges are separate.
el **correo aéreo**	air mail
La mejor posibilidad de mandar una carta a América es por correo aéreo.	The best way to send a letter to America is by air mail.
el **impreso**	printed matter
Las revistas y los periódicos se mandan como impresos.	Magazines and newspapers are sent as printed matter.
telegrafiar	telegraph; wire
En cuanto lleguemos os telegrafiaremos.	As soon as we arrive, we will wire you.
las **señas**	address
Si me da sus señas le mandaré los libros que quiera.	If you give me your address, I'll send you the books that you want.
el **destinatario**	addressee; consignee
Te han devuelto la carta porque el destinatario es desconocido.	They returned the letter to you because the addressee is unknown.
el **remite**	sender; remitter
Me he olvidado de poner el remite.	I forgot to put down the sender's name.

el **remitente** ¿Quién es el remitente del paquete?	sender; remitter Who is the sender of the package?
el **código postal**	zip code
el **giro postal** ¿Prefiere pagar por giro postal o contra rembolso?	postal money order Do you prefer to pay with a postal money order or C.O.D.?
contra rembolso	C.O.D.
Telégrafos	telegraph office
el **télex** Mi padre nos mandó un télex desde Quito.	telex My father sent us a telex from Quito.
el **telefax**; el **fax** Envíennos los documentos por fax.	fax Fax us the documents.

Telephone

la **Telefónica** Perdone, ¿dónde está la central de Telefónica? En España Telefónica provee servicio a todo el país.	Telephone company of Spain; telephone office, exchange Excuse me, where is the main telephone office? In Spain, Telefónica services the entire country.
el **teléfono** Tanto los teléfonos públicos como los privados funcionan mal en España. Es mejor llamar desde Teléfonos que desde una cabina telefónica.	telephone Both the public and the private telephones work poorly in Spain. It's better to call from the telephone office than from a phone booth.
la **cabina telefónica**	(tele)phone booth
la **ficha**	(tele)phone token
el **número de teléfono** ¿Cuál es su número de teléfono?	(tele)phone number What is your phone number?
marcar	dial
llamar (por teléfono)	call; telephone
la **llamada** Estoy toda la mañana esperando una llamada importante.	(telephone) call I've been waiting all morning for an important call.

¡Diga!; ¡Dígame!

Hello! *(used by person answering)*

¡Dígame!—¡Oiga! ¿Está Felisa?
—¿De parte de quién?—De Roberto.
—¿Puedo hablar con Felisa?
—Sí, un momento.

Hello!—Hello, is Felisa there?
—Who's calling, please?—Roberto.
—May I speak to Felisa?
—Yes, just a minute.

¡Oiga!; ¡Oígame!
¡Oiga! El señor Fuertes, por favor.
—Al habla.

Hello; listen; say *(used by caller)*
Hello, may I speak to Mr. Fuertes, please?—Speaking.

estar comunicando
Te he llamado mil veces y siempre estaba comunicando.

be busy
I called you a thousand times, and it was always busy.

sonar
Baja la música porque si no, no oímos si suena el teléfono.

ring
Turn the music down; otherwise, we won't hear if the phone rings.

el **contestador automático**

answering machine

la **conferencia**
¿Para llamar a Valencia hay que marcar el prefijo?—Sí, porque es conferencia.

long-distance call
Do you have to dial the prefix to call Valencia?—Yes, because it's a long-distance call.

Tengo que hacer una llamada urbana y poner una conferencia a Bilbao.

I have to make a local call and place a long-distance call to Bilbao.

la **llamada urbana**

local call

el **prefijo**
Tanto para una conferencia nacional o internacional hay que marcar un prefijo.

prefix; area code
You have to dial a prefix for a long-distance call, whether domestic or international.

al **habla**; al **aparato**

speaking

la **línea**
Por favor señorita, ¡déme línea!

line
Miss, please connect me!

la **comunicación**
Es imposible hablar con Teruel porque de momento no hay comunicación.

connection; communication
It's impossible to call Teruel, because at the moment there's no connection.

descolgar
Como el teléfono estaba descolgado no te pude localizar.

take off the hook
Because the receiver was off the hook, I wasn't able to reach you.

localizar

reach

poner
¡Póngame con la señora Brea, por favor!

connect
Please connect me with Mrs. Brea!

colgar
¡Dolores! ¡Cuelga ya de una vez!

hang up
Dolores! Hang up, at long last!

la guía (telefónica)
En España se puede buscar en la guía el número de teléfono por los apellidos.

telephone book; directory
In Spain, you can find the phone number in the directory under the surname.

Telefónica es la compañía de teléfonos que abarca a toda España.
Telefónica *is the Spanish telephone company that provides coverage to the entire country.*

Print Media

la prensa
Ayer leí en la prensa que va a haber huelga general.

press; newspapers
Yesterday I read in the press that there is going to be a general strike.

el periódico

newspaper

el diario
Hay un diario español que se llama El Periódico.

daily (newspaper)
There's a Spanish daily called "The Newspaper."

la revista
En esta revista hay más anuncios que artículos.

magazine
In this magazine there are more ads than articles.

el anuncio

ad(vertisement); notice; announcement

En Hispanoamérica los anuncios se llaman avisos.

In Spanish America, ads are called "avisos" (notices).

el artículo

article

el editorial
El País publica un editorial cada día.

editorial
El País publishes one editorial each day.

el libro

book

el diccionario

dictionary

leer

read

la página

page

publicar

publish

la editorial
Esa editorial no quiso publicar mi serie de artículos.

publishing house
That publishing house didn't want to publish my series of articles.

la librería

bookstore

los medios de comunicación
Los medios de comunicación pueden influir en la opinión pública.

mass media
The mass media are able to influence public opinion.

influir

influence

la propaganda
¡Mira! Nos han regalado estos bolígrafos de propaganda.

advertising; publicity; promotion
Look, they've sent us these ballpoints as a promotional gimmick.

A pesar de la televisión, los periódicos y las revistas no pierden su popularidad.
Despite the TV, newspapers and magazines have not lost their popularity.

semanal
Cambio 16 es una revista semanal.

weekly
Cambio 16 is a weekly magazine.

el comic; tebeo
Los "comics" para niños se llaman en España "tebeos".

comic (strip)
The comic strips for children are called "tebeos" in Spain.

la publicación
La publicación de esta novela fue un gran éxito.

publication
The publication of this novel was a great success.

la crónica

report; chronicle

el, la periodista
Rosa Montero es periodista y autora.

journalist
Rosa Montero is a journalist and writer.

la redacción
La redacción de este ensayo ha costado mucho trabajo.

editing; editorial staff
Editing this essay was a lot of work.

periodístico, a
Mi hermana ha realizado un trabajo periodístico muy atrevido.

journalistic
My sister has produced a very bold piece of journalism.

atrevido, a

bold; daring

imprimir
Los diarios se imprimen por la noche.

print
Daily newspapers are printed at night.

la imprenta

printing house; press

el editor; la editora
¿Quién es el editor de esta revista?

publisher; publishing house
Who is the publisher of this magazine?

la edición
¿Qué edición del Quijote tienes?

edition
Which edition of Quixote do you have?

el índice

index

el quiosco
Muchos españoles compran el periódico en al quiosco en lugar de suscribirse.

newsstand; kiosk
Many Spaniards buy the newspaper at the newsstand instead of subscribing.

suscribirse

subscribe

agotado, a

out of print

Audiovisual Media

emitir

la **radio**
A Marisa le encanta el programa
de radio de esta emisora.
Como se han terminado las pilas
no podemos oír la radio.

escuchar

la **televisión**; la **tele**
Esta noche ponen una película
policíaca en la tele.
En España se interrumpe la emisión
para los espacios de publicidad.

el **televisor**
Me parece que el televisor está roto
porque la imagen no es clara.—
También puede ser la antena o
el cable.

la **emisora**

el **programa**

las **noticias**
¿Han dicho algo sobre el robo en
las noticias?

la **entrevista**
¿Oíste la entrevista del presidente
del club que emitieron ayer?

entrevistar

la **publicidad**
Hoy en día se hace muchísima
publicidad para cualquier artículo.

interrumpir
En la tele interrumpen las películas
para poner publicidad.

rodar
En mi barrio están rodando una
película.

el **casetero**
Este casetero tiene muy buen sonido.

emit; broadcast; air; show

radio
Marisa likes this station's
radio program very much.
Since the batteries are dead,
we can't listen to the radio.

listen (to)

television; TV
This evening there's a crime film
on TV.
In Spain, broadcasting is
interrupted for commercial breaks.

TV set
I think the TV set is broken,
because the picture isn't clear.—It
could also be the antenna or the
cable connection.

broadcasting station

channel; program

news
Have they said anything about the
theft in the news?

interview
Did you hear the interview with
the club president that was aired
yesterday?

interview

commercial advertising; publicity
Nowadays there's a great deal of
advertising for any item.

interrupt
On TV, movies are interrupted
for commercials.

shoot (film, movie)
In my neighborhood they're
shooting a film.

cassette tape recorder
This cassette tape recorder has a
very good sound.

la **casete**; el **casete**
Angel me ha grabado un casete
con tangos.

cassette
Angel recorded a cassette of
tangos for me.

grabar

record; tape

el **vídeo**; la **videograbadora**
Pepito se ha comprado una
videograbadora pero no tiene
vídeos para ver.

VCR; videorecorder
Pepito bought a VCR, but he
doesn't have any videos to
watch.

la **grabación**

recording

el **disco**

(phonograph) record

el **tocadiscos**
Ya hay nuevos aparatos de alta
fidelidad que producen mejor sonido
que un buen tocadiscos.

record player
There are already new hi-fi
systems that produce a better
sound than a good record
player.

la **emisión**

(radio, TV) show; program;
emission

la **cadena**
En España hay dos cadenas
nacionales, diferentes regionales y
muchas privadas.

television broadcasting station
In Spain there are two state-run
TV stations, several regional
stations, and many private
ones.

el **locutor**; la **locutora**
La locutora de esta emisora tiene
una voz muy agradable.

announcer; speaker
This station's announcer
has a very pleasant voice.

el, la **oyente**

listener; hearer

el **reportero**; la **reportera**
El reportaje del reportero se
publicará en la próxima edición.

reporter
The reporter's report will be
published in the next edition.

el **reportaje**

report; reporting

el, la **corresponsal**
El corresponsal informa sobre
los conflictos internacionales.

correspondent
The correspondent reports on
international conflicts.

la **serie**
Las series argentinas se parecen
mucho a las telenovelas brasileñas.

series
The Argentine soap operas greatly
resemble the Brazilian TV
series.

la **telenovela**

TV series

el **documental**
Algunos documentales son muy
interesantes.

documentary
Some documentaries are very
interesting.

transmitir
Esta tarde transmiten un concierto en
directo por vía satélite.

transmit; broadcast
This afternnoon a concert will be
broadcast live via satellite.

en **directo**

live

el **espectador**; la **espectadora**
Muchos espectadores no están
contentos con el programa de tele.

viewer
Many viewers are not happy with
the TV programming.

la **antena**
Tenemos antena parabólica.

antenna
We have a dish antenna.

la **televisión por cable**

cable TV

el **satélite**

satellite

la **pantalla**
Tienes que limpiar la pantalla porque
no se ve nada.

(TV, computer) screen
You have to clean the screen,
because you can't see anything.

la **imagen**

picture

el **volumen**

volume

el **altavoz**

loudspeaker

la **cinta**
En las emisoras de radio se gastan
muchas cintas para un programa.
Como no tenía ninguna cinta virgen
no te pude grabar el disco.

tape; cassette
At radio stations, many tapes are
used to put together a program.
Since I didn't have a blank tape,
I couldn't tape the record for you.

el **magnetófono**
Jorge cambió su magnetófono por un
reproductor de discos compactos.

tape player
Jorge replaced his tape player
with a CD player.

el **reproductor de discos compactos**

CD player

el **disco compacto (CD)**

CD; compact disc

la **videoteca**
Esta videoteca tiene las últimas
novedades del cine.

video store
This video store has the
latest movies.

Literature

la **cultura**
La cultura española tiene orígenes romanos.

culture
Spanish culture has Roman origins.

cultural
En Barcelona hay actividades culturales muy importantes.

cultural
Very important cultural events are held in Barcelona.

la **literatura**
La literatura española empieza en el siglo XII.

literature
Spanish literature begins in the 12th century.

el **estilo**
Cervantes tenía un estilo muy individual.

style
Cervantes had a very individual style.

diverso, a

diverse; different; various

el **autor**; la **autora**
¿Cómo se llama la autora de esa novela?—No lo sé. Pero es una novelista conocida.

writer; author
What is the name of the author of this novel? —I don't know. But she is a famous novelist.

el **escritor**; la **escritora**

writer

escribir
¿Quién escribió "la Colmena"?
—La escribió Camilo José Cela.

write
Who wrote "The Beehive?"
—Camilo José Cela wrote it.

el **título**

title

el **personaje**
A Juan le gustó mucho el personaje del detective.

figure; character
Juan very much liked the character of the detective.

el **cuento**

tale; story; short story

el **final**
Esta novela tiene un final feliz.

end
This novel has a happy ending.

el **texto**

text

la **novela**
¿En qué capítulo vas de esa novela?

novel
What chapter of the novel are you on now?

el **poema**
Este poema tiene sólo un verso.

poem
This poem has only one verse.

la **crítica**
La crítica no supo apreciar esta obra.

criticism; critics
The critics were unable to appreciate this work.

el **patrimonio**
El patrimonio literario catalán es muy rico.

heritage
The literary heritage of Catalonia is very rich.

la **poesía**

poetry; poem

el **verso**

verse

la **rima**
Los versos que habéis escrito no tienen rima.

rhyme
The verses that you wrote don't rhyme.

el **poeta**; la **poetisa**
Antonio Machado fue un gran poeta español.

poet; poetess
Antonio Machado was a great Spanish poet.

literario, a
El Quijote es la obra literaria española más conocida.

literary
Don Quixote is the best-known Spanish literary work.

el, la **novelista**

novelist

célebre
Unamuno fue un escritor célebre.

famous; celebrated
Unamuno was a famous writer.

el **argumento**
Creo que no has entendido el argumento de la novela.

plot
I think you didn't understand the plot of the novel.

el **diálogo**
Franco prefiere cuentos con poco diálogo.

dialogue
Franco prefers stories with little dialogue.

la **introducción**
Aún tenemos que escribir la introducción de este libro.

introduction
We still have to write the introduction of this book.

el **párrafo**
¿Puedes traducir el primer párrafo de este texto?

paragraph
Can you translate the first paragraph of this text?

el **relato**

narrative; tale

policíaco, a
Me encantan las novelas de detectives y las policíacas.

pertaining to the police
Detective and crime novels fascinate me.

la **estructura**
En el examen tuvimos que analizar la estructura de un cuento.

structure
On the test we had to analyze the structure of a story.

la **interpretación**

interpretation

el **capítulo**	chapter
el **romancero**	Spanish metrical romance; collection of Spanish romances; singer of romances
El romancero es un género literario popular.	The Spanish romance is a literary genre originating among the people.
el **género**	genre
la **leyenda**	legend
Existen muchas leyendas sobre El Cid.	There exist many legends about El Cid.
el **romanticismo**	Romanticism
Zorrilla fue un autor del romanticismo español.	Zorrilla was a writer of the Spanish Romantic Era.
la **cita**	quote
En este ensayo no has marcado las citas.	You haven't marked the quotes in this essay.

Fine Arts

el **arte**
En el Centro Reina Sofía de Madrid se organizan exposiciones de arte.

art
Art exhibitions are held in the Queen Sofía Center in Madrid.

la **exposición**

exhibition

exponer

exhibit

la **galería**
¿Me acompañas a la exposición en la galería de mi tío?

gallery
Are you going with me to the exhibition in my uncle's gallery?

el, la **artista**
Mi abuelo era artista aficionado.

artist
My grandfather was an amateur artist.

el **pintor**; la **pintora**
Nuestro tío es pintor, pero no pinta las casas.

painter
Our uncle is a painter, but he doesn't paint houses.

dibujar

draw

el **cuadro**
Creo que nunca podré comprar un cuadro de Miró.

picture; painting
I think I'll never be able to buy a painting by Miró.

el **escultor**; la **escultora**
En Málaga hablamos con una
escultora muy interesante.

sculptor; sculptress
In Málaga we spoke with a very
interesting scupltress.

la **escultura**
En el Museo Dalí se pueden ver
también algunas esculturas del artista.

sculpture
In the Dali Museum you can also
see some sculptures by the artist.

la **estatua**
Al final de las Ramblas está la
estatua de Colón.

statue
At the end of the Ramblas stands
the statue of Columbus.

el **crítico**; la **crítica**
A veces los críticos de arte no saben
lo que están criticando.

critic
Sometimes art critics don't
know what they are criticizing.

el **monumento**
La ciudad antigua de Toledo es un
monumento histórico.

monument
The old town of Toledo is a
historic monument.

barroco, a

Baroque

románico, a
En Barcelona hay una capilla
románica en la plaza del Pedró.

Romanesque
In Barcelona there is a
Romanesque chapel at Pedró
Plaza.

estético, a

esthetic

el **original**
En El Escorial hay varios originales
de El Greco.

original
In El Escorial there are several
El Greco originals.

restaurar

restore

el, la **dibujante**
Los dibujantes trabajan con lápiz
y carbón.

draftsman; drafter; designer
Draftsmen work with pencil and
charcoal.

la **inspiración**

inspiration

el **retrato**
¿Habéis visto el retrato de mi primo?

portrait
Have you seen the portrait of my
cousin?

el **modelo**

model

el **cartel**
Muchos pintores han dibujado
carteles.
Carteles, no.
En el dormitorio tengo un cartel
de toros.

poster; placard
Many painters have also drawn
posters.
Post no bills.
In the bedroom I have a bullfight
poster.

la **gráfica**

graphic arts; graphics

la **reproducción**	reproduction
Luisa se ha comprado una reproducción de un cuadro de Goya.	Luisa has bought a reproduction of a painting by Goya.
el **diseño**	design; sketch; drawing
diseñar	draw; sketch; design
Paco diseña trajes de baño.	Paco designs bathing suits.
la **pintada**; el **grafiti**	graffiti
He visto unas pintadas antiamericanas.	I have seen some anti-American graffiti.
mudéjar	Mudejar
Los musulmanes en territorio cristiano crearon el arte mudéjar.	Mudejar art was created by Moslems living in Christian territory.
el **Renacimiento**	Renaissance
contemporáneo, a	contemporary

Music and Dance

el **músico**; la **música**	musician
El gran músico Miguel de Falla nació en Cádiz	The great musician Miguel de Falla was born in Cadiz.
el **bailarín**; la **bailarina**	(ballet) dancer; ballerina
Antonio está enamorado de una bailarina de flamenco.	Antonio is in love with a flamenco dancer.
la **banda (de música)**	band
¿Tocas en la banda de música de tu pueblo?	Do you play in your village's band?
el, la **cantante**	singer
¿Habéis oído a la cantante Teresa Berganza?	Have you heard the singer Teresa Berganza?
la **canción**	song
Algunas canciones españolas son muy alegres.	Some Spanish songs are very cheerful.
cantar	sing
Julio no puede cantar porque no tiene voz.	Julio can't sing because he is hoarse.
el **tango**	tango

el **concierto**
El verano pasado fuimos a un
concierto de música clásica.

concert
Last summer we went to a concert
of classical music.

clásico, a

classical

tocar

play

la **música**

music

el **sonido**
Tu guitarra tiene buen sonido.

sound
Your guitar has a good sound.

el **instrumento**
¿Tocas algún instrumento?—Sí,
toco la guitarra, el piano, la flauta,
el violín, la batería y las castañuelas.

(musical) instrument
Do you play an instrument?—Yes,
I play the guitar, piano, flute,
violin, percussion instruments, and
castanets.

la **guitarra**

guitar

el **piano**

piano

la **ópera**
Nunca fui a la ópera.

opera
I've never been to the opera.

el **director de orquesta**;
la **directora de orquesta**
Muchos directores son también
compositores.

orchestra director; conductor

Many directors are also
composers.

el **compositor**; la **compositora**

composer

la **composición**

composition

componer
Granados compuso muchos
conciertos para piano.

compose
Granados composed many
piano concertos.

el **tono**
Siempre que toco el violín me
equivoco de tono.

tone; tune; key
Whenever I play the violin,
I get the wrong key.

la **nota**

(musical) note

el **ritmo**

rhythm

la **orquesta**
Antes todos los domingos tocaba
una orquesta en el parque.

orchestra
Formerly an orchestra played
in the park every Sunday.

el **conjunto**
¿Sabes qué conjunto tocará esta
noche?

(dance) group; (musical) group
Do you know which group will
play tonight?

el **micrófono**

microphone

el **flamenco**
El flamenco puede ser muy triste.

flamenco
The flamenco can be very sad.

la **salsa**	salsa
la **opereta**	operetta
la **zarzuela**	zarzuela
La zarzuela es un género de opereta típica española.	The zarzuela is a type of Spanish operetta.
la **jota**	jota *(traditional dance in Navarre, Aragón, and Valencia)*
el **coro**	choir
A mi padre le gusta el canto de coros.	My father likes choral music.
el **canto**	song; singing
la **melodía**	melody
Esa melodía es muy bonita.	This melody is very lovely.
el **musical**	musical
En el Liceo de Barcelona no representan musicales.	No musicals are presented in the Liceo de Barcelona.
la **flauta**	flute
el **violín**	violin
el **saxofón**	saxophone
la **batería**	percussion instruments
el **órgano**	organ
Algunos curas tocan muy bien el órgano.	Some priests play the organ very well.
las **castañuelas**	castanets

History

la **historia**	history
"La Historia de España" del historiador Vicens Vives es muy importante.	*The History of Spain* by the historian Vicens Vives is very important.
histórico, a	historic
ibérico, a	Iberian
el **imperio**	empire
El Imperio Romano fue muy importante en la cultura mediterránea.	The Roman Empire was very important for the culture of the Mediterranean area.
romano, a	Roman

217

el **emperador**; la **emperatriz**	emperor; empress
la **Edad Media**	Middle Ages
el **moro**; la **mora**	Moor
la **Reconquista**	Reconquest
La Reconquista duró desde el 711 hasta 1492.	The Reconquest of Spain lasted from 711 to 1492.
el **Siglo de Oro**	Golden Age *(16th and 17th centuries)*
el **rey**; la **reina**	king; queen
Los Reyes Católicos, la reina Isabel y el rey Fernando, enviaron a Colón a América.	The Catholic Monarchs, Queen Isabella and King Ferdinand, sent Columbus to America.
el, la **noble**	nobleman; -woman
el **descubrimiento**	discovery
Con el descubrimiento de América empezó la colonización de las nuevas tierras.	With the discovery of America, the settlement of the New World began.
colonizar	colonize; settle
Los españoles y los portugueses colonizaron Iberoamérica.	The Spaniards and the Portuguese colonized Hispanic America.
descubrir	discover
Ya no hay continentes por descubrir.	There are no more continents to be discovered.
conquistar	conquer
Hernán Cortés conquistó México.	Hernán Cortés conquered Mexico.
la **conquista**	conquest
La conquista de la Península Ibérica por los árabes no llegó hasta la región vasca.	The conquest of the Iberian Peninsula by the Arabs did not extend to the Basque region.
la **civilización**	civilization; culture
la **época**	epoch; era; time (period)
La época de mayor pobreza en España fueron los años después de la Guerra Civil.	The period of greatest poverty in Spain was the years after the Civil War.

el **historiador**; la **historiadora**	historian
El historiador Américo Castro escribió las obras más interesantes sobre los judíos en España.	The historian Américo Castro wrote extremely interesting works on the Jews in Spain.
arqueológico, a	archeological
prehistórico, a	prehistoric
En España hay hallazgos prehistóricos.	There are prehistoric finds in Spain.
el **hallazgo**	find
primitivo, a	primitive; original
la **invasión**	invasion
germánico, a	Germanic
el **reino**	kingdom; realm
La capital del Reino Visigodo en el año 560 era Toledo.	The capital of the Visigoth kingdom in 560 was Toledo.
visigodo, a	Visigoth
reinar	reign; rule
el, la **mozárabe**	Mozarab
Los cristianos que permanecieron en territorio no cristiano se llaman mozárabes.	The Christians who remained in non-Christian territory are known as Mozarabs.
expulsar	expel; drive out
hispánico, a	Hispanic
la **aristocracia**	aristocracy
el **conde**; la **condesa**	count; countess
el **marqués**; la **marquesa**	marquis, marquise
el **descubridor**	discoverer
Los descubridores llegaron a América en tres carabelas.	The discoverers came to America in three caravels.
la **carabela**	caravel
descubierto, a	discovered
América fue descubierta en 1492.	America was discovered in 1492.
la **colonización**	colonization; settlement
la **colonia**	colony
Después de la Paz de Utrecht España perdió muchas colonias.	After the Treaty of Utrecht, Spain lost many colonies.
el **esclavo**; la **esclava**	slave
Muchos indios murieron como esclavos.	Many Indians died as slaves.

el **conquistador**	conquerer
Los conquistadores trajeron oro y plata a España.	The conquerors brought gold and silver to Spain.
la **espada**	sword
Las espadas de Sevilla eran famosas.	The swords of Seville were famous.
la **independencia**	independence
la **sucesión**	succession

Religion

la **religión**
Hay que separar la religión de la política.

religion
One has to separate religion from politics.

religioso, a
Leopoldo estudió en un instituto religioso, a pesar de que era ateo.

religious
Leopoldo attended a religious (Catholic) school, although he was an atheist.

creer
Los católicos creen que el Papa siempre tiene razón.

believe
Catholics believe that the Pope is always right.

el **cristiano**; la **cristiana**
Nerón mató a muchos cristianos.

Christian
Nero killed many Christians.

cristiano, a
Las religiones cristianas tienen su origen en Judea.

Christian
The Christian religions have their origin in Judea.

la **Iglesia**
La Iglesia no permite el uso del condón.

Catholic Church
The Catholic Church does not allow the use of condoms.

la **iglesia**
La catedral de Granada es una de las iglesias más grandes de Europa.

church
The Cathedral of Granada is one of the largest churches in Europe.

la **catedral**

cathedral

la **campana**

bell

el **monasterio**
¿Conoces el monasterio de Montserrat?

monastery
Do you know the Monastery of Montserrat?

la **parroquia**

parish

el **cura** — priest; curate; clergyman

el **sacerdote**; la **sacerdotisa** — priest(ess)
Cleopatra fue una sacerdotisa muy guapa. — Cleopatra was a very beautiful priestess.

Dios — God

la **Biblia** — Bible

rezar — pray

la **misa** — mass
En la Edad Media estaba prohibido celebrar misas negras. — In the Middle Ages it was forbidden to hold black masses.

la **limosna** — alms

santo, a — holy; saint
También en las guerras santas mueren muchos inocentes. — In holy wars, many innocent people also die.
Hay dos santos que no llevan "san" delante: Santo Tomás y Santo Domingo. — There are two saints whose names don't begin with "san": Santo Tomás and Santo Domingo.

sagrado, a — holy; sacred

el **ángel** — angel
¿Los ángeles tienen sexo? — Do angels have gender?

el **alma** f — soul
¡De verdad! ¡Lo siento en el alma! — Truly! I feel deeply sorry!

el **espíritu** — spirit

confesarse — confess (to a priest)
Nos confesamos el viernes pasado. — We made confession last Friday.

la **conciencia** — conscience
Hay demasiada gente sin conciencia. — There are too many people without a conscience.

pecar — sin
Adam y Eva pecaron en el paraíso. — Adam and Eve sinned in Paradise.

el **paraíso** — paradise

el **diablo** — devil
Leopoldo no cree que el diablo vive en el infierno. — Leopoldo doesn't believe that the Devil lives in hell.

el **infierno** — hell

el **musulmán**; la **musulmana** — Moslem

la **mezquita** — mosque

islámico, a	Islamic
el **judío**; la **judía**	Jew; Jewess
hebreo, a	Hebrew

ateo, a
atheistic

el **cristianismo**
En el cristianismo hay diferentes confesiones.
Christianity
Within Christianity there are different denominations.

el, la **protestante**
Los protestantes son minoría en España.
Protestant
Protestants are a minority in Spain.

el **católico**; la **católica**
No todos los católicos están en contra del aborto.
Catholic
Not all Catholics oppose abortion.

el **Papa**
El Papa no permite que se casen los curas.
Pope
The Pope does not allow priests to marry.

la **monja**
Mi hermana fue a un colegio de monjas.
nun
My sister went to a convent school.

el **arzobispo**
El Papa nombra a los arzobispos.
archbishop
The Pope names the archbishops.

el **obispo**
El obispo dirá misa el domingo.
bishop
The bishop will say Mass on Sunday.

la **oración**
Antes de clase teníamos que rezar una oración.
prayer
Before class we had to say a prayer.

Cristo
Cristo murió en la cruz.
Christ
Christ died on the Cross.

el **santo**; la **santa**
saint

la **Virgen**
Muchos creyentes rezan a la Virgen o a los Santos.
Virgin Mary
Many believers pray to the Virgin Mary or to the saints.

el **discípulo**
Los discípulos de Jesús fueron los doce apóstoles.
disciple
Jesus' disciples were the Twelve Apostles.

el **apóstol**
apostle

la **comunión**
Hoy toma mi nieto la primera comunión y le regalaré una Biblia.
communion
Today my grandson is making his First Communion, and I'm going to give him a Bible.

el **símbolo**

symbol

el **evangelio**

Gospel(s)

El evangelio forma los primeros
cuatro libros del Nuevo Testamento.

The Gospels form the first
four books of the New
Testament.

la **creación**

creation; Genesis

La creación forma el primer libro del
Antiguo Testamento.

Genesis is the first book
of the Old Testament.

la **confesión**

confession

El cura oye la confesión.

The priest hears the
confession.

el **pecado**

sin

Marta confiesa sus pecados.

Marta confesses her sins.

el, la **creyente**

believer

Los creyentes tienen fe.

Believers have faith.

la **fe**

faith

el **crucifijo**; la **cruz**

crucifix; cross

En todas las iglesias cristianas hay
un crucifijo o una cruz.

In all Christian churches there is a
crucifix or a cross.

la **capilla**

chapel

El bautizo de mi hijo fue en una
capilla.

My son's baptism took place in a
chapel.

el **bautizo**

baptism

el **convento**

convent

En este convento hay una
biblioteca extraordinaria.

In this convent there is an
extraordinary library.

el **milagro**

miracle

Cristo hizo muchos milagros.

Christ performed many miracles.

el **dios**; la **diosa**

god; goddess

el **templo**

temple

Muchos templos aztecas fueron
destruídos durante la conquista de
México.

Many Aztec temples were
destroyed during the conquest
of Mexico.

el **sacrificio**

sacrifice; offering

la **sinagoga**

synagogue

el **hinduismo**

Hinduism

▬▬▬ Manners, Customs, and Celebrations ▬▬▬

la **costumbre**   custom; habit; use

la **fiesta**   party; festivity; holiday
Muchas fiestas españolas se celebran el día del Patrono de la ciudad o del pueblo.

Many Spanish holidays are celebrated on the name day of the patron saint of the town or village.

tradicional   traditional

popular   popular

celebrar   celebrate

el **santo**   name day; saint's day
En España se celebra más el santo que los cumpleaños.

In Spain, name days are celebrated more than birthdays.

el **cumpleaños**   birthday

el **aniversario**   anniversary
¿Dónde celebrásteis vuestro aniversario?

Where did you celebrate your anniversary?

la **corrida de toros**   bullfight
Muchas corridas de toros se hacen durante las fiestas de cada ciudad o región.

Many bullfights are held during the festivals of each city or region.

la **Navidad**   Christmas
¡Feliz Navidad!; ¡Felices Navidades!   Merry Christmas!

Año **Nuevo**   New Year
¡Feliz Año Nuevo!   Happy New Year!

los **Reyes Magos**   Three Wise Men (Epiphany)
En España el día de Reyes se dan los regalos.

In Spain, gifts are presented at Epiphany.

(la) **Semana Santa**   Holy Week
Las procesiones de Semana Santa en Sevilla son famosas.

The Holy Week processions in Seville are famous.

la **procesión**   procession

Una vez al año, los toros corren por las calles de Pamplona.
Once a year the bulls run through the streets of Pamplona.

el **Patrono**; la **Patrona**	patron saint
el **torero**	bullfighter
Los toreros mueren a veces en las corridas.	Bullfighters sometimes die in bullfights.
el **carnaval**	carnival; Mardi Gras
el **San Fermín**	St. Fermín
Los Sanfermines se celebran del uno al siete de julio en Pamplona.	St. Fermín is celebrated from the first to the seventh of July in Pamplona.
las **Fallas**	Fallas
Las Fallas se celebran en Valencia y terminan el día de San José, 19 de marzo.	Fallas are celebrated in Valencia and end on St. Joseph's Day, March 19th.
(la) **Nochebuena**	Christmas Eve
Los españoles colocan ahora en Nochebuena el árbol de Navidad.	Spaniards now put up a Christmas tree on Christmas Eve.
(la) **Nochevieja**	New Year's Eve
Cuando suenan las doce de la noche en Nochevieja los españoles toman doce uvas para tener suerte en el Año Nuevo.	When midnight strikes on New Year's Eve, Spaniards eat 12 grapes in order to have good luck in the New Year.
(la) **Pascua**	Easter
Pentecostés	Pentecost
¿Cuándo es Pentecostés?—No tengo ni idea.	When is Pentecost?—I have no idea.

La Navidad en España y Latinoamérica se ha comercializado como en el resto del mundo.
Christmas in Spain and Latin America has become commercialized as in the rest of the world.

Europe

el **continente**
La tierra está dividida en cinco continentes.

continent
The earth is divided into five continents.

Europa

Europe

europeo, a

European

el **país**
Los países miembros de la Comunidad Europea están en Europa.

country
The member countries of the European Community are in Europe.

limitar
España limita con Francia, Portugal, Gran Bretaña y Marruecos.

bound; border (up)on
Spain borders on France, Portugal, Great Britain, and Morocco.

el **idioma**
En la tierra se hablan muchos idiomas.

language; tongue
Many languages are spoken in the world.

Suecia
Los coches de Suecia son muy seguros.

Sweden
Cars from Sweden are very safe.

sueco, a
Muchos suecos hablan alemán.

Swedish; Swede
Many Swedes speak German.

(la) **Rusia**
Rusia fue parte de la Unión Soviética o URSS durante la mayor parte del siglo XX.
Rusia es un país enorme.

Russia
Russia was part of the Soviet Union or USSR during most of the 20th century.
Russia is an enormous country.

ruso, a
El ruso me parece una lengua muy difícil.

Russian
Russian seems like a very difficult language to me.

Inglaterra

England

inglés; inglesa
Las universidades inglesas son conocidas.

English; Englishman, -woman
The English universities are well known.

Alemania
Alemania estuvo dividida casi 40 años en República Federal (RFA) y República Democrática (RDA).

Germany
For almost 40 years, Germany was divided into the Federal Republic (FRG) and the Democratic Republic (GDR).

alemán; alemana
Los coches alemanes son caros.

German
German cars are expensive.

Suiza
En Suiza no sólo hay bancos.

Switzerland
Banks are not all one finds in
Switzerland.

suizo, a
Los relojes suizos son muy buenos.

Swiss
Swiss clocks and watches are very
good.

Francia
Francia limita con Bélgica, Alemania,
Suiza, Italia y España.

France
France borders on Belgium,
Germany, Switzerland, Italy,
and Spain.

francés; francesa
Los primeros turistas en España
fueron los franceses.

French; Frenchman, -woman
The first tourists in Spain were the
French.

Italia
Carlos se fue a Italia y no quiere
volver.

Italy
Carlos went to Italy and doesn't
want to come back.

italiano, a
La ópera italiana es muy conocida.

Italian
Italian opera is very famous.

España
En España se hablan cuatro lenguas:
el español o castellano, el vasco o
euskera, el gallego y el catalán.

Spain
In Spain four languages are
spoken: Spanish, Basque,
Galician, and Catalan.

español(a)

Spanish; Spaniard

castellano, a

Castilian; Spanish

Portugal
Portugal es un país pequeño con
una gran historia.

Portugal
Portugal is a small country with
a great history.

portugués; portuguesa
Los portugueses y los españoles
no han sido siempre muy amigos.

Portuguese
The Portuguese and the Spaniards
have not always been good
friends.

el **gitano**; la **gitana**	Gypsy
Irlanda	Ireland
Irlanda es desde hace muchos años independiente.	Ireland has been independent for many years.
irlandés; **irlandesa**	Irish; Irishman, -woman
¿Te gusta el café irlandés?	Do you like Irish coffee?
Gran Bretaña	Great Britain
Gran Bretaña fue un imperio enorme.	Great Britain was an enormous empire.
británico, a	British; Britisher
Noruega	Norway
La capital de Noruega es Oslo.	The capital of Norway is Oslo.
noruego, a	Norwegian
No soy noruego pero entiendo muy bien el noruego.	I'm not a Norwegian, but I understand Norwegian very well.
Dinamarca	Denmark
En Dinamarca se produce mucha leche.	In Denmark a great deal of milk is produced.
danés; **danesa**	Danish; Dane
Las playas danesas son muy largas.	The Danish beaches are very long.
Polonia	Poland
En Polonia los inviernos son muy largos.	In Poland the winters are very long.
polaco, a	Polish; Pole
El polaco se parece al ruso.	Polish is similar to Russian.
(los) **Países Bajos**	Netherlands; Holland
En los Países Bajos no hay casi montañas.	In the Netherlands there are almost no mountains.
holandés; **holandesa**	Dutch; Dutchman, -woman
Las flores holandesas se exportan a muchos países.	Dutch flowers are exported to many countries.
Bélgica	Belgium
En Bélgica está la sede de la Comunidad Europea.	The seat of the European Parliament is in Belgium.
belga	Belgian
Los belgas hablan francés y flamenco.	The Belgians speak French and Flemish.

Austria	Austria
En invierno vamos a esquiar a Austria.	In winter we're going to Austria to ski.
austríaco, a	Austrian
Vienna es la capital austríaca.	Vienna is the capital of Austria.
Grecia	Greece
En Grecia hay muchos templos antiguos.	There are many ancient temples in Greece.
griego, a	Greek
Los restaurantes griegos son muy agradables.	Greek restaurants are very pleasant.
Turquía	Turkey
Turquía une el oriente con el occidente.	Turkey links the Orient with the Occident.
turco, a	Turkish; Turk
La comida turca es muy rica.	Turkish food is quite delicious.

America

americano, a	American
El continente americano está compuesto por América del Norte, América Central o Centroamérica y América del Sur.	The American continent consists of North America, Central America, and South America.
América del Norte	North America
norteamericano, a	North American
(los) **Estados Unidos (EE.UU.)**	United States (USA)
Los Estados Unidos tienen grandes puentes y carreteras.	The United States has large bridges and highways.
México (Méjico)	Mexico
De México llegó mucha plata a España.	A lot of silver came to Spain from Mexico.
mexicano, a (mejicano, a)	Mexican
La cocina mexicana es muy picante.	The Mexican cuisine is very spicy.
América Central; **Centroamérica**	Central America

Guatemala	Guatemala
Los países de Centroamérica son Guatemala, Honduras, El Salvador, Nicaragua, Costa Rica y Panamá.	The countries of Central America are Guatemala, Honduras, El Salvador, Nicaragua, Costa Rica, and Panama.
guatemalteco, a	Guatemalan
Los guatemaltecos, hondureños, salvadoreños, nicaragüenses, costarricenses, panameños, bolivianos, dominicanos, colombianos, venezolanos y paraguayos hablan español.	Guatemalans, Hondurans, Salvadorans, Nicaraguans, Costa Ricans, Panamanians, Bolivians, Dominicans, Colombians, Venezuelans, and Paraguayans speak Spanish.
América del Sur	South America
Colombia	Colombia
El café de Colombia se toma también en Europa.	Coffee from Colombia is also drunk in Europe.
colombiano, a	Colombian
Venezuela	Venezuela
Venezuela exporta petróleo.	Venezuela exports petroleum.
venezolano, a	Venezuelan
(el) **Ecuador**	Ecuador
Mi alumno trabaja ahora en Ecuador.	My pupil now works in Ecuador.
ecuatoriano, a	Ecuadorian
Las Islas Galápagos son ecuatorianas.	The Galapagos Islands are Ecuadorian.
(el) **Perú**	Peru
Me gustó mucho Perú y Bolivia.	I liked Peru and Bolivia very much.
peruano, a	Peruvian
Muchos peruanos son indios.	Many Peruvians are Indians.
Bolivia	Bolivia
boliviano, a	Bolivian
La capital boliviana se llama La Paz.	The Bolivian capital is called La Paz.
(el) **Paraguay**	Paraguay
Paraguay es caluroso.	Paraguay is hot.
paraguayo, a	Paraguayan
(la) **Argentina**	Argentina
En Argentina viven muchos italianos.	Many Italians live in Argentina.
argentino, a	Argentine; Argentinian
El tango argentino es muy famoso.	The Argentine tango is very famous.
Chile	Chile
Chile tiene muchas climas.	Chile has many climates.

chileno, a
Los chilenos exportan gran cantidad de cobre, excelentes vinos y productos agrícolas.

Chilean
Chileans export large amounts of copper, excellent wines, and agricultural products.

Hispanoamérica	Spanish America
hispanoamericano, a	Spanish American
Latinoamérica	Latin America
hispanohablante	Spanish-speaking
el, la **hispanohablante**	Spanish speaker
sudamericano, a	South American
el, la **maya**	Maya (people and language)
el **inca**	Inca
el **quechua**	Quechua (language)
el **indio**; la **india**	Indian
la **tribu**	tribe
el **mulato**; la **mulata**	mulatto
el **mestizo**; la **mestiza**	half-breed; mestizo

Los mestizos son de padre blanco y madre india.

Mestizos have a white father and an Indian mother.

azteca	Aztec
Honduras	Honduras
hondureño, a	Honduran
El **Salvador**	El Salvador

El Salvador es un país pequeño y con graves conflictos sociales.

El Salvador is a small country and has serious social problems.

salvadoreño, a — Salvadoran

Nicaragua — Nicaragua

En Nicaragua hay conflictos políticos.

In Nicaragua there are political conflicts.

nicaragüense — Nicaraguan

Costa Rica — Costa Rica

Costa Rica tiene una costa muy bonita.

Costa Rica has a very lovely coast.

costarricense (costarriqueño, a) — Costa Rican

Panamá — Panama

El Canal de Panamá todavía es norteamericano.

The Panama Canal still belongs to the US.

panameño, a	Panamanian
Cuba	Cuba
En Cuba hay playas naturales.	There are natural beaches in Cuba.
cubano, a	Cuban
El tabaco y ron cubanos son famosos en todo el mundo.	Cuban tobacco and rum are famous all over the world.
(la) **República Dominicana**	Dominican Republic
La República Dominicana está en el Caribe.	The Dominican Republic is in the Caribbean.
dominicano, a	Dominican
(el) **Uruguay**	Uruguay
uruguayo, a	Uruguayan
(el) **Brasil**	Brazil
Brasil es el país más grande de Latinoamérica.	Brazil is the largest country in Latin America.
brasileño, a	Brazilian
El carnaval brasileño es más conocido que el cubano.	The Brazilian Carnival is more famous than the Cuban Carnival.

▬▬▬ Africa, Asia, Australia ▬▬▬

África	Africa
africano, a	African
El continente africano, o sea África, está al sur de Europa.	The African continent, or Africa, is south of Europe.
Marruecos	Morocco
Marruecos quiere que Ceuta y Melilla sean ciudades marroquíes otra vez.	Morocco wants Ceuta and Melilla to be Moroccan cities again.
marroquí	Moroccan
árabe	Arabic; Arab
Asia	Asia
China	China
En China hay muchos monumentos históricos.	In China there are many historic monuments.
chino, a	Chinese
Los chinos son un pueblo enorme.	The Chinese have an enormous population.

(el) **Japón**
A Japón pertenecen muchas islas.

Japan
Many islands belong to Japan.

japonés; japonesa
Los productos japoneses son de alta calidad.

Japanese
Japanese products are of high quality.

Australia
Australia junto con otras islas forman un continente que está al sureste de Asia.

Australia
Australia, together with other islands, forms a continent that lies southeast of Asia.

---

asiático, a
El continente asiático limita con Europa al este.

Asiatic; Asian
The Asian continent borders on Eastern Europe.

Israel
En Israel hay muchos conflictos.

Israel
In Israel there are many conflicts.

israelí
Durante nuestras vacaciones conocimos a unos israelíes.

Israeli
During our vacation we met some Israelis.

(la) **India**
La India ocupa casi un continente.

India
India occupies almost a continent.

indio, a
Como Colón se equivocó, los indios viven no sólo en India sino también en América.

Indian
Since Columbus was mistaken, Indians live not only in India, but also in America.

Filipinas

Philippines

filipino, a

Philippine; Filipino; Filipina

Guinea Ecuatorial

Equatorial Guinea

guineano, a

Guinean

Political Systems

(el)**Estado**
Los Jefes de Estado han firmado el acuerdo.

state
The heads of state have signed the agreement.

el **sistema**
Los sistemas políticos no son perfectos.

system
Political systems are not perfect.

la **nación**
El presidente dirigió un mensaje a la nación.

nation; people
The president sent a message to the nation.

el **pueblo**
El pueblo paga las consecuencias de una mala política.

people
The people bear the consequences of a bad policy.

la **república**
En España las primeras repúblicas duraron poco tiempo.

republic
In Spain, the first republics lasted only a short time.

el **régimen**
El régimen franquista era una dictadura.

regime; form of government
The Franco regime was a dictatorship.

la **libertad**
No todos los regímenes respetan la libertad individual.

freedom; liberty
Not all forms of government respect individual liberty.

la **dictadura**

dictatorship

el **dictador**

dictator

la **democracia**
La democracia española existe desde 1975.

democracy
The Spanish democracy has existed since 1975.

el **capitalismo**
El capitalismo se interesa siempre en aumentar la producción.

capitalism
Capitalism is always concerned with increasing production.

el **comunismo**
Durante cuarenta años el comunismo estuvo prohibido en España.

communism
For 40 years, communism was prohibited in Spain.

el **socialismo**
China y Suecia tienen muy distintas formas de socialismo.

socialism
China and Sweden have very different forms of socialism.

liberal
El líder liberal fue presidente hace muchos años.

liberal
The leader of the Liberals was president many years ago.

estatal

pertaining to the state

la **constitución**
La constitución española es
democrática.

constitution
The Spanish constitution is
democratic.

la **igualdad**
La Constitución garantiza la
igualdad de derechos de los
hombres.

equality
The Constitution guarantees the
equality of human rights.

constitucional
Juan Carlos es un rey constitucional.

constitutional
Juan Carlos is a constitutional
monarch.

republicano, a
El gobierno republicano huyó a
Francia.

republican
The republican government fled to
France.

federal
En España no hay Estados federales.

federal
In Spain there are no federal
states.

la **monarquía**
España es una monarquía
parlamentaria.

monarchy
Spain is a parliamentary
monarchy.

parlamentario, a

parliamentary

democrático, a
El gobierno democrático tiene que
luchar contra el terrorismo.

democratic
The democratic government has to
combat terrorism.

el, la **demócrata**
Los demócratas no se van a presentar
a las elecciones.

democrat
The democrats are not going to
run for election.

capitalista
El sistema capitalista funciona con la
libre competencia.

capitalist(ic)
The capitalist system is based
on free competition.

comunista
El Partido Comunista Español tiene
buenas relaciones con el Partido
Comunista Italiano.

communist
The Spanish Communist Party has
good relations with the Italian
Communist Party.

socialista
Los partidos socialistas estuvieron
prohibidos en España durante el
régimen franquista.

socialist
Socialist parties were prohibited in
Spain during the Franco regime.

el **liberalismo**
Los derechos humanos tienen su
origen en el liberalismo.

liberalism
Human rights have their
origin in liberalism.

humano, a

human

la **transición** 1975 es el año de la transición democrática en España.	transition 1975 is the year of the democratic transition in Spain.
progresivo, a El presidente ha presentado una reforma progresiva.	progressive (*adjective*) The president has presented a progressive reform.
progresista Algunos progresistas se vuelven conservadores cuando ganan mucho dinero.	progressive (*noun*) Some progressives become conservative when they earn a lot of money.
la **junta militar**	military junta
suprimir Franco suprimió los principios democráticos.	suppress Franco suppressed democratic principles.
conservador(a)	conservative
el **fascismo**	fascism
el, la **fascista**	fascist
franquista	Francoist
el **caudillo** Franco es conocido en España por el nombre Caudillo.	leader; chief Franco is known in Spain as "El Caudillo."
el **regionalismo**	regionalism
el **centralismo**	centralism

State Institutions

la **Corona** A la Corona de Aragón pertenecían Cataluña, Aragón, Valencia.	crown; kingdom Catalonia, Aragón, and Valencia belonged to the Kingdom of Aragon.
las **Cortes** Las Cortes de Cádiz se crearon en 1812.	Cortes (*royal court and both houses of Parliament*) The Cortes of Cádiz were created in 1812.
el **Congreso** El Congreso de los Diputados reside en Madrid.	Congress The Congress of Deputies is located in Madrid.
el **presidente**	president

el **parlamento**
Los diputados discuten en el parlamento.

Parliament
The deputies debate in Parliament.

el **gobierno**

government

el **ministro**; la **ministra**
Los ministros votaron contra el presidente.

minister
The ministers voted against the president.

nombrar
El Presidente del Gobierno no se nombra sino que se elige.

name; appoint
The president of the government is not appointed, but elected.

el **ministerio**
El Ministerio de Asuntos Exteriores no quiso dar una explicación a la prensa.

ministry
The Ministry of Foreign Affairs did not want to give an explanation to the press.

el **diputado**; la **diputada**

deputy; representative

la **diputación**
Las Diputaciones son instituciones que administran las provincias.

provincial administration
The "Diputaciones" are institutions that govern the provinces.

administrar

administer; govern

el **gobernador**

governor

civil
En España hay gobernadores civiles y militares.

civil; civilian
In Spain there are civilian and military governors.

la **administración**
La administración pública es un mal necesario.

administration
Public administration is a necessary evil.

la **comisión**
El Senado delega funciones en las comisiones.

commission
The Senate delegates functions to the commissions.

---

el **Senado**

Senate

el **senador**; la **senadora**

senator

gobernar

rule; govern

Hacienda

public treasury; tax authorities; internal revenue office

Hacienda me tendrá que devolver los impuestos que pagué de más.

The tax authorities will have to refund me the taxes I paid in excess.

fiscal

fiscal

ministerial
Por orden ministerial se reducirán las ayudas.

ministerial
By ministerial order the subsidies will be reduced.

las **autoridades**
Las autoridades sanitarias recomiendan la vacunación.

authorities
The health authorities recommend the vaccination.

autorizar
El Gobierno no autorizó la huelga.

authorize; approve
The Government did not authorize the strike.

la **burocracia**

bureaucracy

el **departamento**
El departamento de extranjeros es poco comprensivo.

department; office; ministry
The aliens' registration office is not very understanding.

administrativo, a

administrative

el **registro**
Los matrimonios, nacimientos y muertes se inscriben en el Registro Civil.

registry; census; record
Marriages, births, and deaths are recorded at the Registry Office.

el **boletín**

bulletin

el **sector**
Para combatir la inflación debe ahorrar el sector público.

sector
To combat inflation, the public sector has to economize.

la **institución**

institution

delegar

delegate

Police Force and System of Justice

la **comisaría**

police station

la **policía**
La policía debe proteger la seguridad de la población.

police
The police are supposed to protect the safety of the population.

el, la **policía**

policeman, -woman

la **sospecha**
Tengo la sospecha que me están engañando.

suspicion
I suspect that they're deceiving me.

escapar

escape

esconderse	hide
denunciar	denounce; accuse
Me han denunciado injustamente.	They have accused me unjustly.
perseguir	pursue; persecute
El policía prosiguió al ladrón.	The policeman pursued the thief.
detener	detain; arrest
La policía detuvo al asesino.	The police arrested the murderer.
el **acusado**; la **acusada**	accused; defendant
el **fiscal**	district attorney; public prosecutor
el **abogado**; la **abogada**	lawyer
Esta tarde tengo una cita con mi abogado.	This afternoon I have an appointment with my lawyer.
la **ley**	law
el **tribunal**	court
el **juez**; la **jueza**	judge
Los jueces no lo pueden saber todo.	Judges can't know everything.
la **justicia**	justice; right; judge; court of justice
el **Defensor del Pueblo**	ombudsman; people's defender
acusar	accuse
La acusaron de asesinato.	She was accused of murder.
confesar	confess
culpable	guilty
El fiscal demostró que el acusado era culpable.	The district attorney proved that the accused was guilty.
inocente	not guilty; innocent
condenar	condemn
justo, a	just
La pena fue justa.	The punishment was just.
injusto, a	unjust; unfair
El juez fue injusto al dictar la pena.	The judge was unfair when he passed sentence.
castigar	punish
la **cárcel**; la **prisión**	prison; jail
el **prisionero**; la **prisionera**	prisoner

la **Guardia Civil**	Guardia Civil *(Spanish rural police and border guard)*
La Guardia Civil opera principalmente en zonas rurales, fronteras y costas.	The Guardia Civil operates chiefly in rural areas and along the borders and coasts.
el, la **agente (de policía)**	(police) officer
el **comisario**; la **comisaria**	police inspector
Nuestro vecino es comisario de policía.	Our neighbor is a police inspector.
amenazado, a	threatened
Como el policía se sintió amenazado, disparó.	Since the policeman felt threatened, he fired.
amenazar	threaten
la **denuncia**	accusation; denunciation
sospechar	suspect
No sospechamos de nadie.	We don't suspect anyone.
la **persecución**	pursuit; persecution
observar	observe; watch
identificar	identify
el **interrogatorio**	interrogation
supremo, a	supreme
La sede del Tribunal Supremo reside en Madrid.	The seat of the Supreme Court is in Madrid.
el **procedimiento**	procedure; proceeding; process
El procedimiento de la justicia es lento.	The process of justice is slow.
el **juicio**	trial
el, la **testigo**	witness
jurar	swear
juzgar	judge; pass judgement
la **sentencia**	sentence
el **vigor**	force
La nueva ley entra en vigor en enero.	The new law comes into force in January.
legalizar	legalize
la **pena**	penalty; punishment
Al preso le redujeron la pena.	They reduced the prisoner's sentence.

el **castigo**	punishment
legal	legal
la **inocencia**	innocence
la **vigilancia**	guard; surveillance; observation

Political Life

la **política**
No entiendo la política estatal.

policy; politics
I don't understand government politics.

político, a
Las discusiones políticas son a veces muy interesantes.

political
Political discussions are sometimes very interesting.

el **político**; la **política**
Algunos políticos hacen muchas promesas.

politician
Some politicians make a great many promises.

el **partido**

party

la **derecha**
La derecha radical tiene mala fama.

right *(political faction or views)*
The radical right has a bad reputation.

la **izquierda**

left *(political faction or views)*

radical

radical

elegir
¿Ya sabes qué candidato elegir?

elect; vote for; choose
Do you already know which candidate to vote for?

las **elecciones**
¿Cuándo serán las nuevas elecciones?

elections
When will the new elections be?

moderado, a
Las fuerzas moderadas del partido obtuvieron la mayoría absoluta.

moderate
The moderate forces of the party obtained an absolute majority.

la **fuerza**

force

la **mayoría**

majority

la **minoría**
La minoría de los concejales está en contra del alcalde.

minority
A minority of the councilmen are in opposition to the mayor.

el **alcalde**; la **alcaldesa**

mayor

el **concejal**; la **concejala**	councilman; council member
obtener	obtain; get; attain
votar	vote
el **voto** En las últimas elecciones hubo más votos que electores y sólo un candidato.	vote In the last elections there were more votes than voters and only one candidate.
el **elector**; la **electora**	voter
el **candidato**; la **candidata**	candidate
libre Todas las personas son libres.	free All people are free.
protestar Protestamos contra las reformas escolares.	protest We protest against the school reforms.
nacional No se van a aumentar los gastos para la defensa nacional.	national They're not going to increase expenditures for national defense.
público, a Los políticos dependen de la opinión pública.	public Politicians are dependent on public opinion.
la **oposición** La oposición conservadora ganará las próximas elecciones.	opposition The conservative opposition will win the next elections.
la **reforma** El gobierno acordó una reforma fiscal.	reform The government agreed to a tax reform.

acordar	resolve; agree (to, upon)
la **campaña** ¿Quién ha pagado la campaña electoral?	campaign Who paid for the electoral campaign?
electoral	electoral
el **censo electoral** ¿Os habéis inscrito en el censo electoral?	list of voters Have you registered to vote?
prepararse Las campañas electorales se preparan con tiempo.	get ready; make preparations Preparations for the electoral campaigns are made early.
inscribirse	register; enroll

243

la **encuesta**	(opinion) poll
Según las encuestas no hay ningún favorito.	According to the polls, there is no favorite.
el **favorito**; la **favorita**	favorite
representativo, a	representative
la **tendencia**	tendency; trend
partidista	partisan
La actitud del Presidente es partidista.	The President's attitude is partisan.
el **líder**	party leader; leading candidate; leader
la **votación**	voting; vote; balloting
Los resultados de las votaciones se publicarán mañana.	The results of the voting will be made known tomorrow.
la **papeleta de voto**	ballot; voting slip
la **participación**	participation
La participación electoral disminuye.	Attendance at the polls is decreasing.
la **corrupción**	corruption
la **manifestación**	demonstration
Durante la manifestación la policía detuvo a varios manifestantes.	During the demonstration the police arrested several demonstrators.
el, la **manifestante**	demonstrator
la **medida**	measure
Se van a tomar medidas contra el terrorismo.	Measures will be taken against terrorism.
la **intervención**	intervention
la **propuesta**	proposal; offer
El gobierno no acepta la propuesta de la oposición.	The government does not accept the proposal of the opposition.
el **acuerdo**	accord; agreement; pact
proponer	propose
¿Sabes qué propuso la oposición?	Do you know what the opposition proposed?
fundamental	fundamental; principal
La decisión del Parlamento es el tema fudamental.	The decision of Parliament is the primary topic.
la **unión**	union
La Unión General de Trabajadores es un sindicato.	The General Workers' Union is a labor union.

el, la **patriota**	patriot
¡Ten cuidado con los falsos patriotas!	Beware of false patriots!
patriótico, a	patriotic
Los portugueses son más patrióticos que los españoles.	The Portuguese are more patriotic than the Spaniards.
el **nacionalismo**	nationalism
el **racismo**	racism

■■■■ Political Resistance ■■■■

pacífico, a	peaceful
la **revolución**	revolution
Zapata fue muy importante para la revolución mexicana.	Zapata was very important for the Mexican Revolution.
revolucionario, a	revolutionary
En algunos países latinoamericanos hay movimientos revolucionarios.	In some Latin American countries there are revolutionary movements.
luchar	fight
Simón Bolívar luchó por la independencia de Hispanoamérica.	Simón Bolívar fought for the independence of Spanish America.
el **enemigo**; la **enemiga**	enemy
el **terror**	terror
la **guerrilla**	band of partisans
el **guerillero**; **guerrillera**	member of partisan band, guerrilla
el, la **terrorista**	terrorist
El Tribunal Supremo condenó a los terroristas.	The Supreme Court declared the terrorists guilty.
el **terrorismo**	terrorism
la **lucha**	struggle; fight
La lucha contra las drogas es un grave problema.	The war on drugs is a serious problem.
la **bomba**	bomb
La extrema derecha colocó una bomba.	The far right planted a bomb.
estallar	explode

el **fusil**	rifle; gun
disparar	shoot; fire
¡No disparen! ¡Somos amigos!	Don't shoot! We're friends!
el **peligro**	danger
la **seguridad**	security
la **guerra civil**	civil war
La Guerra Civil española duró desde 1936 hasta 1939.	The Spanish Civil War lasted from 1936 to 1939.

la **ideología**	ideology
la **resistencia**	resistance
La resistencia quiere acabar con la dictadura.	The resistance movement wants to put an end to the dictatorship.
la **represión**	repression
La represión franquista llevó a mucha gente a la cárcel.	Francoist repression sent many people to prison.
la **tortura**	torture
Muchas personas sufrieron la tortura de la policía.	Many people were tortured by the police.
torturar	torture
Todavía se tortura a muchos encarcelados en el mundo.	Many prison inmates are still tortured in the world.
el **preso**; la **presa**	prisoner; convict
Amnesty International ayuda a los presos políticos.	Amnesty International helps political prisoners.
el **golpe militar**	military coup
el **golpe de Estado**	coup d'etat
combatir	fight; oppose; struggle
El Gobierno español combatió contra el golpe militar de Franco.	The Spanish Government fought against Franco's military coup.
armado, a	armed
Los terroristas estaban armados con pistolas y fusiles.	The terrorists were armed with pistols and rifles.
la **pistola**	pistol
el **tiro**	shot
explotar	exploit
Dictadores explotan al pueblo.	Dictators exploit the people.
liberar	liberate; (set) free
En 1975 el Gobierno liberó a algunos presos políticos.	In 1975 the Government freed some political prisoners.

la **liberación**	liberation
Los grupos de liberación latino-americana reciben poca ayuda exterior.	The Latin American liberation groups receive little foreign support.

Political Division of Spain

la **provincia**	province
Las provincias españolas tienen gobiernos autónomos por lo que son autonomías o comunidades autónomas.	The Spanish provinces have autonomous governments; hence they are autonomies or autonomous bodies.
la **comunidad**	community; body
la **región**	region
Las regiones autónomas españolas son el País Vasco o Euskadi, Cantabria, Asturias, Galicia, Castilla-León, Madrid, Rioja, Navarra, Aragón, Cataluña, Baleares, el País Valenciano, Murcia, Castilla-La Mancha, Andalucía, Extremadura, Canarias, Ceuta y Melilla.	The autonomous regions of Spain are the Basque Provinces, Cantabria, Asturia, Galicia, Castile-León, Madrid, Rioja, Navarre, Aragon, Catalonia, the Balearic Islands, Valencia, Murcia, Castile-La Mancha, Andalusia, Estremadura, the Canary Islands, and Ceuta and Melilla.
el **País Vasco**; el **Euskadi**; las **Vascongadas**	Basque Provinces
vasco, a	Basque
eusquera	Basque
En las Vascongadas o Euskadi se habla eusquera.	Basque is spoken in the Basque Provinces.
Galicia	Galicia
gallego, a	Galician
Castilla	Castile
Madrid	Madrid
madrileño, a	Madrilenian
aragonés; aragonesa	Aragonese
Aragón	Aragon
Cataluña; **Catalunya**	Catalonia

catalán; **catalana**	Catalan; Catalonian
Baleares	Balearic Islands
valenciano, a	Valencian
andaluz(a)	Andalusian
Andalucía	Andalusia
canario, a	of the Canary Islands; Canary Islander
Canarias	Canary Islands

el **territorio**	territory
la **autonomía**	autonomy
autónomo, a	free; autonomous
la **bandera**	flag; banner
Las provincias autónomas tienen una bandera propia.	The autonomous provinces have their own flags.
regional	regional
Cantabria	Cantabria
cántabro, a	Cantabrian
Asturias	Asturias
asturiano, a	Asturian
La Rioja	Rioja
navarro, a	Navarrese
Navarra	Navarre
murciano, a	of Murcia
Murcia	Murcia
manchego, a	of La Mancha
La Mancha	La Mancha
Extremadura	Estremadura
extremeño, a	Estremenian

International Relations

internacional
Ayer hubo un encuentro internacional de los Ministros de Economía en Madrid.

international
Yesterday an international meeting of ministers for economic affairs was held in Madrid.

la **unidad**
La unidad política española se consiguió con los Reyes Católicos.

unity
Spanish political unity was attained under the Catholic Monarchs.

la **organización**
La OTAN es la Organización del Tratado del Atlántico Norte.

organization
NATO is the North Atlantic Treaty Organization.

la **Comunidad Europea**

European Community

las **Naciones Unidas**

United Nations

los **países en vías de desarrollo**

developing countries

los **países desarrollados**

industrialized countries

la **embajada**
La embajada española en Cuba no quiere tener problemas con el gobierno cubano.

embassy
The Spanish Embassy in Cuba does not want to have problems with the Cuban government.

el **embajador**; la **embajadora**
El embajador de España murió a causa de una bomba.

ambassador; ambassadress
The Spanish ambassador was killed by a bomb.

diplomático, a

diplomatic

la **delegación**
La delegación española firmó el acuerdo secreto.

delegation
The Spanish delegation signed the secret accord.

el **delegado**; la **delegada**

delegate

negociar

negotiate

la **negociación**

negotiation

secreto, a

secret

el **acuerdo**

accord; pact; agreement

el **tratado**

treaty; convention; covenant

el **poder**
El poder debería estar mejor repartido.

power
Power ought to be better distributed.

249

mundial	world
el **pacto**	pact; treaty
¿Qué países firmaron el Pacto Andino?—No tengo ni idea.	Which countries signed the Andean Pact?—I have no idea.
la **OTAN**	NATO
la **sede**	seat
¿Dónde está la sede de la CEE?	Where is the seat of the European Community?
el **comité**	committee
El comité olímpico ha aceptado el catalán para la Olimpiada 1992.	The Olympic Committee allowed the use of Catalan at the 1992 Olympics.
cooperar	cooperate
la **cooperación**	cooperation
La cooperación con la Cruz Roja fue una ayuda importante para Perú.	Cooperation with the Red Cross was a great help for Peru.
el **consulado**	consulate
En Barcelona hay muchos consulados.	In Barcelona there are many consulates.
el **cónsul**; la **consulesa**	consul
El cónsul nos invitó a la recepción.	The consul invited us to the reception.
el **Tercer Mundo**	Third World
la **dependencia**	dependence
la **potencia**	power
Las potencias extranjeras han ayudado a solucionar el problema de la guerra.	The foreign powers have helped solve the problem of war.
independiente	independent
México es un país independiente.	Mexico is an independent country.
la **reunión en la cumbre**	summit conference
intercambiar	exchange
Los embajadores intercambiaron opiniones.	The ambassadors exchanged opinions.
el **intercambio**	exchange
el **secreto**	secret
el, la **espía**	spy
Los espías saben a veces mucho más que los políticos.	Spies sometimes know more than politicians.

el **traidor**; la **traidora**	traitor
exiliarse	go into exile
La mayoría de los intelectuales españoles se exilió después de la Guerra Civil.	The majority of the Spanish intellectuals went into exile after the Civil War.
el **exilio**	exile

War and Peace

la **paz**
Es difícil vivir en paz.

peace
It is difficult to live in peace.

la **guerra**
El pueblo es el que más sufre en las guerras.

war
The people suffer most in wars.

enemigo, a
Este general es enemigo de la democracia.

enemy; hostile; inimical
This general is hostile to democracy.

atacar
Nos atacaron al amanecer.

attack
They attacked us at daybreak.

defenderse
Manuela se defendió contra el atracador.

defend oneself; resist
Manuela resisted the attacker.

defender
El Rey defendió la democracia.

defend
The King defended democracy.

la **mili**
José tuvo que hacer la mili en Melilla.

military service
José had to do his military service in Melilla.

el **objetor de conciencia**

conscientious objector

militar

military

la **defensa**
El Ministro de Defensa visitó la tropa.

defense
The minister of defense visited the troops.

el **ejército**
Algunos soldados piensan que el ejército no es necesario.

army
Some soldiers think the army is not necessary.

el **soldado**

soldier

el **armamento**
El armamento nuclear es un peligro
para todo el mundo.

armament
Nuclear armament is a danger to
the entire world.

nuclear

nuclear

el **arma** *f*
Las armas pueden destruir todo el
mundo.

weapon; arm
Weapons can destroy the entire
world.

destruir

destroy

el **desarme**
Parece que ya empieza el desarme.

disarmament
It seems that disarmament is
already starting.

la **víctima**
Las víctimas de las guerras no son
siempre inocentes.

victim
The victims of war are not always
innocent.

huir
La población huyó ante el peligro de
guerra.

flee
The population fled from the
danger of war.

la **victoria**
Las victorias cuestan vidas.

victory
Victories cost human lives.

la **patria**
En nombre de la patria se hacen
guerras absurdas.

native country; fatherland
Absurd wars are waged in the name
of the fatherland.

el **ataque**
Los enemigos no sobrevivieron
nuestros ataques.

attack
The enemies did not survive our
attacks.

sobrevivir

survive

el **atracador**; la **atracadora**

attacker; aggressor

la **marina**
Alejandro quiere ir a la marina.

Navy
Alejandro wants to join the Navy.

la **infantería**
A Vicente le tocó hacer la mili en
infantería.

infantry
Vicente had to do his military
service in the infantry.

la **aviación**
La aviación alemana destruyó
Guernica.

air force
The German Air Force destroyed
Guernica.

la **base**
Los vecinos de Torrejón protestan
contra la base norteamericana.

base
The inhabitants of Torrejón
protested against the North
American base.

el **general**
El general murió en la guerra.

general
The general died in the war.

el **oficial**	officer
Los oficiales no cumplieron las órdenes.	The officers did not carry out the orders.
la **orden**	order; command (*noun*)
ordenar	order; command (*verb*)
¿Quién ha ordenado que disparen?	Who ordered to open fire?
el **cañón**	cannon; gun
Estos cañones se utilizaron en la Guerra Civil.	These cannons were used in the Spanish Civil War.
utilizar	utilize; make use of
el **cohete**	rocket; missile
Los primeros cohetes se construyeron en Alemania.	The first rockets were built in Germany.
el **tanque**	tank
Francisco sabe conducir un tanque.	Francisco can drive a tank.
la **tropa**	troops; soldiers; force
avanzar	advance
ocupar	occupy
Los españoles piensan que Inglaterra no debe seguir ocupando Gibraltar.	Spaniards think that England should no longer occupy Gibraltar.
la **ocupación**	occupation
Durante la ocupación árabe se construyó la Alhambra.	During the Arab occupation the Alhambra was built.
la **destrucción**	destruction
La destrucción de la tierra se está realizando sin armas.	The destruction of the earth is being accomplished without weapons.
sangriento, a	bloody
la **agresión**	aggression; attack, action
Algunos países están provocando una agresión militar.	Some countries are provoking military action.
provocar	provoke; incite
el **agresor**	aggressor; attacker
Los agresores serán condenados por las Naciones Unidas.	Aggressors will be censured by the United Nations.
invadir	invade
la **guardia**	guard

rechazar	repel; drive back
el **refugio**	refuge; shelter; bunker
No hay refugios atómicos para todo el pueblo.	There are not enough nuclear shelters for the entire population.
el **héroe**; la **heroína**	hero; heroine
El Cid es un héroe para muchos españoles.	El Cid is a hero to many Spaniards.
heroico, a	heroic
La rendición de Granada fue un acto heroico.	The surrender of Granada was a heroic deed.
la **rendición**	surrender; capitulation

El grafiti latino es mas político que el grafiti de países anglosajones.
Latin graffiti is more political than graffiti in Anglo-Saxon countries.

================== **Landscape Forms** ==================

la **tierra** — earth

el **paisaje** — landscape
El paisaje asturiano se parece al suizo. — The Asturian landscape resembles the Swiss.

la **vista** — view
Desde mi habitación tengo una vista maravillosa. — From my room I have a marvelous view.

el **bosque** — woods; forest
En Galicia se quemaron muchos bosques. — In Galicia many forests were destroyed by fire.

el **campo** — field; country
En Castilla hay muchos campos de trigo. — In Castile there are many wheat fields.

la **fuente** — (water) spring; fountain
En los Pirineos hay muchas fuentes. — In the Pyrenees there are many springs.

el **lago** — lake
En España hay más ríos que lagos. — In Spain there are more rivers than lakes.

el **río** — river

desembocar — flow (into); lead (to)
El Ebro desemboca en el Mediterráneo. — The Ebro flows into the Mediterranean.

el **canal** — canal
El Canal de Panamá une el Océano Atlántico con el Pacífico. — The Panama Canal links the Atlantic Ocean with the Pacific.

la **orilla** — bank; shore
La Torre del Oro de Sevilla está a orillas del Guadalquivir. — The Golden Tower of Seville stands on the banks of the Guadalquivir.

la **montaña** — mountain
La montaña más alta de España es el Teide en Tenerife. — Spain's highest mountain is the Teide on Tenerife.

la **sierra** — mountain range; mountains
Este invierno no vamos a esquiar a la sierra. — This winter we're not going to the mountains to ski.

la **cordillera** — mountain range

el **monte**
Mi suegro iba al monte de caza.

mountain; forest; wood
My father-in-law went hunting in
the woods.

el **pico**
¿Habéis subido al pico del Mulhacén?

peak; top; summit
Have you climbed to the top of
Mulhacén?

el **valle**
Cerca del Valle Ansó en Navarra
se puede esquiar.

valley
Near the Ansó Valley in Navarre
you can ski.

la **roca**
Nos subimos a las rocas para tomar
el sol.

rock; cliff
We climbed the rocks to lie in
the sun.

la **cueva**
Las cuevas de Altamira son muy
famosas por sus pinturas
prehistóricas.

cave
The caves of Altamira are renowned
for their prehistoric paintings.

el **desierto**
El desierto de Sahara tiene
una extensión enorme.

desert
The Sahara Desert covers
an enormous area.

el **volcán**

volcano

la **selva**
En Perú hay mucha selva.

virgin forest; jungle
In Perú there is a great deal of
virgin forest.

pantanoso, a
Algunas partes de la selva
son muy pantanosas.

swampy; marshy; miry
Some parts of the virgin forest are
very swampy.

el **pantano**
Franco hizo construir muchos
pantanos en España.

reservoir; dam
Franco had many reservoirs built
in Spain.

la **meseta a (meseta)**
La Meseta Central está en el centro
de la Península Ibérica.

plateau
The Central Plateau is in the
center of the Iberian Peninsula.

pirenaico, a

Pyrenean

la **llanura**
En las llanuras andaluzas se crían toros.

plain; prairie
Bulls are bred on the Andalusian
plains.

la **pampa**
La pampa se extiende desde los Andes
hasta la costa atlántica de Argentina.

pampa; grassland region
The pampa extends from the
Andes to the Atlantic coast of
Argentina.

extenderse

extend; spread

montañoso, a	mountainous
andino, a	Andean
serrano, a	mountain
el **puerto** Cuando nieva se cierran muchos puertos en España.	(mountain) pass When it snows, many passes in Spain are closed.
el **glacial**	glacier
la **cuesta** Para ir al chalet hay que subir aquella cuesta hasta el final.	slope; hill; grade To get to the chalet, you have to climb that slope to the top.
la **pendiente** Cuando tuvimos el accidente nos caímos por esta pendiente.	incline; gradient; drop When we had the accident, we tumbled down this incline.
la **colina** Detrás de esta colina está mi casa.	hill Behind this hill is my house.
la **peña** Desde esta peña se tiene una vista única.	rock; large stone From this rock you have a unique view.
el **peñón** En el peñón de Gibraltar hay muchas monas.	rock; cliff There are many monkeys on the Rock of Gibraltar.
el **polo** La región del polo sur aún está por poblar.	pole The South Pole region has yet to be settled.

Ocean

el **mar**	sea
el **océano** Colón cruzó el Océano Atlántico.	ocean Columbus crossed the Atlantic Ocean.
la **corriente** En el Golfo de Vizcaya hay corrientes peligrosas.	current In the Gulf of Biscay there are dangerous currents.
la **ola** En las playas cantábricas hay olas muy grandes y peligrosas.	wave Along the Cantabrian beaches there are very large and dangerous waves.

la **costa**
La costa mediterránea está muy explotada por el turismo.

coast
The Mediterranean coast is heavily developed for tourism.

mediterráneo, a

Mediterranean

la **cala**
A muchas calas de Ibiza sólo se llega en barca.

bay
Many of Ibiza's bays can be reached only by boat.

la **playa**
A las playas cantábricas no van tantos turistas como a las playas del Mediterráneo.

beach
Not as many tourists go to the Cantabrian beaches as to the beaches of the Mediterranean.

el **cabo**
El Cabo de la Nao está frente a Ibiza.

cape
Cape Nao is opposite Ibiza.

peninsular

peninsular

la **península**
En la península ibérica están España y Portugal.

peninsula
Spain and Portugal are on the Iberian Peninsula.

la **isla**
Las Baleares son las islas Menorca, Mallorca, Cabrera, Ibiza y Formentera.

island
The Balearic Islands are the islands Menorca, Mallorca, Cabrera, Ibiza, and Formentera.

---

el **oleaje**
Virginia se mareó por el fuerte oleaje.

swell; roll; waves
Virginia got seasick from the heavy swell.

la **marea**
Una marea negra contaminó la costa gallega.
Sólo podemos salir del puerto con marea alta y no con marea baja.

tide
An oil slick polluted the Galician coast.
We can leave port only at high tide; we cannot at low tide.

el **estrecho**
El Estrecho de Gibraltar separa el Mar Mediterráneo del Océano Atlántico.

strait; channel
The Strait of Gibraltar separates the Mediterranean from the Atlantic Ocean.

el **istmo**

isthmus

el **litoral**
El litoral del Cabo de Gata no está explotado.

coast; shore
The coast of Cape Gata is not developed.

atlántico, a

Atlantic

Weather and Climate

el **clima**
El clima de las Canarias es
caluroso, en Asturias es fresco
y en las Baleares templado.

climate
The climate of the Canary Islands
is very warm, in Asturias it is
cool, and in the Balearic Islands
it is mild.

caluroso, a

warm; hot

fresco, a

cool; fresh

frío, a

cold

el **calor**
Como no hace mucho calor me tengo
que poner un suéter.
Con este calor no trabaja nadie.
Diego tiene siempre mucho calor y su
mujer en invierno mucho frío.

heat; warmth
Since it's not very warm,
I have to put on a sweater.
In this heat, no one works.
Diego is always very hot, and in
winter his wife is very cold.

el **frío**

cold

el **sol**
Hoy quema el sol de verdad.

sun
Today the sun is really burning.

el **bochorno**
En verano hace un bochorno
increíble en Valencia.

sultry weather; scorching heat
In Valencia it's incredibly
sultry in summer.

hacer
Hoy hace buen tiempo.

be
Today the weather is good.

el **tiempo**

weather

seco, a
En Madrid hace un calor muy seco.

dry
In Madrid there's a very dry heat.

húmedo, a
Julián no soporta el calor húmedo.

humid
Julián can't stand humid heat.

llover
En Bogotá llueve más que en Caracas.

Está lloviendo a mares.

rain
In Bogotá it rains more than in
Caracas.
It's pouring rain.

la **lluvia**
Si cae suficiente lluvia no será
necesario regar los campos.

rain
If enough rain falls, it won't be
necessary to irrigate the fields.

la **gota**
¿Está lloviendo?—No, sólo están
cayendo cuatro gotas.

drop
Is it raining?—No, only a few
drops are falling.

mojarse
¡Coged el paraguas para que no os mojéis!

get wet
Take the umbrella, so that you don't get wet!

nevar
En los Pirineos ya ha nevado.

snow
In the Pyrenees it has already snowed.

la **nieve**
¿Crees que tendremos nieve este invierno?

snow
Do you think we'll get snow this winter?

helar
En invierno se hiela ese lago.

freeze (solid)
In winter the lake freezes over.

helado, a
Sara llegó helada a casa.

frozen; ice cold; icy
Sara came home frozen.

el **granizo**
El granizo ha destruido la cosecha.

hail
Hail has destroyed the harvest.

el **hielo**

ice

el **viento**
Aquí sopla un viento helado.

wind
An icy wind blows here.

espléndido, a
En San Sebastián tuvimos un tiempo espléndido.

splendid; wonderful
In San Sebastián we had splendid weather.

la **nube**
Esta noche se ven todas las estrellas porque no hay nubes.

cloud
Tonight all the stars are visible because there are no clouds.

la **niebla**

fog

nublado, a
Esta mañana el cielo estaba nublado pero por la tarde se despejó.

cloudy; overcast
This morning the sky was overcast, but in the afternoon it cleared up.

cubierto, a
Para mañana se espera en el Pirineo de Navarra cielo cubierto con algunas nevadas y formación de hielo por encima de 800 metros.

covered; cloudy; overcast
For tomorrow, cloudy skies are expected in the Pyrenees of Navarre, with isolated snowfalls and ice formation above 800 meters.

el **cielo**

sky

despejado, a
En el norte de Mallorca habrá cielo despejado, con vientos moderados.

clear; cloudless
In northern Mallorca it will be clear, with moderate winds.

moderado, a

moderate

la **tormenta**

storm; tempest

templado, a — temperate; mild; lukewarm

sereno, a — clear; cloudless; serene

la **temperatura** — temperature
La temperatura media de Logroño en noviembre es de unos cinco grados sobre cero. — The average temperature in Logroño in November is about 5 degrees above 0°C.

el **grado** — degree

el **termómetro** — thermometer
El termómetro marca dos grados bajo cero. — The thermometer registers 2 degrees below 0°C.

marcar — register; record

máximo, a — maximum
Las temperaturas máximas de mañana serán de 24 grados en Tenerife y Las Palmas. — Tomorrow the maximum temperatures on Tenerife and Las Palmas will be 24°C.

mínimo, a — minimum; lowest
La temperatura mínima en Ávila fue el sábado de seis grados bajo cero. — The low in Ávila on Saturday was minus 6°C.

soleado, a — sunny

la **sombra** — shade
Si tienes mucho calor ven aquí a la sombra. — If you're very hot, come here into the shade.

el **parte meteorológico** — weather report
Ya no me fío de los partes meteorológicos. — I don't trust the weather reports any more.

constante — constant
En Canarias el clima es bastante constante. — In the Canary Islands the climate is fairly constant.

la **sequía** — drought
La sequía en Cataluña causó muchos daños en la agricultura. — The drought in Catalonia caused great damage to agriculture.

la **humedad** — humidity
Con esta humedad se nos ha oxidado el coche en poco tiempo. — In this humidity, our car has rusted in a short time.

el **chubasco** — shower; squall
En las Canarias habrá el domingo chubascos que pasarán a llovizna durante la noche. — In the Canary Islands there will be showers on Sunday, changing to drizzle during the night.

inundar — flood; inundate

la **llovizna**
drizzle

despejarse
clear up; become bright and
sunny

el **claro**
clearing; brightening
En todo el Cantábrico habrá niebla
que durante el día pasará a claros con
algunas nubosidades.
Throughout Cantabria there will
be fog, changing during the day
to clearing with isolated cloudiness.

nevado, a
snowy; snow-covered
Nos gusta pasear por los campos
nevados.
We like walking through the
snowy fields.

resbalar
slip
Como había nevado la gente
resbalaba por las calles.
Since it had snowed, people
were slipping in the streets.

la **nevada**
snowfall

la **helada**
frost
Ayer por la noche hubo la primera
helada de este año.
Last night we had the first
frost of the year.

la **tempestad**
tempest; storm
Los barcos no pudieron salir del puerto
por causa de la tempestad.
The ships were unable to leave
port because of the storm.

el **ciclón**
cyclone
El ciclón produjo grandes catástrofes.
The cyclone caused great
catastrophes.

la **calma**
calm
Como hay calma no podemos salir
con el velero.
Because there's a calm, we can't
go out in the sailboat.

soplar
blow
Hoy sopla un viento muy frío.
Today a very cold wind is blowing.

el **temporal**
storm
Durante el temporal se hundieron
todas las barcas.
During the storm all the boats
sank.

la **nubosidad**
cloudiness

el **relámpago**
lightning
A lo lejos se veían los relámpagos y
se oían los truenos de la tormenta.
In the distance the lightning was
seen and the thunder of the storm
was heard.

el **trueno**
thunder

el **rayo**
bolt of lightning
Ayer cayó un rayo en nuestra casa.
¡Menos mal que tenemos un
pararrayos!
Yesterday a lightning bolt struck
our house. Luckily, we have a
lightning rod!

Environmental Problems

ecológico, a
Los ecologistas han presentado un programa ecológico para disminuir la contaminación del aire, del agua y de la tierra.

ecological
Ecologists have proposed an ecological program to decrease air, water, and soil pollution.

el **aire**

air

el **agua** *f*

water

puro, a
En el campo el aire es más puro que en la ciudad.

pure; clean
In the country the air is purer than in the city.

la **tierra**

soil

el **(medio) ambiente**
La contaminación del medio ambiente es un problema cada vez más grave.

environment; atmosphere; air
Environmental pollution is an increasingly serious problem.

la **contaminación**
La contaminación de los mares ha dañado la pesca.

pollution; contamination
The pollution of the seas has hurt fishing.

el **daño**

damage; harm

la **naturaleza**
Hay que proteger mucho más la naturaleza.

nature
Nature has to be protected much more.

la **catástrofe (natural)**

(natural) catastrophe

proteger

protect

natural
Los bosques son el ambiente natural de muchos animales.

natural
Forests are the natural environment of many animals.

conservar
Se debe conservar la selva para las próximas generaciones.

conserve; maintain; preserve
The virgin forest has to be conserved for future generations.

la **energía**
La gente no debe malgastar la energía.

energy
People should not waste energy.

el **terremoto**
Los terremotos producen grandes catástrofes.

earthquake
Earthquakes create huge catastrophes.

el, la **ecologista**

ecologist

la **protección**
La protección de animales y plantas que están condenadas a desaparecer es una tarea de los parques naturales.

protection
The protection of animals and plants that are threatened with extinction is a task of the nature preserves.

desaparecer

Los animales desaparecen cuando no pueden sobrevivir.

disappear; vanish; become extinct
Animals become extinct when they are unable to survive.

perjudicar
Los productos químicos pueden perjudicar la naturaleza.

damage; impair; harm
Chemical products can be harmful to nature.

contaminado, a

contaminated; polluted

contaminar
El tráfico contamina el aire.

contaminate; pollute
Traffic pollutes the air.

dañado, a
La naturaleza está dañada por la contaminación del medio ambiente.

damaged; harmed; impaired
Nature has been harmed by environmental pollution.

el **efecto de invernadero**

greenhouse effect

el **ozono**
El agujero del ozono es una consecuencia de la contaminación del aire.

ozone
The ozone hole is a result of air pollution.

malgastar

waste

la **energía nuclear**
La energía nuclear supone un peligro para la tierra.

nuclear energy
Nuclear energy is hazardous to the world.

la **energía solar**
La energía solar se tiene que desarrollar todavía más.

solar energy
Solar energy is in need of further development.

reciclar
El papel y el cristal se pueden reciclar.

recycle
Paper and glass can be recycled.

el **reciclaje**
Con el reciclaje de algunos productos se pueden ahorrar materias primas.

recycling
Raw materials can be saved by recycling some products.

Basic Concepts

el **animal**

animal

la **raza**
Tefolio tiene un perro de raza.

race; lineage; breed
Tefolio has a purebred dog.

la **pata**
Los pájaros tienen dos patas.

foot or leg of an animal
Birds have two legs.

la **cola**
Los caballos tienen cola pero las
vacas tienen rabo.

tail
Horses have a "cola," but cows
have a "rabo."

el **rabo**

tail

el **ala** *f*
Algunos pájaros no utilizan
las alas para volar.

wing
Some birds don't use their
wings for flying.

picar
Los pollos pican los granos de
maíz cuando comen.
Esta noche me han picado
los mosquitos.

peck; bite, sting
Chickens peck the grains of
corn when they eat.
Tonight the mosquitoes bit me.

el **pico**
Los gallos luchan en las riñas
de gallos con el pico y las
garras.

beak
In cockfights, roosters fight
with their beak and claws.

morder
Este perro no muerde.

bite
This dog doesn't bite.

la **pluma**
Esta paloma debe estar enferma
porque pierde muchas plumas.

feather
This dove must be ill, because
it's losing a lot of feathers.

el **cuerno**
El ciervo macho tiene cuernos
pero no las hembras.

horn
Male deer have horns,
but the females do not.

la **fauna**

fauna

la **res**
El cazador mató una res
hermosa.

beast; head of cattle
The hunter killed a beautiful
beast.

el **rebaño**
El pastor ha vendido su
rebaño.

herd; flock
The shepherd has sold his
flock.

la **cría**
Los leones protegen a sus crías.

brood; litter of animals
Lions protect their young.

el **nido**

nest

el **lomo**
He venido a lomos de una mula.

back
I came here on the back of a
mule.

la **uña**
Esta mula tiene una uña herida.
Los osos tienen uñas muy fuertes.

hoof; claw
This mule has an injured hoof.
Bears have powerful claws.

la **espina**
No me gusta comer pescado por las
espinas.

fishbone
I don't like to eat fish because of
the bones.

el **macho**

male; male animal

la **hembra**

female; female animal

echar de comer; **dar de comer**
Por favor, no echen de comer a los
peces.

feed
Please don't feed the fish.

comer

eat

manso, a
Mis amigos tuvieron un lobo manso.

tame
My friends had a tame wolf.

la **huella**
Los perros perdieron la huella de
la liebre.

track; trace; trail
The dogs lost the hare's trail.

el **olfato**
Los perros policías tienen un
olfato muy educado.

sense of smell
Police dogs have a very well-trained
sense of smell.

Domestic Animals

el **ganado**
En esta finca hay suficiente ganado
para alimentar a todo el pueblo.

cattle
There are enough cattle on
this farm to feed the entire
village.

el **caballo**

horse

el **cerdo**; la **cerda**
Del cerdo se aprovecha todo.

hog; pig; sow
Every part of the hog is put to
good use.

el **cordero**
La carne de cordero tiene un gusto especial.

lamb
Lamb has a special taste.

la **cabra**
La leche de cabra es muy sana.

goat
Goat's milk is very healthful.

la **oveja**
Con la lana de tus ovejas nos podemos hacer dos suéteres.

sheep
We can make ourselves two sweaters with the wool of your sheep.

la **vaca**

cow

la **ternera**
Esta ternera va a ser un toro bravo.

calf
This calf is going to be a fierce bull.

el **toro**
Después de las corridas se puede comprar la carne de toro.

bull
After the bullfights you can buy the meat of the bull.

la **mula**
La mula es un cruce de caballo y burra.

mule
The mule is a cross between a horse and a donkey.

el **burro**; la **burra**

donkey

el **pollo**
Los pollos se crían en granjas.

chicken
Chickens are raised on farms.

el **pájaro**

bird

el **conejo**; la **coneja**

rabbit

el **perro**; la **perra**

dog; bitch

el **gato**; la **gata**
La gata está en celo.

cat
The cat is in heat.

doméstico, a
Los animales domésticos pueden volverse peligrosos.

domestic
Domestic animals can turn dangerous.

inofensivo, a

harmless

bravo, a

wild; untamed; fierce

la **bestia**
La mula y el burro eran tradicionalmente
en España las bestias de carga.

animal; beast
The mule and the donkey were traditionally the beasts of burden in Spain.

el **asno**; la **asna**

donkey; ass

el **buey**
El buey hacía el trabajo más pesado en el campo.

ox; bullock
The ox did the heaviest work in the field.

el **ave** *f* No todas las aves cantan en primavera.	fowl; bird Not all birds sing in springtime.
el **gallo**	rooster; cock
la **gallina** Estas gallinas ponen unos huevos enormes.	hen These hens lay enormous eggs.
cantar	sing
el **pavo**; **pavo real** El pavo real no vuela casi.	turkey; peacock The peacock scarcely flies at all.
ladrar No hemos dormido porque el perro de Curro ha estado ladrando toda la noche.	bark We didn't sleep because Curro's dog barked all night.
en **celo**	in heat; rut; estrus
maullar Este gato sólo maúlla cuando quiere salir a la calle.	meow This cat meows only when it wants to go outdoors.

Wild Animals

el **águila** *f*	eagle
la **mariposa**	butterfly
la **paloma**	dove
el **pato** Hemos echado de comer a los patos y a los cisnes en el lago.	duck We fed the ducks and swans at the lake.
el **león**; la **leona**	lion; lioness
el, la **elefante**	elephant bull; cow
el **mono**; la **mona**	monkey
el **cocodrilo** En Latinoamérica hay bastantes cocodrilos en regiones húmedas.	crocodile There are quite a few crocodiles in humid regions of Latin America.
la **serpiente** Las serpientes son muy silenciosas.	snake; serpent Snakes are very silent.

venenoso, a — poisonous

el **mosquito** — mosquito; gnat

la **mosca** — fly

la **araña** — spider

el **oso**; la **osa** — bear

el **lobo**; la **loba** — wolf; she-wolf

el **zorro**; la **zorra** — fox

el **ratón** — mouse
Vuestro gato ya no caza ratones sino ratas. — Your cat no longer catches mice, but rats instead.

la **rata** — rat

el **pez** — fish

el **tiburón** — shark
Dónde hay delfines no hay tiburones. — Where there are dolphins, there are no sharks.

el **delfín** — dolphin

salvaje — wild; savage
Muchos animales salvajes están desapareciendo. — Many wild animals are becoming extinct.

la **jaula** — cage
En el zoológico viven los lobos y los zorros en jaulas igual que las águilas. — In the zoo wolves and foxes live in cages, just as eagles do.

la **cigüeña** — stork

el **cisne** — swan

el **loro** — parrot
Muchos loros se mueren si no están libres. — Many parrots die if they are not free.

el **ruiseñor** — nightingale

el **insecto** — insect
Los insectos han estropeado la cosecha. — Insects have destroyed the harvest.

el **bicho** — bug; insect; (small) animal
La pulga y la hormiga son bichos que no pican pero muerden. — Fleas and ants are bugs that do not sting, but bite.

la **hormiga** — ant

la **pulga** — flea

la **abeja**
Las abejas producen miel y cera.

bee
Bees produce honey and wax.

el **caracol**
Maruja sabe cocinar unos caracoles muy ricos.

snail
Maruja can prepare delicious snails.

la **rana**
Las cigüeñas se alimentan de ranas y gusanos.

frog
Storks eat frogs and worms.

el **gusano**

worm

la **ostra**
Las ostras son un tipo de concha.

oyster
Oysters are a kind of shellfish.

la **concha**

shell; shellfish; conch

el **pulpo**

octopus; cuttlefish

la **piraña**

piranha

aullar
Cuando estuvimos en los Pirineos oímos aullar a los lobos.

howl
When we were in the Pyrenees, we heard wolves howling.

la **liebre**
Las liebres viven salvajes pero los conejos se crían en granjas.

hare
Hares live in the wild, but rabbits are bred on farms.

el **ciervo**; la **cierva**

deer; stag; hind; doe

Hay numerosas focas en el sur de Chile y Argentina.
There are numerous seals in the south of Chile and Argentina.

Basic Concepts

la **vegetación**
En los Andes se encuentra una vegetación muy variada.

vegetation
In the Andes, a very diverse vegetation is found.

variado, a

diverse; varied

plantar
Todos los años plantamos un limonero.

plant
Every year we plant a lemon tree.

la **raíz**

root

la **semilla**
Muchas semillas son comestibles.

seed
Many seeds are edible.

secar
Las raíces del pino han secado el pozo.

dry; dry out
The roots of the pine have dried up the well.

la **rama**
¡No te subas a esa rama que te vas a caer!

branch
Don't climb on that branch, you're going to fall!

el **ramo**

bouquet; cluster

el **fruto**
El fruto del olivo es la oliva.

fruit
The fruit of the olive tree is the olive.

la **hoja**
En otoño los árboles pierden las hojas.

leaf
In fall the trees lose their leaves.

la **flora**
Hay que proteger más la flora y fauna en todo el mundo.

flora
Flora and fauna need more protection worldwide.

vegetal
El aceite vegetal es mucho más sano que la grasa animal.

vegetable
Vegetable oil is much more healthful than animal fat.

el **grano**

grain (of seed)

la **cáscara**

peel; shell; rind; husk; hull

el **hueso**

stone; pit; core *(stone fruits)*

la **pepita**

pip or seed of fruit

la **corteza**
De la corteza del alcornoque se saca el corcho.
La corteza de la naranja no se come.

bark; peel; rind
Cork is obtained from the bark of the cork tree.
Orange peel is not eaten.

el **tronco** Cuando cortaron el pino vieron que el tronco estaba hueco.	trunk When they cut down the pine, they saw that the trunk was hollow.
hueco, a	hollow
la **ramificación** En el interior de la selva la ramificación de los árboles casi no deja pasar la luz.	branching; ramification In the interior of the virgin forest, the branches of the trees let almost no light through.

■■■ Flowers, Plants, and Trees ■■■

la **flor** El clavel es la flor preferida por Marisa. Los almendros ya están en flor.	flower; blossom; bloom The carnation is Marisa's favorite flower. The almond trees are already in bloom.
la **rosa** Para su cumpleaños le enviaron un ramo de rosas.	rose For her birthday they sent her a bouquet of roses.
la **planta** A María le gusta mucho tener plantas en casa.	plant María likes having plants indoors.
comestible	edible
el **trigo** En Castilla se cultiva mucho el trigo.	wheat In Castile a great deal of wheat is grown.
los **cereales** ¿Ya habéis terminado la cosecha de cereales?	grain Have you already finished the grain harvest?
la **hierba** Con hierbas se pueden curar muchas enfermedades.	herb; grass; weed Many illnesses can be cured with herbs.
la **mata** Las moras crecen en matas.	bush; shrub Blackberries grow on shrubs.
la **mora**	mulberry; blackberry
el **árbol** Tenemos que cortar unas ramas de este árbol para que crezca mejor.	tree We have to cut a few limbs from this tree, so that it will grow better.
frutal En Castellón también hay muchos árboles frutales.	fruit In Castellón there are also many fruit trees.

el **limonero**	lemon tree
el **almendro**	almond tree
el **higo**	fig
El higo es la fruta de la higuera.	The fig is the fruit of the fig tree.
la **higuera**	fig tree
el **olivo**	olive tree
el **pino**	pine
En verano los bosques de pinos se incendian fácilmente.	In summer, pine woods catch fire easily.
la **palmera**	palm tree
¡Mira, esa palmera tiene cocos!	Look! There are coconuts on that palm tree!
el **coco**	coconut

el **clavel**	carnation
el **rosal**	rosebush; rose plant
El rosal ha crecido tanto que ya no se ve el muro del jardín.	The rosebush has grown so much that the garden wall is no longer visible.
el **geranio**	geranium
En nuestro chalet teníamos geranios muy bonitos.	We had very pretty geraniums in our vacation house.
silvestre	wild
En la montaña crecen muchas plantas silvestres.	Many wild plants grow in the mountains.
el **girasol**	sunflower
El aceite de girasol es más barato que el de oliva.	Sunflower oil is cheaper than olive oil.
la **cebada**	barley
el **centeno**	rye
la **avena**	oat
la **seta**	mushroom
Hay que tener mucho cuidado cuando se recogen setas porque algunas son muy venenosas.	You have to be very careful when you gather mushrooms, because some are very poisonous.
la **remolacha**	beet
el **manzano**	apple tree
el **platanero**	banana (tree)
La fruta del platanero es el plátano.	The fruit of the banana tree is the banana.

el **banano**	banana plant
el **mango**	mango tree; mango (fruit)
el **cacao**	cacao tree; cacao
la **caña de azúcar**	sugar cane
el **cactus**	cactus
Juan se pinchó con el cactus.	Juan pricked himself on the cactus.
el **laurel**	bay laurel
Una hoja de laurel da un sabor especial a la comida.	A bay leaf gives food a special taste.
el **romero**	rosemary
la **paja**	straw
La paja aún está en el campo para que se seque.	The straw is still in the field, so that it can dry.
el **prado**	meadow
En el prado hay muchos tréboles.	There is a lot of clover in the meadow.
el **trébol**	clover; clover leaf
el **césped**	lawn; grass; grass plot
Cuesta mucho trabajo y mucha agua para que crezca el césped en el sur de España.	It takes a lot of work and plenty of water for a lawn to grow in southern Spain.
el **alcornoque**	cork tree
el **pinar**	pine grove
El verano pasado se limpió el pinar.	Last summer the pine grove was cleaned up.

Las frutas tropicales crecen por todas partes en América Central.
Tropical fruits grow everywhere in Central America.

City and Village

la **ciudad**	city
Pamplona es una ciudad conocida por sus fiestas.	Pamplona is a city known for its festivals.
la **capital**	capital (city); provincial capital
Lérida es una capital catalana.	Lérida is a Catalan provincial capital.
el **pueblo**	village
Algunas capitales parecen más bien pueblos.	Some capitals look more like villages.
los **alrededores**	environs; outskirts
En los alrededores de Barcelona hay ciudades-dormitorios.	On the outskirts of Barcelona there are bedroom communities.
el **suburbio**	suburb
Las empresas industriales están en los suburbios de Valencia.	The industrial firms are in the suburbs of Valencia.
el **barrio**	part of town; quarter; district
Los vecinos de este barrio han formado una comunidad.	The residents of this district have formed a community of interests.
local	local
Llegaré a Canarias a las tres y media hora local.	I will reach the Canary Islands at 3:30 local time.
situado, a	located; situated
San Sebastián está situada en la costa cantábrica.	San Sebastián is located on the Cantabrian coast.
el **habitante**	inhabitant
¿Cuántos habitantes tiene Salamanca?	How many inhabitants does Salamanca have?
el **ciudadano**; la **ciudadana**	citizen
Los ciudadanos tienen que mantener limpia la ciudad.	The citizens have to keep their city clean.
el **vecino**; la **vecina**	neighbor; resident; inhabitant
el **centro**	center; inner city; downtown
En el centro de Barcelona están las fachadas de Gaudí.	The Gaudí facades are in the center of Barcelona.
la **zona**	zone; area; region

municipal
Los policías municipales llevan
generalmente uniformes azules.

municipal; city
The municipal police generally
wear blue uniforms.

---

la **villa**
Algunas villas españolas mantienen
relaciones con aldeas extranjeras.

small town
Some small Spanish towns maintain
relationships with small villages
abroad.

la **aldea**
En Bolivia algunas aldeas sólo
tienen diez casas.

small village
In Bolivia, some small villages
consist of only 10 houses.

rural
La vida rural es muy tranquila.

rural
Rural life is very peaceful.

rústico, a

country; rustic

la **finca**
Aquello era una finca o una hacienda,
hoy sólo es una ruina.

farmhouse; country estate
That was a country estate or a farm;
today it is only a ruin.

la **hacienda**

farm; ranch; landed property

las **afueras**
Mucha gente vive en las afueras de
la ciudad porque es más tranquilo.

suburbs; outskirts
Many people live in the suburbs
of the city because it is quieter
there.

urbano, a
El alcalde ha presentado
un proyecto de limpieza
urbana.

urban
The mayor has proposed an
urban sanitation project.

la **barriada de chabolas**

slum; shantytown

la **población**
Madrid y Barcelona son las ciudades
de mayor población de España.

population
Madrid and Barcelona are the
most densely populated cities in
Spain.

poblar
Los españoles poblaron parte de
América.

populate
Spaniards populated part of
America.

residir
En verano residen en Benidorm más
turistas que habitantes nativos.

live; reside
In summer, more tourists than
native inhabitants reside in
Benidorm.

nativo, a

native

residente
¿Es usted residente en Cuba?

resident
Are you a resident of Cuba?

| la **urbanización** | development; urbanization |
| Enrique vive en esa urbanización. | Enrique lives in that development. |

■ Buildings ■

el **edificio**
Estos edificios modernos son
horribles.

building
These modern buildings are
horrible.

el **ayuntamiento**
El alcalde ha inaugurado el
nuevo ayuntamiento.

town hall; city hall
The mayor has dedicated the
new city hall.

la **biblioteca**
¿A qué hora abre la biblioteca?

library
What time does the library open?

la **central**
La manifestación de hoy ha sido
contra las centrales nucleares.

main office of a public service
Today's demonstration was
directed against nuclear power
plants.

la **torre**
En Toledo hay muchas torres; por
eso, se dice que es la ciudad de
las torres.

tower; skyscraper
There are many towers in Toledo,
and for that reason it is called the
City of Towers.

el **museo**
En Madrid hay muchos museos
muy importantes.

museum
In Madrid there are many
major museums.

el **castillo**
En España hay muchos castillos de
diferentes épocas.

castle
In Spain there are many castles
from different epochs.

el **cementerio**
En los pueblos los cementerios están
cerca de la iglesia.

cemetery
In the villages, the cemeteries are
near the church.

la **manzana**
Al volver la manzana está el
ayuntamiento.

block (of houses)
Right around the block is the city
hall.

inaugurar
El alcalde inauguró el nuevo
ayuntamiento.

inaugurate; dedicate; open
The mayor dedicated the new city
hall.

el **palacio**
¿En qué palacio viven los Reyes ahora?

palace
What palace do the king and
queen live in now?

el **rascacielos**
Madrid se parece a Nueva York en
los rascacielos.

skyscraper
Madrid resembles New York on
account of the skyscrapers.

la **ruina**

ruin

habitado, a
Estas ruinas fueron habitadas
por los romanos.

inhabited
These ruins were inhabited
by the Romans.

el **acueducto**

aqueduct

el **molino de viento**

windmill

el **alcázar**
El Alcázar de Toledo fue destruido
durante la guerra.

castle; fortress
The Fortress of Toledo was
destroyed during the war.

la **muralla**

rampart; wall of a city

el **(jardín) zoológico**

zoo

Infrastructure

la **infraestructura**

infrastructure

el **camino**
Este parque es tan nuevo que todavía
no han hecho los caminos.

way; path; road
This park is so new that the
paths haven't been laid yet.

la **plaza**
En esta plaza siempre hay mucha
suciedad.

plaza; square
There's always a lot of dirt in this
square.

el **pozo**
El agua del pozo es muy pura.

well
The water from the well is very
pure.

la **piscina**
En Valverde han hecho una piscina
pública muy moderna.

swimming pool
In Valverde a very modern public
swimming pool has been built.

el **puente**
¿Cuántos puentes hay en Sevilla
sobre el Guadalquivir?

bridge
How many bridges across the
Guadalquivir are there in Seville?

el **parque**

park

el **sitio**
En esta ciudad no hubo sitio para
más casas.

place; site; room
In this city there was no room for
more houses.

la **planificación territorial**	area planning
el **callejón**	alley
el **farol**	street lamp
la **fuente** La Plaza de la Cibeles tiene una fuente muy grande.	fountain Cibeles Plaza has a very large fountain.
el **estanque** El estanque del Retiro es muy bonito.	pond The pond in Retiro Park is very lovely.
el **centro comercial** A las afueras de Sabadell hay un centro comercial enorme.	shopping center On the outskirts of Sabadell there is an enormous shopping center.
el **bombero** ¡Llama a los bomberos que hay un incendio en la montaña!	fireman Call the fire department! There's a fire in the mountains!
el **incendio**	fire
el **reactor (nuclear)**	(nuclear) reactor
el **paso subterráneo**	underpass
el **túnel**	tunnel

La urbanización de pueblos pequeños ha sido muy rápida en los últimos 50 años.
Urbanization of small towns has been very fast in the last 50 years.

======= **Miscellaneous** =======

el **tráfico**
En Bogotá el tráfico es un problema.

traffic
In Bogotá traffic is a problem.

registrar
La policía registró un aumento de tráfico en los últimos años.

register; record
In the last few years the police recorded an increase in traffic.

el **accidente**
En la autopista se produjo un accidente muy grave por exceso de velocidad.

accident
A very serious accident resulted from speeding on the expressway.

el **riesgo**
No vale la pena el riesgo de correr tanto.

risk
Driving so fast isn't worth the risk.

chocar
Delante del bar chocaron dos coches pero no hubo heridos.

collide
Two cars collided in front of the bar, but there were no injuries.

el **taller**
Como tengo el coche en el taller, no puedo ir a recogerte a la estación.

workshop
Since I have the car in the workshop, I can't pick you up at the train station.

reparar
Miguel sabe reparar cualquier motor.

repair
Miguel can repair any motor.

conducir
A pesar de saber conducir muy bien no pudo evitar el accidente.

drive (a car)
Although he can drive very well, he was unable to prevent the accident.

el **conductor**; la **conductora**
Raimundo es un conductor prudente.

driver
Raimundo is a careful driver.

el **peatón**
En las carreteras españolas una señal recuerda a los peatones que circulen por su izquierda.

pedestrian
On Spanish highways a sign reminds pedestrians to walk on the left.

atropellar
El siete de julio, San Fermín, me atropelló un toro en Pamplona.

knock down; run over; hit
On July 7th, San Fermín, a bull knocked me down in Pamplona.

circular; **traficar**
A las ocho de la mañana es
casi imposible circular por
Barcelona.

drive
At 8 A.M. it is almost impossible
to drive through Barcelona.

adelantar
Ahora podemos adelantar a ese
camión porque no hay tráfico de
frente.

pass; overtake
Now we can pass this truck, because
there is no oncoming traffic.

girar; **doblar**
Antes de girar tienes que esperar a
que pasen los peatones.

turn
Before turning, you have to wait for
the pedestrians to cross.

---

la **circulación**; **tráfico**
Por las tardes la circulación en
Quito es imposible.

traffic
In the afternoon the traffic in
Quito is impossible.

la **desviación**

detour

el **transporte**
Para el transporte de los
muebles alquilamos un
camión.

transport(ation); moving
For moving our furniture
we rented a truck.

transportar
En mi coche puedo transportar el
armario.

transport
I can transport the cabinet in my
car.

la **señal de tráfico**
Hay que respetar tanto las
señales de tráfico como los
semáforos.

traffic sign
Both traffic signs and traffic
lights have to be observed.

el **semáforo**

traffic light

el **disco**
Alberto cruzó la calle a pesar de
que el disco estaba rojo.

light (phase); disk
Alberto crossed the street
although the light was red.

la velocidad

speed

la **limitación de velocidad**

speed limit

la **auto-escuela**

driving school

el **carnet de conducir**
Si se conduce un coche hay
que llevar el carnet de
conducir.

driver's license
When you drive a car, you have to
carry your driver's license.

el, la **automovilista**

driver

Road and Street Traffic

la **bici**; la **bicicleta**
Perico aún no sabe montar en bicicleta porque es demasiado pequeño.

bicycle; bike
Perico can't ride a bike yet, because he's too small.

el, la **ciclista**
En España muchos conductores no respetan a los ciclistas.

cyclist; bike rider
In Spain, many drivers do not show consideration for cyclists.

la **moto**
En Jerez se organizan carreras de motos.

motorcycle
In Jerez motorcycle races are held.

el **coche**
Después del accidente llevé el coche al taller.

car
After the accident I took the car to the shop.

usado, a
¿Has comprado un coche nuevo o usado?

used
Have you bought a new car or a used one?

el **auto(móvil)**
En Hispanoamérica, excepto en Chile y Argentina, se llama al automóvil "carro".

car, (auto)mobile
In Spanish America, except for Chile and Argentina, the word for automobile is "carro."

el **camión**
Los domingos hay muy pocos camiones por las carreteras.

truck
On Sunday there are very few trucks on the highways.

el **motor**
Enriqueta entiende mucho de motores.

motor; engine
Enriqueta understands a lot about engines.

la **gasolinera**
Ya hay en muchas gasolineras españolas gasolina sin plomo.

gas station
Many Spanish gas stations now carry lead-free gasoline.

la **gasolina**

gas(oline)

el **gasóleo**
Generalmente la gasolina es más cara que el gasóleo.

diesel fuel
Generally gasoline is cheaper than diesel fuel.

arrancar
Como arranca mal el coche, le cambiaré las bujías.

start
Since the car isn't starting well, I'm going to change the spark plugs.

frenar
Tuvimos que frenar en seco para no atropellar el burro.

brake
We had to brake suddenly to avoid hitting the donkey.

el **freno**
Los frenos de tu moto funcionan
muy mal.

brake
The brakes of your motorcycle are
very bad.

la **rueda**
Me han robado las cuatro ruedas.

wheel; tire
All four of my tires were stolen.

derecho
Para ir a la playa siga por aquí
derecho.

straight ahead
To get to the beach, keep going
straight ahead.

seguir

keep going; driving

torcer
Perdone, ¿cómo voy a la Sagrada
Familia?—Tuerza aquí a la derecha
y continúe derecho hasta el final
de la calle.

turn
Excuse me, please, how do I get to
Sagrada Familia Church?—Turn
right here and keep driving straight
ahead to the end of the street.

parar
El autobús para Gerona, ¿para
aquí?

stop
Does the bus to Gerona stop
here?

el **taxi**

taxi

el, la **taxista**

taxi driver

el **autobús**
Para ir a las Ramblas puede tomar el
autobús o ir en metro.

bus
To get to Ramblas, you can take the
bus or go by subway.

la **parada**
Para ir al centro, ¿es esta parada?

stop
Is this the right stop to go
downtown?

pasar
¿A qué hora pasa el próximo
autobús para Guadalajara?

pass; go
What time is the next bus
for Guadalajara?

acelerar

accelerate; speed up

la **póliza del seguro**
¿Lleva usted la póliza del seguro?

insurance certificate
Do you have the insurance
certificate with you?

el **cinturón de seguridad**
En carreteras y autopistas españolas
es obligatorio llevar el cinturón de
seguridad.

safety belt
On Spanish highways and
superhighways, wearing a safety
belt is required by law.

aparcar; **estacionar**
¡Aquí no puede aparcar!

park
You can't park here!

el **estacionamiento**
Estacionamiento prohibido.

parking
No Parking.

la **multa**	fine
la **avería** La Guardia Civil le ayudará si tiene una avería.	breakdown The Guardia Civil will help you if you have a breakdown.
la **grúa** La grúa se llevó mi coche porque estaba mal aparcado.	tow truck My car was towed because it was improperly parked.
estropeado, a El embrague de mi coche está estropeado, por eso no le entran bien las marchas.	defective; damaged The clutch of my car is damaged, and that is why the gears are hard to shift.
la **marcha**	gear
la **matrícula** El coche tiene matrícula de Barcelona.	registration The car has a Barcelona registration.
la **placa** La placa de tu moto está sucia.	license plate The license plate of your motorcycle is dirty.
cegar De noche me ciegan los faros de los coches.	blind At night the car headlights blind me.
el **faro**	(car) light; headlight
el **embrague**	clutch
la **bujía**	spark plug
el **depósito**; **tanque** Por favor, lléneme el depósito y míreme el aceite.	(gas) tank Please fill the tank and check the oil for me.
el **bidón (de gasolina)**	(gas) canister
el **neumático** Lleváis los neumáticos muy gastados. Será mejor que los cambiéis antes del viaje.	tire Your tires are very worn. It will be better to replace them before the trip.
la **presión**	pressure
el **volante** No coja el volante si ha bebido.	steering wheel Don't get behind the wheel if you've been drinking.
el **maletero**	trunk
el **claxon**; **bocina**	horn
el **velo(motor)**	motorbike; motor-assisted bicycle

| el **casco** | (crash) helmet |

Rail Traffic

el **metro**
Lo más rápido para ir al centro es
el metro.

subway; metro
The fastest way to go downtown is
the subway.

el **ferrocarril**
En Ibiza no hay ferrocarril.

railroad
In Ibiza there is no railroad.

el **tren**
El tren procedente de Málaga entra
en la vía cuatro.

train
The train from Malaga arrives on
track 4.

la **estación**
¿Dónde está la estación central?
—Al lado del ayuntamiento.

train station
Where is the main train station?
—Next to the town hall.

el **billete**
Los billetes de diez viajes para el
autobús se venden en los estancos.

ticket
Bus tickets good for 10 trips are
sold in tobacco stores.

la **ida**
Como a la vuelta Pedro me lleva en su
coche, sólo tengo que tomar el tren
de ida.

(journey) way there
Since Pedro is taking me in his
car on the way back, I only
have to take the train on the way
there.

la **vuelta**
Déme un billete de ida y vuelta para
Córdoba.

return trip; (journey) way back
Please give me a round-trip ticket
to Córdoba.

hacer transbordo
¿Hay que hacer transbordo para
ir de Segovia a Cáceres?

transfer
Do you have to transfer to go
from Segovia to Caceres?

el **horario**
Hemos estado mirando el horario
de trenes pero no hemos entendido
nada.

schedule
We've been looking at the train
schedule, but we didn't understand
anything.

la **vía**
Ahora entra el tren para Aranjuez
por la vía tres.

track
The train to Aranjuez is now
arriving on track 3.

el **andén**
¿De qué andén sale el tren para Irún?

platform
From which platform does the train
to Irún leave?

la **reserva**
¿Cuánto es la reserva de asiento?
—No lo sé, pregunte en la
ventanilla dos.

reservation
What does a seat reservation cost?
—I don't know. Ask at window 2.

la **ventanilla**

(ticket) window

el **asiento**

seat

el **tranvía**
Desde hace muchos años ya no
existen tranvías en Valencia.

streetcar; tram
There haven't been any streetcars in
Valencia for many years.

el **enlace**

connection; tie; link

la **correspondencia**
Este tren no tiene correspondencia
con el expreso de Santander.

connection
This train doesn't make connection
with the express to Santander.

procedente
El tren procedente de Bilbao llegará
con una hora de retraso.

coming from
The train from Bilbao will
arrive one hour late.

el **expreso**

express train

el **rápido**

fast train; vestibule train

el **Talgo**

intercity (train)

las **cercanías**
el tren de cercanías

surroundings; neighborhood
suburban (short-distance) train

el **suplemento**

supplement

el **vagón**
¿Qué vagones lleva el rápido a Vigo?
—Lleva un coche-restaurante y
coches-literas.

railroad car; coach
What cars does the fast train to
Vigo have?—A dining car and
couchette cars.

el **coche-cama**
¿Puedo sacar reserva para el coche-
cama?

sleeping car
Can I make a reservation for the
sleeping car?

el **coche-litera**

couchette car

el **coche-restaurante**

dining car

el **compartimento**

compartment

la **RENFE**
RENFE significa "red nacional de
ferrocarriles españoles".

Spanish state railroad system
RENFE means "Spanish national
railroad network."

el **revisor**; la **revisora**

conductor

la **consigna**

railroad checkroom

■ Aviation and Shipping ■

el **avión**
En Latinoamérica el avión muchas veces es la única posibilidad de trasladarse.

airplane; aircraft
In Latin America, the airplane is often the only way to travel.

aéreo, a
Algunas compañías aéreas son famosas por sus retrasos.

air; aerial
Some airlines are famous for their delays.

el **aeropuerto**
En el aeropuerto de Zaragoza hay problemas con la aviación militar norteamericana.

airport
At the Zaragoza airport there are problems with the U.S. Air Force.

el **vuelo**
El vuelo de Mallorca a Valencia es muy corto.

flight
The flight from Mallorca to Valencia is very short.

volar
Cuando se vuela sobre las nubes, se puede ver el sol.

fly
When you fly above the clouds, you can see the sun.

aterrizar
¿Ya ha aterrizado el avión de Acapulco?

land
Has the plane from Acapulco already landed?

despegar
Antes de despegar las azafatas explican las instrucciones de seguridad.

take off
Before takeoff the stewardesses explain the safety instructions.

la **azafata**

stewardess; flight attendant

el **auxiliar de vuelo**

steward; flight attendant

el **capitán**
En nombre del capitán les damos la bienvenida a bordo.

captain
On behalf of the captain, we welcome you on board.

a **bordo**

on board; aboard *(ship; airplane)*

el **pasajero**; la **pasajera**
Los pasajeros con destino a Cádiz diríjanse a la puerta número trece.

passenger
Passengers traveling to Cádiz are requested to go to gate 13.

embarcarse
¿A qué hora os tenéis que embarcar?

check in; board *(ship)*
What time do you have to board?

desembarcar
Los pasajeros acaban de
desembarcar en Palma.

disembark; go ashore
The passengers have just
disembarked in Palma.

el **barco**
Un viaje en barco es muy agradable si
no hay tempestad.

ship
A voyage can be very pleasant
if no storm arises.

el **puerto**
El transbordador de Ibiza acaba
de llegar al puerto de Barcelona.

port
The Ibiza ferry has just arrived
in the port of Barcelona.

el **pasaje**
¿Has sacado ya el pasaje?

passage; fare
Have you already bought the ship
ticket?

el **transbordador**
De Melilla sale un transbordador
para Málaga.

ferry
From Melilla a ferry goes to
Malaga.

marítimo, a
Muchos transportes de
Latinoamérica se realizan por vía
marítima.

maritime; marine; sea
Many shipments from Latin
America are made by sea.

la **aviación**

aviation

la **navegación**
La navegación aérea ha aumentado
en los últimos años.
Es necesario para la navegación
por alta mar una brújula.

navigation; voyage
Air traffic has increased
in recent years.
For oceangoing navigation,
a compass is necessary.

la **brújula**
Los marineros se orientan con la
brújula.

(ship's) compass
Sailors get their bearings with a
compass.

orientarse

find one's way; get one's
bearings

la **escala**
¿Este vuelo a Buenos Aires es directo
o hace escala en Asunción?

stopover; port of call
Is this a direct flight to Buenos
Aires, or does it make a stopover
in Asunción?

directo, a
¿Hay combinación de metro directa
al Paseo de la Castellana?

direct
Is there a direct subway connection
to Paseo de la Castellana?

el **destino**
El vuelo con destino a Santa Cruz
se retrasa media hora.

destination
The flight to Santa Cruz is
delayed half an hour.

retrasarse

be delayed; late

el **helicóptero**
Nunca he subido a un helicóptero.

helicopter
I've never been inside a helicopter.

la **nave**
Los aviones se reparan en naves enormes.

hangar
Planes are repaired in enormous hangars.

el **marinero**
Los marineros están en todos los puertos en casa.

sailor; seaman; mariner
Sailors are at home in every port.

marino, a
Su abuelo era capitán de barco y siempre llevaba un uniforme marino.

marine; sea; nautical
His grandfather was a ship's captain and always wore a nautical uniform.

la **proa**

bow; prow

la **popa**

stern; poop

la **cubierta**

deck

navegar
Es difícil navegar por aguas desconocidas.

navigate; sail; steer
It is difficult to sail through unknown waters.

la **barca**
En el Retiro de Madrid hay barcas para pasear por el estanque.

boat
In Madrid's Retiro Park, there are boats for sailing on the lake.

el **ancla** *f*

anchor

el **nudo**

knot

el **yate**
Este verano hemos pasado las vacaciones a bordo de un yate.

yacht
This summer we spent our vacation aboard a yacht.

el **naufragio**
El naufragio de muchos barcos es debido al desconocimiento de las aguas.

shipwreck
Many shipwrecks are due to unfamiliarity with the waters.

el **náufrago**; la **náufraga**
Los náufragos fueron rescatados por la marina de guerra.

shipwrecked person
The shipwrecked people were rescued by the Navy.

rescatar

rescue

Traffic Routes

la **calle**
En esta calle a todas horas hay mucho tráfico.

street
There's always a lot of traffic on this street.

la **avenida**
La Diagonal es la avenida que cruza Barcelona.

avenue
La Diagonal is the avenue that passes through Barcelona.

atravesar
¡Nunca atraviese la avenida cuando el semáforo esté en rojo!

cross; go through
Never cross the avenue when the traffic light is red!

el **cruce**
Este cruce fue peligroso porque no había semáforo.

crossing; crossroads
This crossing was dangerous because there was no traffic light.

cruzar
Vamos a cruzar la calle por el paso de peatones.

cross; pass through
We're going to cross the street at the pedestrian crossing.

la **carretera**
En las carreteras españolas hay una limitación de velocidad.

highway
On Spanish highways there is a speed limit.

la **autopista**
En España hay que pagar peaje en las autopistas.

superhighway; expressway
In Spain, you have to pay a toll on superhighways.

la **curva**
¡Cuidado con esta curva! Es muy peligrosa.

curve
Careful! This curve is very dangerous.

las **obras**

construction work; site (*always plural in this meaning*)

La carretera está cortada por obras.

The highway is closed for construction work.

cortar
Han cortado la calle de Alcalá por una manifestación.

close
Alcalá Street is closed because of a demonstration.

la **entrada**
¿Dónde está la entrada al garaje del hotel?

entrance
Where is the entrance to the hotel garage?

la **salida**
Venimos tarde porque nos equivocamos en la salida de la autopista.

exit
We're late because we took the wrong superhighway exit.

la **acera**
En verano las aceras de los pueblos están ocupadas por señoras que hacen labores.

sidewalk
In summer the village sidewalks are occupied by women who do needlework.

el **aparcamiento**; **estacionamiento**
He estado buscando dos horas aparcamiento y al final he aparcado mal.

parking place
I've been looking for a parking place for two hours, and finally I parked in a no parking zone.

el **paso de peatones**
Casi me atropellan en el paso de peatones.

pedestrian crossing
I was almost run over in the pedestrian crossing.

la **zona azul**
Cuando se aparca en la zona azul hay que comprar un billete en un automático y dejarlo visible en el coche.

limited parking zone
When you park in the limited parking zone, you have to buy a ticket from an automat and leave it in a visible position in your car.

el **automático**

automat

el **peaje**
A veces no merece la pena utilizar la autopista porque el peaje es muy caro.

toll
Sometimes it's not worth it to use the superhighway, because the tolls are very high.

el **tránsito**
El tránsito de Valencia ha mejorado con la autopista.

transit; traffic; passing
Passing through Valencia has become easier with the superhighway.

¡Y dicen que el manejo calma los nervios!
And they say that driving relaxes you!

el **planeta**	planet
la **estrella**	star
Las estrellas brillan en noches claras.	On clear nights, the stars sparkle.
brillar	shine; sparkle; glitter
el **espacio**	(outer) space
El espacio aún no se conoce bien.	Outer space is still not well known.
el **mundo**	world
Todavía no hemos descubierto otros mundos habitados.	We haven't discovered other inhabited worlds yet.
la **tierra**	earth
La tierra es el planeta azul.	Earth is the blue planet.
solar	solar
En nuestro sistema solar hay un sol.	In our solar system there is one sun.
el **sol**	sun
la **luna**	moon
Esta noche hay luna llena.	Tonight there's a full moon.
el **elemento**	element
el **origen**	origin
el, la **astronauta**	astronaut
¿Quiénes fueron los primeros astronautas que fueron a la luna?	Who were the first astronauts who went to the moon?
espacial	space
Las naves espaciales no son perfectas.	Spaceships are not perfect.
el **satélite**	satellite
El partido de fútbol será transmitido vía satélite.	The soccer game will be transmitted by satellite.
el **universo**	universe
En el universo todos los planetas parecen igual de pequeños.	In the universe, all the planets seem equally small.
terrestre	terrestrial; earthly
El agua cubre la mayor parte de la superficie terrestre.	Water covers the majority of the earth's surface.
la **astronomía**	astronomy

la **puesta de sol**
¿Sabes a qué hora es la puesta de sol
y la puesta de luna?

sunset
Do you know when sunset and
moonset are?

la **puesta de luna**

moonset

la **salida del sol**
Nos levantamos a la salida del
sol para ir a pescar.

sunrise
We got up at sunrise to go fishing.

el **crepúsculo**
Estuvimos trabajando en el campo
hasta el crepúsculo.

twilight; dawn; dusk
We worked in the field until dusk.

la **oscuridad**
Las noches que no hay luna, la
oscuridad da miedo.

darkness
On the nights when there's no
moon, the darkness is frightening.

la **atmósfera**
La contaminación del aire daña la
atmósfera.

atmosphere
Air pollution harms the
atmosphere.

atmosférico, a
Un cambio atmosférico puede
destruir la tierra.

atmospheric
An atmospheric change can
destroy the earth.

la **cosmografía**
En la cosmografía se estudian
diferentes modelos del origen del
universo, los elementos y las
materias cósmicas.

cosmography
In cosmography, different models
of the origin of the universe,
the elements, and cosmic matter
are studied.

cósmico, a

cosmic

la **nave espacial**

spaceship

la **estación espacial**

space station

"¡Shhh! ¡Están tocando la sonata Claro de Tierra!"
"Shhh! They are playing the Earthlight Sonata!"

━━━━━━━━━━━━━━━ **Colors** ━━━━━━━━━━━━━━━

el **color**
¿De qué color vas a pintar tu coche?

color
What color are you going to paint your car?

en **colores**

multicolored

claro, a
¿Te gustan más los colores claros o los oscuros?

light
Do you like light or dark colors more?

oscuro, a

dark

gris
En casa tengo una alfombra gris clara.

gray
At home I have a light gray carpet.

azul
Hay andaluces con pelo negro y ojos azules.

blue
There are Andalusians with black hair and blue eyes.

lila
Carmen tiene una blusa y un pantalón lila muy bonitos.

lilac
Carmen has a very pretty lilac blouse and slacks.

violeta
Margarita quiere teñirse el pelo color violeta.

violet
Margarita wants to dye her hair violet.

marrón
Virginia tiene un suéter marrón.

brown
Virginia has a brown sweater.

amarillo, a

yellow

verde
Catalina se ha comprado unos zapatos verde oscuro.

green
Catalina has bought a pair of dark green shoes.

negro, a
El negro está de moda.

black
Black is in fashion.

blanco, a
José quiere vender su coche blanco.

white
José wants to sell his white car.

rojo, a
¿Te gustan las rosas rojas?
—No, prefiero los claveles rosas.

red
Do you like red roses?
—No, I prefer pink carnations.

incoloro, a
¿Tiene crema para zapatos incolora?

colorless
Do you have colorless shoe cream?

el **brillo**
Antes esta estantería estaba mate pero ahora tiene mucho brillo.

shine; gloss
Formerly this bookcase was mat, but now it has a high gloss.

mate

mat; dull; lusterless

beige
A Emilio no le gusta el beige.

beige
Emilio doesn't like beige.

pardo, a
Por las noches no todos los gatos son pardos.

dark gray; brown
At night not all cats are gray.

rosa

pink

encarnado, a
Ofelia lleva un pendiente encarnado.

red; flesh-colored
Ofelia wears a red earring.

color naranja
Tomás tenía una boina color naranja.

orange
Tomás had an orange beret.

dorado, a

gold(en)

plateado, a

silver(y)

Shapes

el **círculo**
¿Sabes dibujar un círculo sin compás?

circle
Can you draw a circle without a compass?

cuadrado, a
Como no teníamos sitio hemos cambiado la mesa ovalada por una cuadrada.

square
Since we didn't have enough room, we exchanged the oval table for a square one.

ovalado, a

oval

la **línea**
El juez de línea estaba ciego durante el partido.

line
The line referee was blind during the game.

la **raya**
Tengo un pijama a rayas.

stripe
I have striped pajamas.

la **punta**
Se ha partido la punta del lápiz.

tip; point
The pencil tip has broken off.

puntiagudo, a
¡Ten cuidado con ese cuchillo puntiagudo!

sharp; pointed
Be careful with that sharp knife!

redondo, a
Los discos son redondos y planos.

round(ed)
Records are round and flat.

plano, a

flat

la **esquina**
Pablo te está esperando en la esquina.

corner
Pablo is waiting for you at the corner.

la **forma**
Estas tazas tienen una forma horrible.

shape; form
These cups have a horrible shape.

formar
En el cabo las rocas forman una cueva.

form
At the cape, the rocks form a cave.

la **cruz**
Las personas que no saben escribir firman con una cruz.

cross
People who can't write sign their name with a cross.

la **bola**
Nuestro profesor siempre juega con una bola de cristal.

ball; globe
Our teacher always plays with a glass ball.

la **esfera**
Desde la tierra la luna tiene forma de esfera.

sphere; globe; ball
From the earth, the moon looks globe-shaped.

la **pirámide**
Julián tiene altavoces en forma de pirámide.

pyramid
Julián has pyramid-shaped loudspeakers.

recto, a
Esta pared no está recta.

straight
This wall is not straight.

el **rectángulo**

rectangle

el **triángulo**
Luis se ha hecho una mesa en forma de triángulo, o sea triangular.

triangle
Luis has made a table in the shape of a triangle, that is, triangular.

triangular

triangular

el **tamaño**
¿De qué tamaño desea los sobres?

size
What size envelopes do you want?

el **arco**
En esta iglesia hay unos arcos románicos.

arch; arc; bow
There are Romanesque arches in this church.

la **columna**
En la entrada de mi casa han puesto dos columnas.

column; pillar
At the entrance of my house two columns have been put up.

la **cúpula**

dome; cupola

el **cubo**
¿Cuántas esquinas tiene un cubo?

cube
How many angles does a cube have?

el **cilindro**

cylinder

llano, a
Este campo es tan llano como para construir una casa.

flat; smooth
This land is flat enough for building a house.

Millones de obras de arte son inspiradas por la fe.
Millions of works of art are inspired by faith.

▬▬▬ Miscellaneous Concepts ▬▬▬

la **cosa**
thing

la **materia prima**
raw material
México es un país rico en materias primas.
Mexico is a country rich in raw materials.

el **material**
material
¿De qué material está hecho ese puente?
What material is that bridge made of?

auténtico, a
genuine; authentic
Marisa tiene una blusa de seda china auténtica.
Marisa has a blouse of genuine Chinese silk.

líquido, a
liquid
La gasolina está compuesta por diferentes productos líquidos.
Gasoline is made up of different liquid products.

frágil
fragile; breakable
¿Hay materiales más frágiles que el cristal?
Are there materials more fragile than glass?

la **materia**
matter; substance; stuff

estar compuesto, a
be composed; made up; consist

el **combustible**
fuel

inflamable
flammable; inflammable
La pólvora no sólo es inflamable sino que explota.
Gunpowder is not only flammable, but it also explodes.

arder
burn
Algunas sustancias orgánicas arden con poca llama y mucho humo.
Some organic substances burn with a small flame and lots of smoke.

la **llama**
flame

el **humo**
smoke

la **sustancia**
substance

orgánico, a
organic

la **fibra**
fiber

el **líquido**
liquid

turbio, a
muddy; turbid

transparente	transparent
visible	visible
delicado, a	delicate
sólido, a	firm; solid
eléctrico, a	electric(al)

■■■■■ Substances of Plant and Animal Origin ■■■■■

el **cuero**
Juan se ha comprado una chaqueta de cuero.

leather
Juan has bought himself a leather jacket.

la **piel**

leather; fur; hide

la **seda**
La seda y el terciopelo son muy difíciles de limpiar.

silk
Silk and velvet are very hard to clean.

el **algodón**
Me gusta llevar ropa de lana o algodón.

cotton
I like to wear wool or cotton clothing.

la **lana**

wool

la **grasa**
Tienes que ponerle grasa a esta puerta para que no haga ruido.

oil; fat; grease
You have to oil this door so that it doesn't squeak.

la **madera**
De madera se hacen muchas cosas como por ejemplo papel.

wood
Many things are made from wood—for example, paper.

el **barro**

mud; clay

el **corcho**

cork

el **papel**

paper

biológico, a

biologic(al)

el **ante**

buckskin; suede

el **caucho**
Las primeras ruedas eran de caucho.

rubber
The first tires were made of rubber.

la **caña de bambú**

bamboo

la **leña**
La madera del pino es demasiado buena como para hacer sólo leña.

firewood
Pinewood is too good to be used only as firewood.

la **franela** No sé si ponerme el traje de franela.	flannel I don't know whether to wear the flannel suit.
el **terciopelo**	velvet
el **marfil** Se han matado muchos elefantes por causa del marfil.	ivory Many elephants have been killed for their ivory.
la **cera**	wax
el **cartón** Es mejor que envíes los regalos en una caja de cartón.	cardboard; pasteboard It's better to send the gifts in a cardboard box.
el **vapor**	steam; vapor

▬▬▬ Mineral and Chemical Substances ▬▬▬

la **goma** La goma es un producto artificial y elástico.	gum; rubber; glue Gum is an artificial and elastic product.
elástico, a	elastic
artificial	artificial
el **diamante** El cristal se corta con un diamante.	diamond Glass is cut with a diamond.
la **piedra** ¡No tires piedras a los perros!	stone Don't throw stones at the dogs!
el **oro** He cambiado la cadena de oro por una de plata.	gold I have exchanged the gold chain for a silver one.
la **plata**	silver
el **metal** El hierro, el cobre y el estaño son metales.	metal Iron, copper, and tin are metals.
el **acero** El acero de Toledo es famoso.	steel Steel from Toledo is famous.
el **hierro** El hierro se funde en hornos.	iron Iron is melted in furnaces.

el **carbón**
En Asturias hay importantes minas de carbón.

coal; carbon
In Asturias there are important coal mines.

el **cemento**
Para construir una casa se necesita cemento, hormigón, arena, yeso, grava, mármol, y vidrio.

cement
To build a house you need cement, concrete, sand, plaster, gravel, marble, and glass.

la **arena**

sand

el **vidrio**; **cristal**

glass

el **gas**
La cocina de gas es a veces mejor para cocinar.

gas
The gas stove sometimes is better for cooking.

el **petróleo**
Como ha subido el precio del petróleo también ha subido el gasóleo y la gasolina.

crude oil
Since the price of crude oil has risen, diesel fuel and gasoline have also increased in cost.

el **plástico**

plastic

sintético, a

synthetic

químico, a

chemical

---

el **mineral**
Algunos minerales son importantes para la industria.

mineral
Some minerals are important for industry.

atómico, a

atomic

oxidado, a

oxidized

oxidarse

oxidize; rust

la **esmeralda**

emerald

el **brillante**
Este brillante es un diamante de mucho valor.

diamond; brilliant; sparkler
This brilliant is a very valuable diamond.

el **aluminio**

aluminum

el **plomo**
En mi casa hay tubos de plomo.

lead
In my house there are lead pipes.

el **bronce**
Han hecho un monumento de bronce al rey.

bronze
A bronze monument has been erected to the king.

plateado, a

silver-plated

el **hormigón**
Este hormigón tiene más arena que cemento.

concrete
This concrete contains more sand than cement.

el **yeso**	plaster
Tape los agujeros con yeso.	Close up the holes with plaster.
la **grava**	gravel
el **mármol**	marble
El baño es de mármol.	The bathroom is made of marble.
el **cobre**	copper
el **estaño**	tin
el **azufre**	sulfur
el **fósforo**	phosphorus
En Hispanoamérica se llama fósforos a las cerillas.	In Spanish America matches are called "fosforos."
el **arsénico**	arsenic
la **pólvora**	gunpowder
la **porcelana**	porcelain
el **vidrio**	glass
¡Cuidado con este paquete que contiene vidrio!	Be careful with this package! It contains glass.
el **alambre**	wire
la **chapa**	plate; sheet (of metal)
la **laca**	lacquer; shellac
La laca y el plástico son productos químicos.	Lacquer and plastic are chemical products.
el **nilón**	nylon
el **butano**	butane
el **oxígeno**	oxygen
El agua se compone de oxígeno e hidrógeno.	Water is composed of oxygen and hydrogen.
el **hidrógeno**	hydrogen
el **nitrógeno**	nitrogen
El nitrógeno es importante para el abono de las plantas.	Nitrogen is important for fertilizing plants.
el **cloro**	chlorine
El agua de la piscina tiene cloro.	The water in the swimming pool is chlorinated.
el **mercurio**	mercury
España es el productor de mercurio más importante de Europa.	Spain is Europe's major producer of mercury.

Numbers

el **número**
Todavía no me sé tu número.

number; numeral
I haven't memorized your number yet.

cero

zero

uno; **un**; **una**

one; a; an

dos

two

tres

three

cuatro
Es tan cierto como dos y dos son cuatro.

four
It's as sure as two and two make four.

cinco
No cojas los huevos de cinco en cinco.

five
Don't take five eggs at a time.

seis

six

siete

seven

ocho
Ocho y ocho son dieciséis.

eight
Eight and eight are 16.

nueve

nine

diez

ten

once

eleven

doce

twelve

trece

thirteen

catorce

fourteen

quince

fifteen

dieciséis; **diez** y **seis**

sixteen

diecisiete

seventeen

dieciocho

eighteen

diecinueve

nineteen

veinte

twenty

veintiuno; **veintiún**; **veintiuna**
Nací el día 21 de Mayo, tengo veintiún años y me han regalado veintiuna rosas.

twenty-one
I was born on May 21, I am 21 years old, and I got 21 roses as a present.

veintidós

twenty-two

303

veintitrés	twenty-three
veinticuarto	twenty-four
veinticinco	twenty-five
veintiséis	twenty-six
veintisiete	twenty-seven
veintiocho	twenty-eight
veintinueve	twenty-nine
treinta	thirty
treinta y uno; **treinta y un**; **treinta y una**	thirty-one
treinta y dos	thirty-two
cuarenta	forty
cincuenta	fifty
sesenta	sixty
setenta	seventy
ochenta	eighty
noventa	ninety

cien; **ciento**
De ciento uno a ciento noventa y nueve se usa "ciento".
He comprado cien conejos y cien gallinas.

one hundred
From 101 to 199, "ciento" is used.
I have bought 100 rabbits and 100 hens.

ciento uno; **un**; **una**

one hundred one

doscientos, as
¡Imagínate, tengo doscientos libros!

two hundred
Imagine, I have 200 books!

trescientos, as — three hundred

cuatrocientos, as — four hundred

quinientos, as — five hundred

seiscientos, as — six hundred

setecientos, as — seven hundred

ochocientos, as — eight hundred

novecientos, as
¿Cuántos marcos te dan por novecientas pesetas?

nine hundred
How many German marks do you get for 900 pesetas?

mil
En mil novecientos noventa y uno me tocó la lotería.

one thousand
In 1991 I won the lottery.

dos mil	two thousand
un millón	one million
mil millones	one billion

1°; 1ª; primer; primero, a
En primer curso fui el primero.
La primera vez me entusiasmé pero
al segundo día me desilusioné.

first; in the first place
In first grade I was first in my class.
The first time I was enthusiastic, but
on the second day I was
disappointed.

2°; 2ª; segundo, a   second

3°; 3ª; tercer; tercero, a   third

4°; 4ª; cuarto, a   fourth

5°; 5ª; quinto, a   fifth

6°; 6ª; sexto, a   sixth

7°; 7ª; séptimo, a   seventh

8°; 8ª; octavo, a   eighth

9°; 9ª; noveno, a   ninth

10°; 10ª; décimo, a   tenth

11°; 11ª; undécimo, a   eleventh

12°; 12ª; duodécimo, a   twelfth

**13°; 13ª; décimotercer;
décimotercero, a**   thirteenth

General Concepts

dividir
9 dividido por 3 son 3.

divide
9 divided by 3 is 3.

multiplicar
2 multiplicado por 3 son 6.

multiply
2 times 3 is 6.

sumar
¿Quién sabe sumar 2 más 2?

add
Who can add 2 plus 2?

restar
Clara sabe restar muy bien.

subtract
Clara can subtract very well.

ser
11 más 2 son 13.

make; be
11 plus 2 makes 13.

último, a
A última hora vienen las prisas.

last
At the last minute everything has
to go quickly.

siguiente

following; next

sucesivo, a
Al día siguiente y los sucesivos
dormí mal.

successive
The next day and the days
thereafter I slept badly.

---

la **cifra**
De lejos no puedo leer estas cifras.

figure; number
I can't read these figures from a
distance.

la **numeración**
No entiendo esta numeración.

numeration; numbering
I don't understand this numbering.

numerar
¿Has numerado las cajas?

number; enumerate
Have you numbered the boxes?

penúltimo, a
No se bebe nunca la última copa
sino siempre la penúltima.

next to last; penultimate
One never drinks the last glass,
but always the next to last.

precedente

prior; preceding

seguido, a

continued; successive; direct

posterior
El Siglo de Oro es posterior al
Renacimiento.

later; subsequent
The Golden Age comes after the
Renaissance.

Weights and Measures

el **milímetro**
¿Cuántos milímetros mide un
centímetro?

millimeter
How many millimeters are in a
centimeter?

el **centímetro**

centimeter

el **metro**
Esta casa tiene cien metros cuadrados.
—¿Lo has medido con el metro?

meter; measuring tape, stick
This house has 100 square
meters.—Have you measured it
with the measuring stick?

el **kilómetro**
¿Faltan muchos kilómetros para
Granada?

kilometer
Is it many more kilometers to
Granada?

el **cuarto**	quarter
Déme un pan de cuarto.	Give me a quarter kilo of bread.
la **mitad**	half
¿Quieres la mitad de mi bocadillo?	Would you like half of my sandwich?
medio, a	half
el **par**	pair
Julio se ha comprado un par de pantalones.	Julio has bought himself a pair of trousers.
pesar	weigh
¿Cuánto pesa este melón?	How much does this melon weigh?
el **peso**	weight; scale
Vamos a comprarnos un peso para controlar mejor nuestro peso.	We're going to buy a scale to control our weight better.
el **gramo**	gram
Déme doscientos gramos de queso.	Please give me 200 grams of cheese.
el **kilo(gramo)**	kilo(gram)
Pónganos medio kilo de patatas.	Please give us half a kilo of potatoes.
la **tonelada**	ton
Este coche pesa casi una tonelada.	This car weighs almost a ton.
el **litro**	liter
Ayer nos tomamos dos litros de vino comiendo.	Yesterday we drank two liters of wine at dinner.
el **pedazo**	piece
el **trozo**	piece

medir	measure
la **milla**	mile
En el mar se miden las millas.	At sea, one measures in miles.
la **medida**	measurement
¿Tomasteis las medidas de la cocina?	Have you taken the measurements of the kitchen?
el **metro cúbico**	cubic meter
la **hectárea**	hectare
¿Cuántas hectáreas miden sus campos?	How many hectares do your fields measure?
la **docena**	dozen
¡Póngame una docena de langostinos!	Give me one dozen crayfish!

el **barril**	barrel; keg
pesado, a	heavy
Esta caja es demasiado pesada para ti.	This box is too heavy for you.
ligero, a	light
Este vino es muy ligero.	This wine is very light.
el **volumen**	volume

Concepts of Quantity

más
Lucas es el más listo, por lo menos tanto como su hermana.

more; most
Lucas is the smartest, at least as smart as his sister.

más que, de
Braulio come más que todos nosotros juntos.
Este coche es más caro que el vuestro.

Fidadelfo tiene más de 60 años.

more than
Braulio eats more than all of us together.
This car is more expensive than yours.
Fidadelfo is over 60 years old.

demasiado, a

too; too much

mucho, a
A mis fiestas vienen siempre muchos amigos.

much; many
Many friends always come to my parties.

mucho
Aquí no trabajamos mucho.

much; very
Here we don't work much.

tanto, a
No esperábamos tanta gente.

so much; so many
We weren't expecting so many people.

tanto ... como
Luis no es tan alto como Carlos.

as ... as
Luis is not as tall as Carlos.

bastante
¿Has comido bastante o quieres más?
—Gracias, creo que ya he comido demasiado.

enough
Have you eaten enough or would you like more?—Thank you, I think I've already eaten too much.

menos
Este invierno es menos frío que el anterior.

less
This winter is less cold than the previous one.

menos que, de
Luisa tiene menos libros que Carlos.
¿Tienes más de 30 años?—Sí, pero menos de 40.

less; fewer than
Luisa has fewer books than Carlos.
Are you over 30?—Yes, but under 40.

poco, a
Fernando tiene pocas ganas de trabajar.
¿Me da un poco de queso?

little; few; some
Fernando has little desire to work.
Will you give me some cheese?

poco
Los profesores ganan poco en
Perú.

little
Teachers earn little in Peru.

más o menos

Arreglar el coche me va a costar
más o menos un sueldo.

about; approximately; more or
less
Repairing the car is going to
cost me about a month's
wages.

solo, a

alone

juntos, as
Los hijos y los padres juntos forman
una familia.

together
Together parents and children
form a family.

la **parte**
La tercera parte de la novela es
muy emocionante.

part
The third part of the novel
is very thrilling.

todo
Entiendo todo lo que me has explicado.

everything
I understand everything you've
explained to me.

todo, a
Beatriz se ha comido todo el
chocolate.
Todos estos niños son mis hijos.

all; whole
Beatriz has eaten all the
chocolate.
All these boys are my sons.

entero, a
¿Os habéis comido el melón entero?
—No, aún queda medio.

entire
Have you eaten the entire melon?
—No, there's still half left.

el **doble**
Este trabajo me ha costado el doble
de tiempo y esfuerzo de lo que
esperaba.

double
This job took me double the
time and effort I expected.

doble
Déme un brandy doble.

double
Give me a double brandy.

incluso, a

included; including

el **total**
¿Cuánto es en total?

total
How much is it in all?

lleno, a
No pudimos entrar porque la
discoteca estaba llena.

full
We couldn't go in because the
discotheque was full.

el **por ciento** — percent

vacío, a — empty
Esta botella está vacía; — This bottle is empty;
tendré que abrir otra. — I'll have to open another.

quedar — remain; be left

faltar — be lacking; be needed
Nos faltan mil pesetas para — We need 1000 pesetas to
poder pagar la cuenta. — be able to pay the tab.

algo — something
¿Quieres tomar algo?— — Do you want something to drink?
No, no quiero nada. — —No, I don't want anything.

la **cantidad** — quantity; amount
¡Qué cantidad de arroz has hecho! — What a huge quantity of rice
you've made!

bastar — suffice; be enough
Dos kilos me bastan. — Two kilos are enough for me.

suficiente — sufficient; enough
Tenemos suficiente trabajo para todo — We have enough work for the
el año. — entire year.

insuficiente — insufficient; inadequate
Este trabajo ha resultado insuficiente. — This work has turned out to be
inadequate.

ambos, as — both

numeroso, a — numerous
Numerosas personas vieron el — Numerous people saw the
accidente. — accident.

por lo menos — at least

al menos — at least
Al menos me podrías ayudar. — At least you could help me.

a lo sumo — at most
Vinieron pocos amigos, a lo sumo — Few friends came, at most 15.
quince.

incluir — include

excluir — exclude

reducido, a — limited; small; narrow
Sólo hemos invitado a un grupo — We have invited only a limited
reducido. — group.

excepto

excepting; except

escaso, a
Este mes voy escaso de dinero.

scarce; little; limited
This month I'm short of money.

contain
Este paquete contiene veinte cigarillos.

contener
This pack contains 20 cigarettes.

el **contenido**
¡Cuidado! El contenido de ese
bidón es inflamable.

contents
Caution! The contents of that
drum are flammable.

el **montón**
Tengo un montón de cosas por hacer.
Hay un montón de ropa que lavar.

heap; pile; mass
I have a heap of things to do.
There's a pile of laundry to be
washed.

en **parte**
Reconozco que en parte tienes
razón.

in part
I admit that you are right in
part.

aparte de
Aparte de lo que me has pedido,
¿te mando algo más?

aside from; besides
Besides what you asked me
for, shall I send you anything
else?

el **promedio**

average

el **todo**
No comprendimos del todo
lo que querías decir.

whole; total; entirety
We didn't entirely understand
what you wanted to say.

el **porcentaje**
¿Qué porcentaje de alemanes vienen
todos los años a España?—No sé,
¿un dos por ciento?

percentage
What percentage of Germans come
every year to Spain?—I don't know,
about 2 percent, possibly?

el **exceso**

excess

excesivo, a

excessive

sobrar
¿Ha sobrado mucha comida?

be in excess; be left over
Was much food left over?

completar

complete

cargar
¿Cuántos litros carga tu coche?

load; charge; carry; ship
How many liters does your car
take?

la **masa**
Al fútbol van masas de espectadores.

mass; crowd (of people)
Crowds of spectators go to soccer
games.

relleno, a	stuffed; filled
vaciar	empty
¡No vacíes el cenicero en la calle!	Don't empty the ashtray into the street!

Llena

Demasiado

Poco

Vacía

Más que   Menos que

Tanto como

Length and Size

la **altura**
El Teide mide 3.718 metros de altura.

altitude
Teide has an altitude of 3,718 meters.

alto, a
¿Cuál es la montaña más alta de España?

tall; high
Which is Spain's highest mountain?

bajo, a
Las antiguas casas de campo son muy bajas.

low
The old farmhouses are very low.

profundo, a
El Mar Mediterráneo no es tan profundo como el Océano Pacífico.

deep
The Mediterranean is not as deep as the Pacific Ocean.

grande
El tío Paco no compraba helados muy grandes.
Verónica me ha regalado un gran libro.

large; big; great; grand
Uncle Paco didn't buy very large ice creams.
Verónica has given me a great book as a present.

pequeño, a
Esta casa es pequeña para tanta gente.

small; little
This house is too small for so many people.

el **ancho**
El armario tiene dos metros de ancho.

width; wide
The cabinet is 2 meters wide.

el **largo**
Clara quiere cambiar el largo del vestido.

length; long
Clara wants to alter the length of the dress.

estrecho, a
En los pueblos hay calles muy estrechas.

narrow
In the villages there are very narrow streets.

enorme
La Sagrada Familia es una iglesia enorme.

enormous; gigantic
The Sagrada Familia is an enormous church.

la **profundidad**
¿Cuánta profundidad tiene esta cueva?

depth
What is the depth of this cave?

hondo, a
Algunos pozos de petróleo son muy hondos.

deep
Some oil wells are very deep.

la **longitud**

length; longitude

el, la **gigante**
Aurelio es un gigante en comparación con sus padres.

giant
Aurelio is a giant in comparison to his parents.

el **nivel**
Valencia está al nivel del mar.

level
Valencia is at sea level.

fino, a
Esta cuerda es demasiado fina para atar el paquete.

thin; fine
This string is too thin for tying up the package.

la **extensión**
España tiene una extensión de casi medio millón de kilómetros cuadrados.

extent, length; dimension; volume
Spain has an area of almost half a million square kilometers.

extenderse
Los Pirineos se extienden del Cantábrico hasta el Mediterráneo.

extend
The Pyrenees extend from the Cantabrian Sea to the Mediterranean.

la **superficie**
La menor parte de la superficie de la tierra la ocupan los continentes.

surface
The lesser part of the earth's surface is occupied by the continents.

Place

el **lugar**
Todavía no conocía este lugar tan bonito.

place; site; town
I did not yet know this very pretty place.

¿dónde?
¿Dónde estarán mis papeles?

where?
Where are my papers likely to be?

donde
Ésta es la casa donde nació Velázquez.
En esta casa es donde vivió Dalí.

where; in which
This is the house in which Velazquez was born.
This is the house where Dali lived.

estar
be located

el **lado**
side

Al otro lado de la calle hay una
farmacia.
On the other side of the street
there is a pharmacy.

al lado (de)
next door; near at hand

El mercado central está al
lado del ayuntamiento.
The central market is
next door to the town hall.

junto a
next to; by; beside

Hemos dejado el coche junto al tuyo
para luego no tener que buscarlo.
We left the car next to yours, so that
we wouldn't have to look for it
later.

enfrente (de)
opposite; across (from)

Enfrente de la escuela hay
una parada de autobús.
Across from the school
there is a bus stop.

frente a
(directly) facing

Frente a la oficina hay un bar muy
barato.
Facing the office there is a very
inexpensive bar.

en
in; on

En la mesa sólo hay dos tazas.
There are only two cups on the
table.

El regalo está en el paquete.
The gift is in the package.

encima de
on; upon

¡No pongas los pies encima de la mesa!
Don't put your feet on the table!

sobre
on; upon; over; above

Gerardo te ha dejado las llaves sobre
la mesa.
Gerardo left the keys on the table
for you.

Los pájaros volaban sobre nuestras
cabezas.
The birds flew over our heads.

debajo de
under; beneath

El gato está debajo del coche.
The cat is under the car.

derecho, a
right

Carolina se ha roto la mano derecha.
Carolina has broken her right
hand.

a la derecha
right; to the right

Vamos a correr la mesa un poco a
la derecha.
We're going to slide the table a
little to the right.

izquierdo, a
left

Tomás sólo sabe escribir con la
izquierda.
Tomás can only write with his left
hand.

a la izquierda
left; to the left

Para ir al ayuntamiento tiene que
torcer la siguiente calle a la
izquierda.
To get to the town hall, you have
to turn left at the next street.

delante (de)
Delante del cine hay una cola enorme.

before; in front (of)
In front of the movie theater there is a huge line.

atrás
Deja la maleta atrás, en el coche.

back; behind
Leave the suitcase behind, in the car.

detrás (de)
Detrás de aquellas montañas está el mar.

behind; in back (of)
Behind those mountains is the sea.

alrededor de
Alrededor de la casa hemos plantado pinos.

about; around
Around the house we've planted pines.

por
¡Vamos a tomar algo por aquí!

Lisa pasea por la calle sola.

by; through; for
Let's drink something here-abouts!

Lisa strolls through the street alone.

aquí; acá
Aquí en la costa el clima es muy agradable.
¡Miguel, ven acá!

here
Here on the coast the climate is very pleasant.
Miguel, come here!

ahí
Ahí está Correos.

there
There is the post office.

allí; allá
¿Conoces la señora que está allí?
—¿Cuál?—Ésa que está allá.

there
Do you know the woman there?
—Which one?—That one over there.

hallarse
Madrid se halla en Castilla.

be (in a place)
Madrid is in Castile.

instalarse

establish oneself; settle

central
Miguel vive en un barrio central.

central
Miguel lives in a central part of town.

céntrico, a
Las Ramblas están en una zona céntrica de Barcelona.

central; focal
The Ramblas are in a central area of Barcelona.

horizontal

horizontal

vertical
Es mejor guardar los discos en posición vertical.

vertical
It's better to store records in a vertical position.

paralelo, a

parallel

la **posición**
¡Poned el tocadiscos en posición horizontal!

position
Put the record player in a horizontal position!

depositar
He depositado las joyas en la caja fuerte del hotel.

deposit
I've deposited the jewelry in the hotel safe.

la **mitad**
¿Corto el pan por la mitad?

middle
Shall I cut the bread through the middle?

el **rincón**
He buscado los libros por todos los rincones y no los he encontrado.

corner
I've looked in every corner for the books, and I haven't found them.

fuera (de)
Fuera está haciendo un frío terrible.
Jorge vive fuera de la ciudad.

outside (of)
It is terribly cold outside.
Jorge lives outside the city.

exterior
Hay que pintar las paredes exteriores de la casa.

exterior; outer
The exterior walls of the house have to be painted.

interior
La reforma interior del piso ha sido muy barata.

interior; inner
The interior renovation of the apartment was very inexpensive.

superficial
La herida de Ventura es sólo superficial.

superficial
Ventura's injury is only superficial.

superior
En el piso superior viven mis abuelos.

upper; higher; superior
My grandparents live in the upper apartment.

inferior
Las camisas están en el cajón inferior.

lower; inferior
The shirts are in the lower drawer.

aparte
¡Pon este libro aparte!

aside; separately
Put this book aside!

el **fondo**
Al fondo de la foto se ven los padres de Mayte.

background
In the background of the photo are seen Mayte's parents.

separar
El Estrecho de Gibraltar separa a España de África.

separate
The Strait of Gibraltar separates Spain from Africa.

unir
El Peñón de Ifach y el de Calpe están unidos por un istmo.

unite; join; link
The Rock of Ifach and the Rock of Calpe are linked by an isthmus.

por todas partes
Por todas partes vimos carteles de la Olimpiada.

everywhere
Everywhere we saw posters for the Olympics.

317

en todas partes
En verano hay mucha gente en todas partes.

everywhere
In summer there are many people everywhere.

en ninguna parte
No encuentro en ninguna parte mis gafas y ya he buscado por todas partes.

nowhere; not anywhere
I can't find my glasses anywhere, and I've looked everywhere.

el **agujero**

hole

Direction

la **dirección**

direction

¿adónde?
¿Adónde vas de vacaciones?

where (to)?
Where are you going on vacation?

adonde

where

hasta
Continúen hasta el final de esta calle, allí verán el monumento.

till; until; to; as far as
Go to the end of the street; you'll see the monument there.

a
Dolores va a comprar.
Leopoldo hizo un viaje a Chile.
A la salida de la autopista hay una gasolinera.
Marisa fue al cine con Quique.

to; in; at; by; for
Dolores is going to go shopping.
Leopoldo made a trip to Chile.
At the superhighway exit there is a gas station.
Marisa went to the movies with Quique.

hacia
Este autobús va hacia León.

toward; to; near
This bus is going to León.

para
El tren para Huelva sale a la una de la tarde.

for; to; toward
The train to Huelva departs at 1 P.M.

¿de dónde?
¿De dónde venís a estas horas?

where from?; whence?
Where are you coming from at this time of day?

de
Mi amiga viene de Sevilla.

from; of; by
My girlfriend comes from Seville.

desde
Desde nuestras ventanas veíamos la montaña.

from
From our windows we saw the mountains.

adelante
Por este camino no podemos seguir adelante; hay que volver atrás.

ahead; forward; farther on
We can't go any farther on this road; we have to turn back.

derecho
Perdón, el cine Rialto ¿está cerca de aquí?
—Sí, muy cerca. Siga esta calle derecho, gire la primera a la derecha y, luego, la segunda a la izquierda.

straight ahead
Excuse me, is the Rialto movie theater near by?
—Yes, very near. Follow this street straight ahead, turn right at the first street and then left at the second.

contra
El camión chocó contra un autobús.

against
The truck crashed into a bus.

el **norte**
Al norte de España está la cordillera cantábrica y al noreste la pirenaica.

north
In the north of Spain are the Cantabrians, and in the northeast, the Pyrenees.

el **sur**
Al sur de Galicia está Portugal.

south
Portugal is south of Galicia.

el **este**
Navarra está al este del País Vasco.

east
Navarre is east of the Basque Provinces.

el **oeste**
Al oeste de Cataluña está Aragón.

west
Aragon is west of Catalonia.

occidental
Alemania estaba dividida hasta 1990 en Alemania Occidental y Alemania Oriental.

western; west
Until 1990 Germany was divided into West Germany and East Germany.

el **occidente**
El sol sale por oriente y se pone por occidente.

west
The sun rises in the east and sets in the west.

oriental

eastern; oriental

el **oriente**

east; orient

Distance

la **distancia**
¿Qué distancia hay entre Tarragona y Huesca?

distance
What is the distance between Tarragona and Huesca?

cerca (de)
Perdone, ¿está cerca de aquí el Palacio de la Moncloa?—No, está lejos.

near; close (to)
Excuse me, please, is Moncloa Palace near by?—No, it's far away.

lejos (de)

far (away, off, from); distant (from)

acercar a
La cultura acerca a los pueblos.

bring or place nearer
Culture brings the peoples closer.

alejarse
¡No te alejes de la orilla!

move away; withdraw
Don't go away from the riverbank!

entre
Entre tú y yo hay una confianza absoluta.

between; among
Between you and me there exists absolute trust.

a través de
Marcos consiguió trabajo a través de un amigo.

through; across
Marcos found work through a friend.

próximo, a
El chalet próximo al nuestro es de mi prima.

next; nearest; neighboring
The vacation house next to ours is my cousin's.

marcharse

go away; leave

---

cercano, a
Aranjuez es un pueblo cercano de Madrid.

near; close
Aranjuez is a village near Madrid.

lejano, a
Tengo una casa en un rincón lejano.

distant; far; remote
I have a house in a remote place.

apartarse
¡Apártese, por favor, aquí hay sitio para dos coches!

withdraw; move aside; depart
Please move over, there's enough room for two cars here.

la proximidad
Antes de llegar al mar se siente su proximidad.

closeness; proximity
Before you reach the sea, you sense its nearness.

el extremo
Marisa se sentó a un extremo de la mesa.

extreme; farthest end
Marisa sat down at one extreme of the table.

el horizonte
Cuando los barcos desaparecieron en el horizonte las madres y mujeres de los pescadores volvieron a casa.

horizon
When the ships had disappeared on the horizon, the fishermen's mothers and wives returned home.

■ Time ■

a
¿A qué hora empieza el teatro?
—El teatro empieza a las ocho y media.
Se levantan al amanecer.

at
What time does the theater begin?
—The theater begins at 8:30.
They rise at daybreak.

medio, a
La conferencia duró media hora.

half
The meeting lasted half an hour.

el cuarto
¿Qué hora es?—Es la una y cuarto.

¡Son ya las diez y cuarto! A las cinco
menos cuarto tengo una cita.

quarter
What time is it?—It's a quarter
after one.
It's already a quarter after four! At
a quarter to five I have an
appointment.

dentro de
Dentro de dos días acabaré este trabajo.

in; within
I will finish this job in two days.

de ... a
Julio trabaja de ocho a tres en verano.

from ... to; until
In summer Julio works from eight
to three.

desde ... hasta
La biblioteca está cerrada desde
las dos hasta las cinco.

from ... to; until
The library is closed from two
until five.

desde
Pablo está esperándote desde la una.

since; from
Pablo has been waiting for you
since one.

entre
Podemos vernos entre las seis y
las siete.

between
We can see each other between six
and seven.

hasta
Hoy trabajamos hasta las nueve
y media.

until; till
Today we work till 9:30.

la hora
¿A qué hora llegáis?
¿Qué hora es?—Son las ocho menos
cinco.
Perdone, ¿tiene hora?—No, lo siento.

hour; time
What time do you arrive?
What time is it?—It's five to eight.

Excuse me, do you have the time?
—I'm sorry, no.

menos
Tengo que tomar el autobús a las
ocho menos veinte para no
llegar tarde.

minus; less
I have to take the bus at twenty
to eight so that I don't arrive late.

y
El avión para Mallorca sale a las
diez y cinco, o sea que tenemos
que estar en el aeropuerto a las
nueve y pico.

plus; after
The plane to Mallorca leaves at five
after ten, so we have to be at the
airport shortly after nine.

---

el **cuarto de hora**
Laura saldrá dentro de un
cuarto de hora de la oficina.

quarter hour
Laura will leave the office in a
quarter of an hour.

hacia
Te recogeré hacia las ocho.

toward; about; near
I'll pick you up about eight
o'clock.

hasta que
Mi abuela me guarda una pipa
hasta que sea mayor.

until
My grandmother is keeping a pipe
for me until I'm older.

para
¿Para cuándo necesita el coche?

(at the latest) by
By when do you need the car?

por
José se ha ido por un año a
Argentina.

for
José has gone to Argentina for a
year.

el **minuto**
Esto está hecho en cinco
minutos.

minute
It will be done in five
minutes.

el **segundo**
Mi reloj se atrasa cinco segundos
cada día.

second
My watch loses five seconds every
day.

el **punto**
Son las tres en punto.

point; dot
It's three o'clock on the dot.

atrasarse

lose time; be late

ir atrasado, a
Tu reloj va atrasado.

(be) run slow
Your watch is slow.

atrasado, a
Tenemos mucho trabajo
atrasado.

behind; back
We have a lot of work
piled up.

ir adelantado, a

(be) run fast

▰▰▰ **Day** ▰▰▰

el **día**
En invierno los días son muy cortos
porque hasta las nueve no es de día.

day
In winter the days are very short,
because it doesn't get light until
nine o'clock.

Algún día os acordaréis de mis
consejos.
El verano pasado estuvimos
quince días en Lima.

Someday you'll remember my
advice.
Last summer we were in Lima for
two weeks.

diario, a
El trabajo diario puede ser muy
aburrido.
Soledad tiene que tomar dos pastillas
a diario.

daily
One's daily work can be very
boring.
Soledad has to take two tablets
daily.

mañana
Esta mañana ha nevado un poco.

morning
This morning it snowed a little.

la **mañana**
Mañana por la mañana tendré que ir
al médico.

tomorrow
Tomorrow morning I have to go to
the doctor.

el **mediodía**
No cerramos a mediodía.

midday; noon
We don't close at midday.

la **tarde**
Te llamé por la tarde pero
no estuviste en casa.

afternoon
I called you in the afternoon,
but you weren't home.

la **noche**
Los vecinos han estado de fiesta toda
la noche.
A las cinco ya es de noche en invierno.

night
The neighbors partied all night
long.
In winter it's already dark at five
o'clock.

anoche
Anoche vi una película muy
emocionante en el cine.

last night
Last night I saw a very thrilling
film at the movies.

la **medianoche**
En verano las terrazas de
los cafés están llenas a
medianoche.

midnight
In summer the cafe terraces
are full at midnight.

ayer

yesterday

hoy

today

nocturno, a	nocturnal; night
anteayer	day before yesterday
Anteayer estuvo lloviendo todo el día y ayer empezó a hacer frío.	The day before yesterday it rained all day, and yesterday it turned cold.
la **víspera**	eve; day before
pasado mañana	day after tomorrow
Pasado mañana podré recoger el reloj.	I can pick up the clock the day after tomorrow.
la **madrugada**	dawn; early morning
De madrugada salimos de Vigo y llegamos a mediodía a Madrid.	We left Vigo at daybreak and reached Madrid at noon.
el **amanecer**	dawn; daybreak
cotidiano, a	daily

Days of the Week and Dates

la **semana**	week
La semana pasada invitamos a Nicolás y Rosa a cenar.	Last week we invited Nicolás and Rosa to dinner.
el **lunes**	Monday
Trabajo los lunes, martes y miércoles.	I work on Monday, Tuesday, and Wednesday.
el **martes**	Tuesday
el **miércoles**	Wednesday
el **jueves**	Thursday
En España hay una revista que sale los miércoles y se llama El Jueves.	In Spain there's a magazine that comes out on Wednesday and is called *Thursday*.
el **viernes**	Friday
¡Hasta el viernes que viene!	See you next Friday!
el **sábado**	Saturday
el **domingo**	Sunday
la **fecha**	date
¿Qué fecha es hoy?—Hoy es 31 de enero de 1996.	What is today's date?—Today is January 31, 1996.
¿a cuántos?	what's today?
¿A cuántos estamos?—Estamos a miércoles, doce de diciembre.	What's today?—Today is Wednesday, December 12.

el **fin de semana**	weekend
El próximo fin de semana será la fiesta de Roberto.	Roberto's party will be next weekend.
a partir de	from ... on; starting from
A partir del martes no hay clases.	From Tuesday on there will be no classes.
el **día laborable**	workday
el **día festivo**	holiday

Months

el **mes**	month
Honorio estuvo dos meses en Honduras.	Honorio was in Honduras for two months.
mensual	monthly
enero	January
Bernardo tiene cumpleaños el once de enero.	Bernardo's birthday is January 11.
febrero	February
En febrero aún hace frío.	In February it is still cold.
marzo	March
A primeros de marzo nos vamos a Grecia.	In early March we're going to Greece.
abril	April
A mediados de abril tendrás que devolver los libros.	In mid-April you will have to return the books.
mayo	May
A finales de mayo hay que pagar esta factura.	At the end of May this bill has to be paid.
junio	June
julio	July
agosto	August
Agosto es el mes más caluroso.	August is the hottest month.
septiembre	September
octubre	October
noviembre	November

diciembre	December

a primeros de	at the beginning of
a principios de A principios de mes vivo como un rey.	at the beginning of At the beginning of the month I live like a king.
a mediados de	in the middle of
a finales de A finales de marzo ya no es fácil reservar apartamentos para el verano.	at the end of At the end of March it is no longer easy to reserve apartments for the summer.

Year

el **año** El año tiene cuatro estaciones, doce meses y 365 días.	year The year has four seasons, 12 months, and 365 days.
la **estación (del año)**	season
la **primavera** En primavera muchas plantas están en flor.	spring In spring, many plants are in flower.
el **verano** El verano pasado estuvimos en Málaga.	summer Last summer we were in Malaga.
el **otoño** El otoño es muy bello en Madrid.	autumn; fall Fall is very lovely in Madrid.
el **invierno** En Sierra Nevada ya ha llegado el invierno porque nevó ayer.	winter In the Sierra Nevada winter has already begun, because it snowed yesterday.

anual El seguro del coche se puede pagar anual o por semestres, o trimestres o mensualmente.	annual; yearly Car insurance can be paid annually, semiannually, quarterly, or monthly.
el **semestre**	semester; half year

el **trimestre**	quarter (year)
el **calendario**	calendar
el **siglo** Mi abuela nació a principios de este siglo.	century My grandmother was born at the beginning of this century.
antes de (Jesu)cristo Los Romanos llegaron a España el año 300 a.C.	B.C. The Romans came to Spain in 300 B.C.
después de (Jesu)cristo El filósofo Seneca murió en Roma en el año 65 d.C.	A.D. The philosopher Seneca died in Rome in A.D.65.

Periods of Time

el **tiempo**
El tiempo pasa volando cuando
se tiene muchas cosas que hacer.

time
Time flies when one has a lot to do.

¿cuánto tiempo?

how long?

en
En el siglo XIX empezó la
revolución industrial.

in
The Industrial Revolution
began in the nineteenth century.

hace
Hace un año nos vemos.

ago
One year ago we started meeting.

pasado, a
La semana pasada hubo un
atentado en Sabadell.

past; last
Last week there was an
assault in Sabadell.

pasar
¿Cómo ha pasado el fin de semana?

spend (time); pass
How did you spend the weekend?

mientras
Mientras pones la mesa
la comida está hecha.
¿Qué ha ocurido mientras tanto?

He limpiado la casa mientras que tú
te has divertido con los amigos.

while; whereas
While you're setting the table,
the meal will be ready.
What has happened in the
meantime?
I cleaned the house while you were
enjoying yourself with your friends.

durante
¡No fumad durante la clase!

during
Don't smoke during class!

tardar
Estamos preocupados porque el niño tarda en volver a casa.

delay; take a long time; be late
We're worried because the boy is late coming home.

durar
¿Cuánto dura la película?

last
How long does the film last?

estar haciendo
Este junio está haciendo frío.
Estaba leyendo cuando sonó el teléfono.

be doing (something)
It is cold this June.
I was reading when the phone rang.

ir a hacer
¡Vamos a ver!
Voy a terminar de limpiar la casa.

be going to do (something)
We'll see!
I'm going to finish cleaning the house.

el **futuro**
No conocemos nuestro futuro.

future
We don't know our future.

presente
En la situación presente será mejor esperar.

present
In the present situation it's probably better to wait.

la **actualidad**
En la actualidad hay muchos problemas por solucionar.

present time
At the present time there are many problems to solve.

actual
¿Cómo se llama el actual presidente de Panamá?

present; current
What is the name of Panama's current president?

la **duración**
Esta cinta tiene una duración de tres horas.

duration
This tape has a playing time of three hours.

coincidir

coincide

eterno, a
Esta serie de televisión parece eterna.

eternal; everlasting
This TV series seems to go on forever.

anterior
Me gustaba más tu casa anterior.

previous; earlier; former
I liked your previous house better.

breve
Nuestra visita fue muy breve porque teníamos mucha prisa.

brief; short
Our visit was very brief because we were in a great hurry.

entretanto
Estuve cinco años en Chile y entretanto he perdido el contacto con mis amigos españoles.

meanwhile; in the meantime
I was in Chile for five years, and in the meantime I lost contact with my Spanish friends.

el **rato**   short time; while; moment
Dentro de un rato va a llamarme Isidro.   Isidro will call me in a moment.

de **antemano**   beforehand; in advance
Ya sabíamos de antemano que   We knew beforehand that you
llegarías tarde.   would come late.

recién   recently; lately; newly

Points in Time

¿cuándo?   when?

cuando   when
Cuando vengas, te daré el regalo.   When you come, I'll give you the
                                            present.

Cuando llegué a casa, no había nadie.   When I got home, no one was
                                            there.

antes   before; formerly
En este país antes todo era diferente.   Before, everything was different in
                                            this country.

desde hace   since
Desde hace dos años estoy   For two years I've been
buscando este libro.   looking for this book.

hace poco   a short time ago
Hace poco vi a Clara.   I saw Clara a short time ago.

desde que   since; ever since
Desde que estamos aquí hace   Since we've been here, the
muy buen tiempo.   weather's been very good.

acabar   finish
¿Cuándo acabas la carrera?   When do you finish your studies?

acabar de   have just
Acabamos de llegar a casa.   We have just come home.

terminar   end; conclude
¿Cuándo terminan sus vacaciones?   When is your vacation over?

dejar de   stop; quit
Roberto ha dejado de fumar.   Roberto has stopped smoking.

el **momento**   moment
En este momento no me acuerdo   At the moment I don't remember
qué tenía que hacer.   what I was supposed to do.
De momento no podemos ayudarles.   At the moment we can't help you.

ahora
Ahora nos vamos a la playa.

now
Now we're going to the beach.

de **repente**
De repente se abrió la puerta y
entró un hombre.

suddenly
Suddenly the door opened
and a man entered.

ocurrir
El accidente ocurrió el lunes.

occur; happen
The accident occurred on
Monday.

ahora mismo
Quieren hablar ahora mismo con
el jefe.
Iba a llamarte ahora mismo.

right now; at once; just now
They want to speak with the boss
at once.
I was just now going to call you.

empezar
¿A qué hora empiezas a trabajar?

begin; start
What time do you start work?

comenzar
La misa comienza a las ocho de
la mañana.

commence; begin
Mass begins at 8 A.M.

pronto
¡Adiós Luisa! ¡Hasta pronto!

soon
Goodbye, Luisa! See you
soon!

enseguida; en seguida
En seguida le traigo la cuenta.

at once; right away
I'll bring you the bill right
away.

luego
¿Qué vais a hacer luego?

afterwards; later; next
What are you going to do
afterwards?

después
Después de comer tomamos el café.

after; afterward
After eating we drink coffee.

al **principio**
Al principio creía que eras su hermana.

at first; at the start
At first I thought you were his
sister.

después (de) que
Después de que hayas terminado de
comer, ¡lava los platos!

after
After you've finished eating,
wash the dishes!

antes (de) que
Tenemos que buscar un hotel antes
de que sea de noche.

before
We have to look for a hotel
before nightfall.

tan pronto como
¡Escríbeme tan pronto como puedas!
Tan pronto como hayas leído el
libro, ¡devuélvemelo!

as soon as
Write me as soon as you can!
As soon as you've read the
book, give it back to me!

producirse
Se ha producido un accidente en
la autopista.

come about; happen
An accident has happened on
the superhighway.

a la vez
Por favor, no hablen todos a la vez.

at one time; simultaneously
Please, don't all talk at the same
time.

inmediato, a
Gracias a la intervención inmediata de
la policía se evitó una catástrofe.

immediate
Thanks to the immediate
intervention of the police, a
disaster was prevented.

de pronto
Íbamos por la calle,
cuando de pronto
nos llamó alguien.

suddenly
We were walking along the street
when suddenly someone
called out to us.

el **fin**
Aún no sabemos dónde estaremos
el fin de mes.

end
We don't know yet where we'll
be at the end of the month.

entonces
El jefe me explicó entonces por
qué el negocio va mal.

then; at that time
Then the boss explained to me
why business is poor.

parar
Está lloviendo quince días sin parar.

stop
It has been raining for two weeks
without stopping.

el **instante**
La policía llegó al instante de sonar
la alarma.

instant; moment
The police came the instant the
alarm sounded.

ponerse
A las tres me he puesto a trabajar.

begin; start
At three o'clock I started
working.

en **cuanto**
En cuanto haga más calor, vamos a
la playa.

as soon as
As soon as it's warmer, we'll go to
the beach.

acontecer
En la política actual acontecen
pocos hechos positivos.

happen; come about
Few positive things are happening
in politics today.

el **acontecimiento**

event

el **suceso**
Recientemente la prensa trae muchos
sucesos desagradables.

event
Lately the press has carried news of
many unpleasant events.

recientemente

recently; lately

■ **Frequent Occurrences** ■

siempre
always

siempre que
Siempre que te veo, has adelgazado más.
whenever
Whenever I see you, you've become thinner.

seguir
Esta noche tenemos que seguir trabajando un rato.
continue; keep on
This evening we have to continue working for a while.

continuar
¡No continuaré la novela hasta julio!
continue; go on
I won't continue the novel until July.

continuo, a
En este cine hay sesión continua.
continuous; constant; steady
In this movie theater there are continuous showings.

nunca
No hemos ido nunca a Sevilla.
never
We've never been to Seville.

jamás
¡Jamás te prestaré dinero!
never
I will never lend you money!

frecuente
No es frecuente que los alumnos no vengan a clase.
frequent; usual
It is not usual for the students to be absent from class.

la **vez**
Llamamos varias veces pero no contestó nadie.
¿Es la primera vez que está en España?—No, ya he estado muchas veces aquí.
turn; time; occasion
We called several times, but no one answered.
Is this the first time you've been in Spain?—No, I've been here many times.

pocas veces
Pocas veces te he visto tan enfadado.
seldom; rarely
I've seldom seen you so angry.

de vez en cuando
De vez en cuando me gusta quedarme en casa pero a veces no tengo otra posibilidad.
occasionally; from time to time
Occasionally I like to stay home, but sometimes I have no option.

cada vez
Cada vez que te veo estás más gordo.
each time; every time
Every time I see you, you're fatter.

la **frecuencia**	frequency
a **menudo** ¿Vas a menudo al cine?—No, apenas.	often; frequently Do you go to the movies often?—No, rarely.
raro, a Esto es un libro muy raro.	rare This is a very rare book.
de nuevo Este trabajo hay que hacerlo de nuevo.	again; once more This work has to be done again.
suceder ¿Quién sucederá al Presidente González?	follow; succeed Who will succeed President González?
la **continuación**	continuation
poco a poco El enfermo va mejorando poco a poco.	little by little; gradually The patient is improving gradually.
la **mayoría de las veces** La mayoría de las veces tienes razón.	most of the time Most of the time you're right.

▬▬▬▬ Subjective Estimates of Time ▬▬▬▬

ya Emilia ya tiene dos hijos.	already Emilia already has two children.
a tiempo ¿Llegaste a tiempo o ya la tienda estaba cerrada?	on time; in time Did you arrive in time, or was the store already closed?
ya no Ya no tenemos ganas de jugar.	no longer We no longer want to play.
aún Aún no me han pagado.	yet I haven't been paid yet.
todavía Todavía hace buen tiempo en septiembre.	still In September the weather is still good.
apenas Apenas tenemos tiempo para dormir.	scarcely; hardly We hardly have time to sleep.

estar listo, a
El equipaje está listo para el viaje.

be ready
The luggage is ready for the trip.

tarde
¡Vámonos que ya es tarde!

late
Let's go! It's already late.

temprano
Juanjo se levanta todos los días temprano para hacer deporte.

early
Juanjo gets up early every morning to engage in sports.

despacio
Por favor, hable un poco más despacio para que le entienda mejor.

slowly
Please speak a little more slowly so that I can understand you better.

deprisa
¡Deprisa, Marisa, que llegas tarde!

quickly
Quickly, Marisa! You'll be late!

rápido, a
Emilia es muy rápida para algunas cosas.

rapid; quick; swift
Emilia is very quick in some things.

lento, a
Este tren es demasiado lento.

slow
This train is too slow.

---

por fin
¡Por fin lo hemos conseguido!

at last; finally
We've done it at last!

por último

ultimately; finally

acabarse
¡Se acabó!

end; be over
That's enough of that!

Modal Expressions

así
¡Así es la vida!
¡No te pongas así!

so; thus; like this or like that
Thus is life!
Don't behave like that!

¿cómo?
¿Cómo está usted?

how?
How are you?

hasta
He perdido todo, hasta mis llaves.

even
I've lost everything, even my keys.

la **manera**
¡No hay manera de localizarte!

manner; way; mode
There is no way to reach you!

de manera que
De manera que no has terminado el trabajo porque estuviste jugando al tenis.
Organiza tu trabajo de manera que no pierdas el tiempo.

so that; so as to; so then
So then you haven't finished the work, because you were playing tennis.
Organize your work so that you don't lose time.

de otra forma
No sé cocinar de otra forma.

in another way; differently
I can't cook any other way.

de (tal) forma que
Pinta el armario de forma que no se note.

so that; so as
Paint the cabinet so that it is not noticeable.

el **modo**
Trabaja de modo que no te canses.

way; manner; mode
Work in such a way that you don't tire.

deber
Deben ser las cuatro.

must; ought; should
It must be 4 o'clock.

hay que
Hay que ser más puntual.

one has to; you have to
You have to be more punctual.

tener que
Tenéis que daros prisa para no llegar tarde.

must; have to
You have to hurry, so that you don't arrive late.

general
En general estamos satisfechos con su servicio.

general
In general, we are satisfied with your service.

generalmente

generally

en especial
A Marta le gusta leer, en especial novelas policíacas.

especially
Marta likes to read, especially mystery novels.

normal

normal

poder
Esta tarde no nos podemos ver.

be able; can; may
This afternoon we can't see each other.

¡qué . . . !
¡Qué bonito es aquel
barco!

how . . . !
How beautiful that
ship is!

sobre todo
Han subido mucho los precios, sobre todo el pescado está muy caro.

above all
The prices have risen a great deal; fish, above all, is very expensive.

sólo
Prefiero trabajar sólo por las mañanas para estar con mis hijos.

only
I prefer to work only in the morning, in order to be with my children.

aproximado, a
En esta estadística sólo hay resultados aproximados.

approximate
These statistics contain only approximate results.

particular

particular; special

efectivo, a
Este medicamento es muy efectivo contra el resfriado.

effective
This medication is very effective against colds.

en el fondo
En el fondo, Luis es una buena persona.

at heart; at bottom
At heart, Luis is a good person.

en principio
En principio no estamos de acuerdo con ustedes.

in principle
In principle we are not in agreement with you.

exclusivo, a
En este comercio se venden productos muy exclusivos.

exclusive
In this shop very exclusive products are sold.

total
En esta oficina hay un desorden total.

total; complete
In this office there's total chaos.

por lo visto
Por lo visto no has aprendido nada.

apparently
Apparently you have learned nothing.

único, a
Este libro es único.

unique; only
This book is unique.

haber de
He de buscar una solución.

have to; must
I must find a solution.

de esta forma
No sé cómo puedes vivir de esta forma.

so; in this way
I don't know how you can live in this way.

incluso
Ayer nevó incluso en Sevilla.

even
Yesterday it snowed even in Seville.

no . . . más que
No tenemos más que llamar a Vicente para que nos recoja.

only
We have only to call Vicente for him to pick us up.

Degree and Comparison

casi
Tu abuela tiene casi cien años.

almost
Your grandmother is almost 100 years old.

de ninguna manera
No iremos de ninguna manera a la exposición.

not at all; by no means; in no way
By no means will we go to the exhibition.

en absoluto
¿Le molestamos?
—No, en absoluto.

absolutely; not at all.
Are we bothering you?
—No, not at all.

mucho
Me gusta mucho la blusa que llevas.

very much; a great deal
I very much like the blouse you're wearing.

muy
Puerto Rico es muy hermoso.
¿Te encuentras mal? Estás muy pálido.

very
Puerto Rico is very beautiful.
Do you feel ill? You're very pale.

tan
Pensábamos que la cola no sería tan larga.

so
We thought the line wouldn't be so long.

tan . . . como
Eduardo es tan listo como su tío.

(just) as . . . as
Eduardo is as clever as his uncle.

tanto
El médico me ha dicho que no trabaje tanto.

so much
The doctor told me I shouldn't work so much.

tanto, a
Hace tanto calor que no puedo dormir.

so much
It is so hot that I can't sleep.

tanto, a . . . como
Jamás he visto tanta gente como en este concierto.

as much . . . as
I've never seen as many people as at this concert.

como
La familia de mi amigo es como
la mía.

like; as
My friend's family is like mine.

la **diferencia**
Entre las provincias españolas hay
diferencias en las costumbres.

difference
There are differences in
customs among the Spanish
provinces.

diferente
Los hombres no son tan diferentes
como a veces parece.

different
Men are not as different
as it sometimes seems.

distinto, a
To abrigo es distinto del suyo
aunque sea de la misma marca.

distinct; clear; different
Your coat is different from
his, although it's the same
make.

igual
¿Quieres un café o un té?—Me
es igual.

equal; even
Would you like coffee or
tea?—It's all the same
to me.

parecido, a
Esos zapatos son parecidos
a los que lleva Dolores.

similar
Your shoes are similar to the
ones Dolores is wearing.

que
Mi casa es más pequeña que la tuya.

than
My house is smaller than yours.

también
El señor Vázquez habla inglés,
francés y también portugués.

also; too
Mr. Vázquez speaks English,
French, and also Portuguese.

tampoco
Marta no viene a la fiesta y
tampoco su hermana.

neither; not either
Marta isn't coming to the party,
and neither is her sister.

apenas
Miguel apenas conoce a su primo
Rafael.

barely; scarcely
Miguel scarcely knows his cousin
Rafael.

intenso, a
A Saladino le encantan los colores
intensos.

intense; strong; vivid
Saladino adores vivid colors.

extremo, a
Carlos no soporta las
temperaturas extremas.

extreme
Carlos can't tolerate
extreme temperatures.

comparable
Estas motos no son comparables.

comparable
These motorcycles are not
comparable.

distinguir
No distingo los hermanos
gemelos de la señora Blandes.

distinguish; tell apart
I can't tell Mrs. Blandes's
twin brothers apart.

más bien
Esto no es cuero, más bien será
plástico.

rather; more likely
This isn't leather; more likely, it's
plastic.

máximo, a
¿Cuál fue su máxima victoria
en estos campeonatos?

greatest
What was your greatest victory
in these championships?

mínimo, a
¡No habéis hecho el más mínimo
esfuerzo para no suspender estos
exámenes!

least
You haven't made the least effort
to avoid failing these tests!

menor
El médico me ha prohibido el menor
movimiento.
El menor defecto en estas instalaciones
puede causar una catástrofe.

smallest; least; slightest
The doctor has forbidden me to
make the slightest movement.
The least defect in this facility
can cause a catastrophe.

mayor
Nuestros mayores gastos este
año han sido los salarios.

greatest; main, principal
Salaries have been our greatest
expenses this year.

realmente

really

por poco
Por poco me caigo.

almost; early
I nearly fell.

principal

principal; main

Cause, Effect, Aim, Purpose

¿a qué?
¿A qué habéis venido?

what for?; for what purpose?
For what purpose did you come
here?

la **causa**

cause; reason

causar
El terremoto causó la muerte
de muchas personas.

cause
The earthquake caused the
death of many people.

como
Como llegamos tarde al cine
no había entradas.

since; as
Since we got to the movies late,
there were no more tickets.

conducir
Este programa económico
condujo a la crisis.

lead
This economic program
led to a crisis.

el **medio**
Los medios de comunicación
han mejorado con el fax.

means; medium
The means of communication
have improved with the fax.

el **motivo**
¿Cuál fue el motivo para
cerrar la tienda?

motive; cause; reason
What was the reason for
closing the store?

la **razón**
¿Qué razón te dio el jefe
para despedirte?

reason
What reason did the boss give
you for your dismissal?

para
Este regalo es para tus padres.
Carmen se va a Vigo para
estar con su familia.

for; (in order) to
This gift is for your parents.
Carmen is going to Vigo to
be with her family.

¿para qué?
¿Para qué vas a lavar el coche si va
a llover?—Para que esté limpio.

what for?
What are you washing the car for,
when it's about to rain?—So that it
will be clean.

para que

so that

por
Jaime no se casa por amor,
sino por el dinero de Clara.
Toma esta flor, por simpatía.

Por mi puedes irte.

for; for the sake of; through
Jaime is not marrying for love,
but for Clara's money.
Take this flower, in the name of
friendship.
For all I care, you can go.

¿por qué?
¿Por qué no fuisteis a la conferencia?
—Porque no tuvimos tiempo.

why?
Why didn't you come to the lecture?
—Because we didn't have time.

porque

because

resultar
La venta de la casa ha resultado
un buen negocio.
Angel no encontró a sus amigos
porque resulta que se habían ido
al teatro.

result; turn out (to be)
The sale of the house has turned
out to be a good deal.
Angel didn't find his friends,
because it turns out that they had
gone to the movies.

a causa de
Muchos caballos murieron a
causa de una enfermedad
desconocida.

on account of; because of
Many horses died on account
of an unknown disease.

la **consecuencia**
Las consecuencias de la
contaminación del aire son muy
graves para los habitantes de esta
ciudad.

consequence
The consequences of air pollution
are very serious for the inhabitants
of this city.

debido a
Debido a la ayuda de muchos países,
la población sobrevivió el invierno.

owing to; on account of
Owing to the assistance of many
countries, the population survived
the winter.

depender
Depende del tiempo que haga
mañana que vayamos a esquiar
o no.

depend
It depends on tomorrow's weather
whether we go skiing or not.

el **efecto**
Estas pastillas no hacen el efecto
deseado.

effect
These pills don't have the desired
effect.

gracias a
Gracias a los ordenadores podemos
trabajar mucho más rápido.

thanks to
Thanks to computers, we can
work much faster.

determinado, a

determined; definite

el **objeto**
El objeto de nuestros estudios es
crear nuevos productos, por eso
trabajamos tanto.

object; aim; purpose
The purpose of our studies is to
create new products; that is
why we work so hard.

el **fin**

end; object; purpose

por eso; por esto

therefore; for this reason

por lo tanto
Marta tiene que terminar este trabajo
para mañana, por lo tanto no irá a
la boda.

therefore
Marta has to finish this work by
tomorrow, therefore she will not
go to the wedding.

puesto que
Te voy a pedir un favor, puesto
que eres mi amigo.

since; inasmuch as; because
I'm going to ask you a favor,
since you're my friend.

en vano

in vain

la **casualidad**
¿Por casualidad eres hermano de
Vicente?

chance
Are you by any chance Vicente's
brother?

State and Change

aumentar
Este año hemos aumentado
el volumen de negocios.

augment; increase; enlarge
This year we have increased our
turnover.

subir
Los precios siguen subiendo mucho.

rise; climb
Prices continue to climb sharply.

bajar
Ayer bajó el precio de la
gasolina dos pesetas.

sink; drop; fall
Yesterday the price of gasoline
dropped two pesetas.

caer
La nieve cae lentamente.

fall
The snow falls slowly.

cambiar
Con los años han cambiado
sus costumbres.

change
Their habits have changed
with the years.

cambiarse
El paisaje mediterráneo
ha cambiado mucho.

change
The Mediterranean landscape
has changed greatly.

nuevo, a

new

viejo, a

old

volverse
Tu hermana se ha vuelto muy lista.

become
Your sister has become very clever.

ponerse
Creo que voy a ponerme enfermo.

become; get
I think I'm getting sick.

desarrollarse
La industria en España se desarrolló
mucho en los últimos años.

develop
Industry in Spain has developed
greatly in the last few years.

el **desarrollo**
Los niños necesitan buenos
alimentos para su desarrollo.

development
Children need good food for
their development.

estar

be; be located

Juan está en la oficina.
Carmelo estuvo muy enfermo.

Juan is in the office.
Carmelo was very ill.

ser
Mariano es actor.

be
Mariano is an actor.

hay
¿Qué hay de nuevo?
En los Correos hay unas
cartas para ti.

there is; there are
What's new?
There are some letters for you at the
Post Office.

mejorar(se)
La situación política no ha
mejorado en Nicaragua.
Paco no se ha mejorado de su gripe.

recover; improve
The political situation in
Nicaragua has not improved.
Paco has not recovered from his
flu.

agravarse
Se está agravando nuestra
situación económica.

get worse; more serious
Our economic situation
is getting worse.

el **resultado**

result

la **situación**

situation; position

resuelto, a

solved; resolved

acostumbrado, a

accustomed; used

roto, a
El televisor estuvo quince días roto.

broken
The TV was broken for two
weeks.

la **reparación**

repair

romperse
Se me han roto los zapatos.

break (down)
My shoes are in need of repair.

quedar
Media casa ha quedado por pintar.

remain; be left
Half the house remains to be
painted.

salir
Este dibujo te ha salido muy
bien.

leave; come out
Your drawing came out very
well.

volver (a)
Esta mujer me vuelve loco.
Gerardo ha vuelto a romper la
ventana.

turn; do again
This woman drives me crazy.
Gerardo has broken the window
again.

el **aumento**
El aumento del paro es un
problema muy difícil.

increase; rise
The rise in unemployment is
a very difficult problem.

la **circunstancia**
Las circunstancias de su muerte
se están investigando.

circumstance
The circumstances of his death
are being investigated.

el **lío**
¡Vaya lío!

mess; confusion
What a mess!

el **proceso**

process

convertirse
Este joven se ha convertido en un
especialista importante.

turn into; become
This young man has become
an important specialist.

hacerse
Paquita se ha hecho católica.

become
Paquita has become a Catholic.

modificar

modify; change

disminuir
El número de alumnos de este
curso ha disminuido mucho.

diminish; lessen
The number of pupils in
this course has diminished
greatly.

el **estado**
La enferma estuvo en un estado
crítico.
Mi mujer está en estado.

state; condition
The patient was in a critical
condition.
My wife is pregnant.

existir
En esta sociedad existen graves
problemas.

exist
In this society there exist serious
problems.

la **existencia**
La existencia de esta empresa está en
juego.

existence
The existence of this company is
at stake.

el **progreso**
Mis alumnos han hecho un gran
progreso en español.

progress
My pupils have made great
progress in Spanish.

la **realidad**
La realidad puede ser muy
triste.

reality
Reality can be very sad.

la **alternativa**

alternative

transformar

transform

variar
En Andalucía el clima puede variar
bastante.

vary; change
In Andalusia the climate can be
quite variable.

surgir

appear; arise; issue

inmóvil

motionless; fixed

estropearse

get out of order; get damaged

reducir
Los impuestos han sido reducidos
en un cinco por ciento.

reduce; decrease
Taxes have been decreased to 5
percent.

sustituir
Hay que sustituir el motor de la
lavadora por otro nuevo.

replace; substitute
The motor of the washing
machine has to be replaced with a
new one.

abrirse

open

■ Articles ■

el, la
El señor Martín cuida mucho la gata.

the *(m. sing. and f. sing.)*
Mr. Martín takes good care of the cat.

los, las
Los niños están jugando con las pelotas.

the *(m. pl. and f. pl.)*
The children are playing with the balls.

lo

No me gusta hacer siempre lo mismo.

the *(neuter; only before substantized adjectives, pronouns, and numerals)*
I don't like doing the same thing all the time.

al *a + el*
Este autobús va al centro.
No estés tanto tiempo al sol.

in; to the
This bus goes to the center of town.
Don't stay so long in the sun.

del *de + el*
La farmacia del señor Sotelo está abierta.

of the
Mr. Sotelo's pharmacy is open.

un; una
Déme un periódico y una revista.

a; an
Please give me a newspaper and a magazine.

unos; unas
Quisiéramos unos lápices y unas libretas.

some
We would like some pencils and notebooks.

■ Personal Pronouns ■

yo
Yo soy Rafael, ¿y tú?

I
I'm Rafael, and you?

me
¡No me digas!
¿No me conoces?
¿Dígame?—¿Está Carola?—No, no la he visto.—Dígale, por favor, que estoy buscándola desde ayer y que tengo que darle una noticia importante.—Bien se lo diré. —¡No se olvide! —Me lo apuntaré.

me; to; for me; myself
You don't tell me!
Don't you know me?
Hello!—Is Carola there?—No, I haven't seen her.—Please tell her that I've been looking for her since yesterday and that I have important news for her.—Fine, I'll tell her.—Don't forget! —I'll make a note of it.

mí
Este regalo es para mí.

me
This gift is for me.

conmigo
¿Quién viene conmigo a la playa?

with me
Who's coming with me to the beach?

tú

you

te
¿Te devolvió Miguel el libro?
Te recojo de la fábrica.
¿Te vas al cine ahora?

you; to you; yourself
Did Miguel return the book to you?
I'll pick you up at the factory.
Are you going to the movies now?

ti
A ti no te conozco.

you
You I don't know.

contigo
María irá contigo a Sevilla.

with you
María will go with you to Seville.

él
Isabel y Tomás son muy simpáticos,
pero él tiene más gracia que ella.
Con él puedes contar.

he; him
Isabel and Tomás are very nice,
but he is funnier than she.
You can count on him.

le
Dile que vuelvo mañana.

him
Tell him that I'm returning
tomorrow.

le; lo
A Juan no lo he visto.
No le hemos visto hace días.
¿Qué le parece este reloj?—No sé,
lo encuentro muy caro.

him; it
Juan, him I haven't seen.
We have not seen him for days.
What do you think of this watch?
—I don't know. I find it very
expensive.

ella
El reloj se lo he regalado a ella.

she; her
I gave her the watch as a present.

le
Le he dicho que se tome vacaciones.

her
I told her she should take a
vacation.

la
A Lucía no la veo.
La película la encuentro muy divertida.

her; it
Lucia, her I don't see.
I find the film very entertaining.

usted; Ud.
Dígale usted a la señora Marco que
se puede marchar a casa.
La palabra usted se puede acortar
"Ud." o "Vd.".
A Vd. no la conozco.
¿Puedo ir con Ud.?

you
Tell Mrs. Marco that she can go
home.
The word "usted" can be
abbreviated as "Ud." or "Vd."
I don't know you.
May I go with you?

le
¿Qué le duele?

you
What hurts (you)?

le; lo
A usted no le (lo) recuerdo.

you
I don't remember you.

la; le
¿Cuándo puedo llamarla?

you
When can I call you?

ello
No hace falta hablar de ello.

it
There's no need to talk about it.

le
Le doy mucha importancia a la
puntualidad.

it
I attach great importance to
punctuality.

lo
¿Dónde están mis gafas?—No lo sé.

it
Where are my glasses?—I don't
know.

nosotros, as
Nosotras nos vamos a la fiesta
de Luis, ¿y vosotros?

we; us
We (women) are going to Luis's
party, and you (men)?

nos
En verano nos gusta estar junto al mar.

us; to us; ourselves
In summer we like being near the
sea.

Nos veremos el próximo año.
Nos levantamos a las dos.

We'll see each other next year.
We get up at 2 o'clock.

vosotros, as

you

os
Os llamamos pero no estabais.

you; to you; yourselves
We called you, but you weren't
there.

Os damos lo que queréis.
¡Os laváis poco!

We're giving you what you wanted.
You don't wash very much!

ellos
Ellos son los primos de José.
Este libro es para ellos.

they; them; to them *(m.)*
They are José's cousins.
This book is for them.

les
¡Dales a los niños un helado!

them; them; to them
Give the children an ice cream!

los; les
¿Has llamado a los empleados?
—Sí, les he dicho todo lo necesario.

them; to them
Have you called the employees?
—Yes, I've told them everything
necessary.

ellas
Ellas van a la playa, nosotros no.

them; them; to them *(f.)*
They're going to the beach; we're
not.

les
Las enfermeras han protestado
porque no les pagan suficiente.

them; to them
The nurses have protested because
they aren't paid enough.

las
No las llamamos porque era tarde.

them
We didn't call them because it was late.

ustedes; Uds.
¿Ustedes hablan todos español?
Con ustedes no se puede discutir.

you
Do you all speak Spanish?
It's impossible to discuss anything with you.

les
Señoras y señores, les damos
la bienvenida.

you
Ladies and gentlemen,
we bid you welcome.

les; los
Estimados pasajeros, les saludamos
a bordo de nuestro avión.

you
Ladies and gentlemen, we welcome
you aboard our aircraft.

las
¡Qué sorpresa, señoras! ¡No
las había visto nunca por aquí!

you
What a surprise, ladies! I've
never seen you here before.

se

Marisa se ducha todos los días.
Los niños se han bebido un refresco.

oneself; herself; himself; itself;
themselves; each other
Marisa showers every day.
The children have drunk a cold
beverage.

se

¿Se lo has dado?

to him; to her; to them; to you
(*singular and plural before
personal pronouns in the accusative*)
Have you given it to him?

sí

Andrés sólo piensa en sí mismo.

himself; herself; yourself; itself;
oneself; themself; yourselves
Andrés thinks only of himself.

consigo

with oneself (himself, etc.)

▄▄▄▄▄ Demonstrative Pronouns ▄▄▄▄▄

**este; esta; estos; estas; éste;
ésta; éstos; éstas**
Esta fruta está muy buena.—
¿Cuál? ¿Ésta?

this; these; this one; these

This fruit is very good.—
Which? This one?

**ese; esa; esos; esas; ése; ésa;
ésos; ésas**
Ese coche de ahí es como el mío.
El chico, ése de ahí, es mi primo.

that; those; that one; those

That car there is like mine.
The boy, that one there, is my
cousin.

Quisiera ver esas faldas.—¿Éstas?—
Sí, ésas.

I would like to see those skirts.—
These?—Yes, those.

aquel; aquella; aquellos; aquellas;
aquél; aquélla; aquéllos; aquéllas

that (over there); those (yonder);

that one; the former; those

Aquel día hizo un frío terrible.
Allí está mi pueblo, aquél al pie de la montaña.

On that day it was terribly cold.
There is my village, that one at the foot of the mountains.

esto
Esto no me gusta.

this
I don't like this one.

eso
¿Qué es eso?

that
What is that?

aquello
Aquello sí que fue bonito.

that
That was really lovely.

Interrogative Pronouns

¿cuántos, as?
¿Cuántos apellidos tienen los españoles?

how many?; how much?
How many surnames do Spaniards have?

¿cuánto?
¿Cuánto cuesta este libro?

how much?
How much does this book cost?

¿cuál?; ¿cuáles?
¿Cuál es la capital de Extremadura?

¿Cuál de vosotros me ayuda?

which (one)?; what?
What is the capital of Estremadura?

Which of you will help me?

¿quién?, ¿quiénes?
¿De quién es esta maleta?
¿Quiénes son tus amigos?

who?; whom?; whose?
Whose is this suitcase?
Who are your friends?

¿qué?
¿Qué desea usted?

what?
What do you want?

Relative Pronouns

que
La mujer que me ha saludado es la madre de Virginia.

who; that
The woman who greeted me is Virginia's mother.

que
Juan todavía no me ha devuelto el disco que le presté.

whom; that
Juan still hasn't given me back the record that I loaned him.

el, la, los, las que
Todos los que quieran
pueden venir al entierro.

he; she; those who
All those who wish can
come to the funeral.

el, la cual; los, las cuales
Este es el libro del cual te he hablado.

which; who
This is the book about which I've
told you.

quien; quienes

who; whom; he who; those who;
whose

Jaimito fue quien rompió la tele.

Jaimito was the one who broke the
TV.

cuyo; cuya; cuyos; cuyas
Esta es la familia cuyos
hijos viven en Lima.

whose
This is the family whose
children live in Lima.

lo que
Ya no me acuerdo de
lo que te dije ayer.

what; that which
I no longer recall what
I said to you yesterday.

lo cual
Teresa nos invitó a un helado,
lo cual no era necesario.

which
Teresa invited us for an ice cream,
which was not necessary.

semejante

similar; like; such; of that kind

Indefinite Pronouns

alguien
¿Ha venido alguien a recoger el
paquete?

somebody; someone
Has someone come to pick up the
package?

**algún; alguno; alguna; algunos;
algunas**
¿Alguno de vosotros va a comprar el
periódico?
Algún día me iré para no volver.

some, any; some people

Is any of you going to buy the
newspaper?
Someday I'll leave and not come
back.

Algunas veces preferimos estar en
casa que salir con los amigos.

Sometimes we prefer staying at
home to going out with friends.

cada
Cada día nuestra situación es más
crítica.

each; every
Every day our situation is more
critical.

cada uno, cada una
Cada uno de los niños recibirá
un regalito.

each one; every one
Each one of the children will
receive a small gift.

cualquier; cualquiera

any(one); anybody; some(one);
somebody

Este trabajo lo puede hacer cualquier
aprendiz.

Any trainee can do this work.

Pablo se ha comprado una revista
cualquiera.

Pablo has bought some newspaper.

lo demás; los, las demás

the rest; the others; the remaining
(ones)

De esta novela sólo me ha gustado el
principio, lo demás no vale la pena
leerlo.

Of this novel I liked only the
beginning; the rest is not worth
reading.

¿Cuándo vienen los demás?

When are the others coming?

mismo, a

same; self (same)

Nosotros mismos te recogemos del
puerto.

We ourselves will pick you up at
the port.

el **mismo**; la **misma**

the same (one)

Este es el mismo modelo que el tuyo.

This is the same model as yours.

lo **mismo**

the same (thing)

Esta mujer siempre dice
lo mismo cuando os ve.

This woman always says the
same thing when she sees you.

nadie

nobody, no one, none

Nadie sabía dónde estaban las llaves
del coche.

No one knew where the car keys
were.

ningún; ninguno; ninguna

no; not one; not any

Aquí no hay ningún hotel.

There is no hotel here.

Ninguno de vosotros quiso
acompañarle.

Not one of you wanted to
accompany her.

tal

such (a, an)

¡Jamás he visto tal cosa!

I've never seen such a thing!

todo el mundo

everyone; everybody

Todo el mundo sabe que
España es muy grande.

Everyone knows that
Spain is very large.

varios, as

various, some, several

Te hemos escrito varias cartas
pero no has contestado.

We have written you several
letters, but you haven't answered.

cierto, a

certain; true

Ciertas noticias deberían
salir más en la prensa.

Certain news should appear
more often in the press.

Las noticias ciertas deberían salir
más en la prensa.

True news should appear more
often in the press.

otra cosa

something else

Hablando de otras cosas,
¿cómo están tus hijos?

To talk about something else,
how are your children?

351

Prepositions

a
Llama a Miguel para que venga.
A ellos no les gusta hablar.
No nos vamos a Málaga.
Iremos a las cuatro.

to; in; at; by; for; of; on
Call Miguel, so that he'll come here.
They don't like to talk.
We're not going to Málaga.
We'll go at 4 o'clock.

con
Carlos va con Marta al teatro.

Tienes que pintar la mesa con un
pincel.
Isabel vive con Tomás en un piso
pequeño.
El señor Lobos ha sido muy amable
conmigo.

with
Carlos is going with Marta to the
theater.
You have to paint the table with a
brush.
Isabel lives with Tomás in a small
apartment.
Mr. Lobos has been very friendly
to me.

para
Estos dulces son para los niños.
Haz el trabajo para mañana.
Salgo para Cádiz.

for; to; in order to; toward
These sweets are for the children.
Do the work for tomorrow.
I'm leaving for Cádiz.

por
Hemos comprado esta casa por
medio millón.
¿Cuánto es por persona?
Te pasa por tonta.

Trabajo por la noche.
Pasará por León.
Le enviamos los documentos por
avión.

by; for; through; at; across; about; per
We bought this house for half a
million.
How much is it per person?
That happens to you through
stupidity.
I work at night.
He will pass through León.
We are sending you the documents
by air mail.

sin
No salgas a la calle sin abrigo
porque hace frío.

without
Don't go out without your coat,
because it's cold.

a pesar de
A pesar del mal tiempo hemos
hecho una excursión.

despite
Despite the bad weather,
we made an outing.

además de
Esta tienda es, además de cara, mala.

besides; as well; too
This shop is not only poor, but
expensive as well.

ante
No supimos qué hacer ante
una situación tan extraña.

in the presence of
We didn't know what to do in the
face of such a strange situation.

en vez de
Déme un bolígrafo negro
en vez de este azul.

instead of; in place of
Give me a black ballpoint
in place of this blue one.

en cuanto a
En cuanto a nuestra amistad,
no ha cambiado nada.

as for; as regards
As for our friendship,
nothing has changed.

respecto a
Respecto a tu propuesta debo decirte
que no puedo visitarte.

with respect to; with regard to
With regard to your proposal, I
must tell you that I cannot visit
you.

según
Según el contrato no tenemos
que pagar la reforma.

according to
According to the contract, we
don't have to pay for the
renovation.

Conjunctions

aunque
Aunque no tengo ganas, iré a tu casa.

Aunque sea tarde no podremos irnos
a casa.

(al)though; notwithstanding; even if
Although I don't want to, I will go
to your house.
Even if it's late, we won't be able
to go home.

como si
Ponte cómodo, como si
estuvieras en tu casa.

as if
Make yourself comfortable,
as if you were at home.

y
Me han regalado un sombrero y un
abrigo.

and
They have given me a hat and a
coat.

e
Javier e Isabel se casaron hace cuatro
años.

and *(before i- and hi-)*
Javier and Isabel married four
years ago.

o
¿Quieres vino tinto o blanco?

or
Would you like red wine or white?

u
Un día u otro llegará la carta.

or *(before o- and ho-)*
Sooner or later the letter will arrive.

pero
Quisiera acompañaros a la estación
pero no tengo tiempo.

but
I would like to accompany you to
the train station, but I don't have
time.

que
Deseamos que se mejoren pronto.

that
We hope that you get well soon.

si
Si estás enfermo quédate en la cama.
Carmen quiere saber si vienes a
comer.

if; in case; whether
If you are ill, stay in bed.
Carmen wants to know whether
you're coming to eat.

si no
Manda la carta urgente si no,
no llegará a tiempo.

otherwise
Send the letter express, otherwise
it won't arrive in time.

sino
Ese no es Mariano sino su hermano
mayor.

but; except; besides; only
That isn't Mariano, but his older
brother.

(en) caso (de) que
En caso que no estemos en casa,
llamad al vecino.

in case
In case we aren't at home, ring at
the neighbor's house.

ni ... ni ...
O sea que no te gusta ni la carne ni
el pescado.

neither ... nor
So, you like neither meat nor fish.

sin embargo
No hablé con el director, sin embargo
pude hablar con la actriz.

however; nevertheless
I didn't speak with the director;
however, I was able to speak with
the actress.

sin que
Juana se fue sin que la oyéramos.

without
Juana left without our hearing her.

mientras
Mi mujer madruga mientras
que yo me levanto tarde.

while; whereas
My wife rises early,
while I get up late.

Los indios representan una importante fuerza social en Perú, Ecuador,
Bolivia y Paraguay.
*Native Americans are an important social force in Perú, Ecuador, Bolivia,
and Paraguay.*

Americanisms

Latin American Spanish exhibits a number of special characteristics in the areas of pronunciation, vocabulary, and grammar. This chapter presents some of the most common Americanisms of Spanish-speaking Latin America. The following list is organized according to the themes and subject matter of the first 41 chapters. The Americanisms are listed in the first column, the Spanish versions of the Iberian Peninsula in the second, and the English equivalents in the third.

Personal Data

la **cédula**	el documento de identidad	identification card

The Human Body

la **pera**	la barbilla	chin
pararse	ponerse de pie	stand up
estar parado, a	estar de pie	stand
voltear	volver	return; come back
apurarse	darse prisa	hurry
estar/andar apurado, a	tener prisa	be in a hurry
agarrar	coger	grasp; seize; take
botar	tirar, echar	throw (away)
jalar; halar	tirar	pull
prender	encender	light; turn on (light)
la **peluquería**	la peluquería de señoras	ladies' hairdresser
la **barbería**	la peluquería de caballeros	barber shop

Health and Medicine

el **resfrío**	el resfriado	cold
los **lentes**	las gafas	(eye)glasses
la **tapadura**	el empaste	filling

Eating and Drinking

la **manteca**	la mantequilla	butter
la **crema**	la nata	cream
el **salame**	el salchichón	salami
la **papa**	la patata	potato
el **durazno**	el melocotón	peach
la **banana**	el plátano	banana
el **damasco**	el albaricoque	apricot
la **frutilla**	la fresa	strawberry
el **ananás**	la piña	pineapple
la **arbeja**; la **arveja**	el guisante	pea
los **frijoles**	las judías	beans
tomar	beber	drink
alegrón	bebido, a	tipsy
el **cigarro**	el puro	cigar
el **fósforo**	la cerilla	match
la **cigarrería**	el estanco	tobacco shop
el **changuito**	el carrito	shopping cart
el **sartén**	la sartén	frying pan
el **sándwich**	el bocadillo	sandwich

Clothing

el, la **marchante**	el, la cliente	customer
la **vitrina**; la **vidriera**	el escaparate	show window
lindo, a	bonito, a	pretty
el **terno**; el **flus**; el **vestido**	el traje	suit
el **pulóver;** el **suéter**	el jersey	sweater, pullover
el **saco**	la chaqueta	jacket

357

el **piyama**	el pijama	pajamas
el **corpiño**	el sujetador	bra
angosto, a	estrecho, a	tight, narrow
el **cierre zipper**; el	la cremallera	zipper
cierre relámpago		
el **taco**	el tacón	heel

Living Arrangements

el **departamento**	el piso	apartment
la **pieza**, la **habitación**	el cuarto	room
la **baranda**	la barandilla	railing
el **botón**	el interruptor	switch
la **ampolleta**; el **foco**	la bombilla	light bulb
el **balde**	el cubo	pail
el **bidón de basura**	el cubo de basura	garbage pail
tapado, a	atascado, a	clogged
el **plomero**; la **plomera**	el fontanero; la fontanera	plumber
la **heladera**; la **nevera**	el frigorífico	refrigerator
la **cobija**; la **frazada**	la manta	blanket
cambiarse	mudarse de casa	move

Human Characteristics

flojo, a	vago, a	lazy

Feelings, Instincts, Drives

enojarse	enfadarse	become angry
enojado, a	enfadado, a	angry

■ Expressing Thoughts, Feelings, or Perceptions ■

fuerte	alto, a	loud
cómo no	por supuesto	of course; naturally

■ Making Evaluations ■

chévere	formidable	great; super

■ Social Relations ■

¡Nos vemos!	¡Hasta luego!	See you later!

■ Education and Training ■

el **liceo**	el instituto	high school; secondary school
la **prueba**	el examen	exam; test
aplazar	suspender	fail
quedar aplazado, a	quedar suspendido, a	to fail a course

■ Professional Life ■

el **chofer**	el chófer	chauffeur; driver

■ Economics ■

el **patrón**	el jefe	boss
la **mercadería**	la mercancía	merchandise
el **contador**; la **contadora**	el, la contable	bookkeeper; accountant

Finance

la **plata**	el dinero	money
el **sencillo**	el suelto	(small) change
en **concreto**	al contado	cash

Professional Tools and Office Items

la **piola**	la cuerda	cord; rope; string

Use of Leisure Time

el **boleto**	la entrada	admission ticket

Sports

la **cancha**	el campo de deportes	playing field

Tourism

el **pasaje**	el viaje	trip; journey
la **estadía**	la estancia	stay
la **valija**	la maleta	suitcase
la **visa**	el visado	visa
la **carpa**	la tienda de campaña	tent

Means of Communication

el **directorio de teléfonos**	la guía telefónica	telephone book; directory

las **cartas detenidas**	la lista de correos	general delivery
la **carta registrada**	la carta certificada	registered letter
la **estampilla**	el sello	stamp

Media

el **radio**	la radio	radio
el **altoparlante**	la altavoz	loudspeaker
el **aviso**	el anuncio	(ad)vertisement; notice; announcement
el **noticioso informativo**	las noticias	news

The Organization of Government

la **corte**	el tribunal	court

Vegetable Kingdom

la **grama**	el césped	lawn; grass; grass plot

Transportation and Traffic

el **tránsito**	el tráfico	traffic
el **carro**	el coche; el auto	car; (auto)mobile
el **baúl**	el maletero	trunk
la **chapa**	la placa	license plate
manejar	conducir	drive (a car)
enceguecer	cegar	blind
doblar	torcer; girar	turn
parquear	aparcar; estacionar	park
la **playa**	el estacionamiento	parking place
la **bomba**	la gasolinera	gas station
andar en bicicleta	montar en bicicleta	ride a bicycle
el **bus**	el autobús	bus
el **coche-dormitorio**	el coche-cama	sleeping car
el **vagón-restaurante**	el coche-restaurante	dining car

el **compartimiento**	el compartimento	compartment
la **combinación**	el enlace	connection
la **boletería**	la ventanilla	(ticket) window
el **boleto**	el billete	ticket
el **ferry-boat**	el transbordador	ferry
la **vereda**	la acera	sidewalk
dañado, a	estropeado, a	defective; damaged

Substances and Materials

el **concreto**	el cemento	cement

Statements of Quantity

liviano, a	ligero, a	light

Space and Time

acá	aquí	here
allá	allí	there
el **día feriado**	el día festivo	holiday
demorar(se)	tardar	be late
ahorita	ahora	now
recién	recientemente	recently
a la mañana	por la mañana	in the morning
a la tarde	por la tarde	in the afternoon
a la noche	por la noche	at night

Manner

malograrse	estropearse	get damaged; out of order

Mercado al aire libre en un pequeño pueblo boliviano.
Open market in a small Bolivian town.

Uruguay es de suelo ondulado y desprovisto de montañas, pero cuenta con
muchos ríos.
*Uruguay's land is undulated and without mountains, but rivers are
plentiful.*

Index of All Spanish Key Words

All the basic vocabulary words appear in **boldface letters**. The more advanced terms are set in normal-type letters.

deseo 120
desesperado, a 96
desgracia 131
desgraciadamente
115
desierto 256
desigualdad 143
desilusionado, a 96
desilusionarse 96
desmayarse 41
desnudarse 65
desnudo, a 66
desorden 87
desordenado, a 92
despacio 334
despacho 81
despedida 139
despedir 159
despedirse 139
despegar 287
despejado, a 260
despejarse 262
despensa 81
despertador 83
despertarse 24
despido 160
despierto, a 27
despistado, a 92
despreciar 130
después 330
después de
(Jesu)cristo 327
después (de) que
330
destinatario 201
destino 288
destornillador 178
destrucción 253
destruir 252
desventaja 131
desviación 281
de tal forma que 335
detalle 115
detective 157
detener 240
detergente 72
determinado, a 341
de todos modos 121
detrás (de) 316
deuda 172

deudor, deudora
173
de vez en cuando 332
devolver 141
día 323
diablo 221
día feriado 362
día festivo 325
día laborable 325
diálogo 212
diamante 300
diapositiva 188
diario 205
diario, a 323
diarrea 42
dibujante 214
dibujar 213
dibujo 149
diccionario 205
diciembre 326
dictado 149
dictador 235
dictadura 235
dictar 149
didáctico, a 153
diecinueve 303
dieciocho 303
dieciséis 303
diecisiete 303
diente 16
diez 303
diez y seis 303
diferencia 338
diferente 338
difícil 149
dificultad 131
Diga 203
Dígame 203
digerir 18
digestión 18
Dinamarca 229
dinámico, a 108
dinero 173
Dios 221
dios, diosa 223
diplomático, a 108,
249
diputación 238
diputado, diputada
238

dirección 14, 200, 318
directo, a 288
director 185
director, directora
148
director de orquesta,
directora de
orquesta 216
*directorio de
teléfonos* 360
dirigir 162
dirigirse a 140
disciplina 192
discípulo 222
disco 209
disco 281
disco compacto
(CD) 210
discoteca 182
discriminar 143
disculpa 116
disculpar 115
disculparse 115
discurso 112
discusión 112
discutir 112
diseñar 215
diseño 215
disfrutar 195
disgusto 96
disminuir 344
disparar 246
disponer 144
distancia 319
distinguido, a 139
distinguir 339
distinto, a 338
distracción 182
distraerse 183
distraído, a 110
diversión 182
diverso, a 211
divertido, a 109, 182
divertirse 182
dividir 305
divisas 176
divorciado, a 13
divorciarse 133
divorcio 133
doblar 361

P

V